# Bible Country

Crusader Gate at Caesarea.

Early morning haze over
the Sea of Galilee,
in Hebrew "Kinneret."

# Bible Country

A JOURNEY
THROUGH THE
HOLY LAND

Woodrow Michael Kroll

ACCENT
IMPERIALS

ACCENT BOOKS
Denver, Colorado

# Bible Country

## ACCENT ♛ IMPERIALS

A division of Accent Publications, Inc.
12100 W. Sixth Avenue
P.O. Box 15337
Denver, Colorado 80215

Copyright © 1982 Woodrow Michael Kroll
Printed in the United States of America

Library of Congress Catalog Card Number 81-69782
ISBN 0-89636-060-1

Photo Credits: Woodrow Michael Kroll, Jerry Wilke, Walter W. Meyer, Connie Gruen, Rev. Harvey A. Anderson, Larry Lundstrom, Violet T. Pearson, Rev. Richard Stoehr, James Rix, Holy Land Exhibit, Mpls., Minn., Israel Government Tourism Administration, NASA

Book Design: Koechel/Peterson Design, Mpls., Minn.

# CONTENTS

*To my children,*
*Tracy, Tim, Tina and Tiffany*

# PREFACE

I was nineteen at the time. It was my first trip abroad. Six others and I had shipped our car to Ostend, Belgium and from there we drove it across Europe, through Greece and Turkey and even through Syria and Lebanon on our way to the Holy Land. Then we turned around and drove back through Europe and throughout the British Isles. It was too good to be true, the adventure of a lifetime.

You would expect after visiting Paris, London, Zurich, Rome and Athens all the same summer that surely one of these great cities would loom large in my mind and dominate my memory. That's what you would expect, but you'd be wrong. Even repeated visits to each of these cities have not made the impression on me that one city has. What city has more style than the stylish capitals of Europe? What city dwarfs all others in importance? What is the most unforgettable city on earth? There's no question about it. JERUSALEM.

The dream of every Christian I know is someday to visit the Holy Land. It has been said that ten days in the Holy Land are worth a semester in a seminary, but for one who has studied in half a dozen seminaries I can say that, for me, this is an understatement. The most useful understanding of the archaeology, history and geography of the Bible came to me from the many journeys I have made to the Holy Land. Likewise, I can describe things to you in word pictures, but the only way for you really to absorb the land of the Bible is to see it firsthand.

This handy book is designed to be of benefit both to the traveler and to the dreamer. That's important, because dreamers somehow have the habit of becoming travelers. This is an armchair guide to the Holy Land. As you sit before your fireplace in an easy chair, your feet stretched out before you, this guide will transport you in mind and spirit to the hills of Galilee and the mountains of Judaea. You will live the Holy Land experience as best you can without actually being there. But when that exciting day comes when your 747 jet lands in the Promised Land, and it surely will, you won't want to leave this book behind. It will then be an invaluable guide to you as you sit in an air-conditioned coach on a plush seat, your feet stretched out before you.

There is simply no place on earth like the Holy Land. It never loses its luster. After I had been to Jerusalem at least a dozen times before, I arrived after dark one night champing at the bit to get to the Old City. I was so tired, however, that I decided to wait until the morning, but couldn't sleep at all that night because of the excitement! Jerusalem the golden, the city of God. It's unlike any other city in the world, as the Holy Land is unlike any other place in the world.

Although we have highlighted the places of most interest to Christians, nonetheless this guide to the Holy Land will be of real value to others as well. It is my prayer that it will not just bring you to a greater appreciation of the land of the Lord, but to the Lord of the land as well. May it contribute to the holy life of all who read it and may your Holy Land experience be an exciting one.

Woodrow Michael Kroll
*Bible School Park, New York*

Galilee Sunrise.

# A Journey Through the Holy Land

# CHAPTER 1

# A Cycle Complete

HISTORY OF THE HOLY LAND

*"And the Lord said to Abram . . . Lift up now thine eyes, and look from the place where thou art northward, and southward, and eastward, and westward: For all the land which thou seest, to thee will I give it, and to thy seed for ever"* (Genesis 13:14-15).

SHALOM! SALAM! HELLO! In Israel you'll hear all three greetings simultaneously. They welcome you in Hebrew, Arabic, and English to one of the oldest/newest nations on earth. This Promised Land, given to Abraham and his descendants, is one of incredible contrasts. Here lie the ruins of the world's ancient civilizations, the Phoenician, Philistine, Hebrew, Nabatean, Roman, and Greek, yet amid these ruins rise the skyscrapers of Tel Aviv, Jerusalem, and Haifa. Here sun bathers frolic in the subtropical heat of Eilat and ski the slopes of Mount Hermon in the same season. With the annual inflation rate soaring over one hundred percent, the haggling shopkeeper of Old Jerusalem seemingly has a hand-to-mouth existence. Still at night he slides into the family Mercedes exuberant at the day's profits. In a land where Hebrew, Arabic, Yiddish, English, French, German, Polish, and Russian are commonly spoken, a land which abounds with artifacts, excavations and amateur archaeologists, a land which Mark Twain described as "forbidding desolation" yet today blossoms like a rose, in this land as in no other the Christian can relive Bible history, retrace Bible geography, and recapture Bible familiarity.

The history of this troubled land reads like the rough draft of *War and Peace*, with the accent on war. Since the day the LORD God made the Genesis 13 promise to Abraham, invaders from far and near have trampled the grain of Israel's fields. See the outline overview of her history which graphically displays Israel's checkered dominance.

**Jerusalem, central in the Holy land and the most unforgettable city on earth.**

## The conquerors of Canaan over the centuries include:

### THE JEWS (2000-587 B.C.)

1900 B.C.  Abraham the patriarch enters Palestine, then known as Canaan for it was controlled by Amorites and Canaanites.

1630 B.C.  Jacob moves patriarchal family to Egypt to be with Joseph.

1250 B.C.  Joshua and the Israelites re-enter the land of Canaan. Some date this event to 1400 B.C.

1200 B.C.  Philistines invade the land from Crete.

1025 B.C.  Saul crowned Israel's first king.

1004 B.C.  David ascends to the throne of Israel.

965 B.C.  Solomon succeeds David as Israel's king.

920 B.C.  Israel divided into Northern and Southern tribes.

721 B.C.  Assyrians capture Samaria, capital of Northern tribes. Captives taken, vanish into the pages of history.

### THE BABYLONIANS (605-562 B.C.)

587 B.C.  Nebuchadnezzar, king of Babylon, sacks Jerusalem, capital of the Southern tribes, and takes Judah captive.

### THE PERSIANS (549-332 B.C.)

539 B.C.  Cyrus, king who conquered Babylonia, decrees that Jewish captives may return to homeland. Repatriation begins.

### THE GREEKS (332-167 B.C.)

334 B.C.  Alexander the Great vanquishes Palestine. After his death Ptolemies and Seleucids rule the land.

175 B.C.  The Seleucid king, Antiochus IV Epiphanes, desecrated the temple altar by offering a pig on it.

### THE HASMONEANS (167-63 B.C.)

167 B.C.  Aged priest Mattathias and his sons revolt against the Seleucids. The Maccabees give nearly a century of peace to Palestine.

### THE ROMANS (63 B.C.-A.D. 330)

63 B.C.  Roman general Pompey conquers Palestine.

40 B.C.  Parthians capture the land from Rome in a surprise attack.

39 B.C.  Herod the Great expels the Parthians, reigns until 4 B.C. Jesus Christ is born during his reign.

30 A.D.  Approximate date of Christ's crucifixion.

66 A.D.  Jewish zealots revolt against Roman rule.

70 A.D.  Jerusalem sacked and burned by Roman general Titus.

73 A.D.  Masada, last zealot stronghold, falls to the Romans.

132 A.D.  Under Bar Kokhba the Jews revolt a second time unsuccessfully.

### THE BYZANTINES (313-634)

313 A.D.  Constantine issues the Edict of Milan bringing freedom of worship to all religions. Constantinople (Byzantium) made capital of eastern half of Roman Empire. Christianity flourishes.

614 A.D.  Persians retake Palestine, 33,877 people slain. Christian churches destroyed.

### THE ARABS (634-1099)

632 A.D.  Mohammed, the prophet born in Mecca in 570, dies but his religion spreads over the Arab world.

1009 A.D.  Al-Hakim, the mad Fatimid Caliph, begins persecution of Christians and Jews in the Holy Land. The Church of the Holy Sepulchre among the 30,000 Christian buildings destroyed.

### THE CRUSADERS (1099-1291)

1099 A.D.  Jerusalem captured by the Crusaders.

1187 A.D.  Saladin routs the Christian Crusaders at the Horns of Hattin in Galilee. Christian influence gone from Palestine.

1263 A.D.  Mameluke Sultan Baybars of Egypt continues to capture remaining Crusader strongholds.

## THE MAMELUKES (1291-1517)

1291 A.D.  Acre, the last Christian bastion of the Crusader period falls to the Moslems. The land becomes a backwater province of Damascus.

1400 A.D.  Mongol invasion is only partially successful and the Egyptian Mamelukes regain control of Palestine until they are destroyed in 1517 by the Ottoman army of Selim I.

## THE TURKS (1517-1917)

1517 A.D.  Turkish Ottoman Empire begins 400 year control of Palestine.

1799 A.D.  Napoleon unsuccessfully attempts to make Palestine part of his growing empire.

1917 A.D.  Jerusalem liberated from the Turks by the Allies of World War I under General Allenby.

## THE JEWS (1917-     )

1917 A.D.  The Balfour Declaration recognizes the historic connection between the Jewish people and Palestine, pledges support for a national home for the Jews.

1922 A.D.  The League of Nations confirms the British Mandate over Palestine.

1947 A.D.  The United Nations partitions Palestine between Israel and Jordan.

1948 A.D.  On May 14th the State of Israel is established, the British withdraw, Israeli-Arab war begins. War ended July 18th.

1956 A.D.  Egypt nationalized the Suez Canal. On July 26, 1956 Israel attacks and occupies nearly all the Sinai but later withdraws to 1949 armistice lines.

1967 A.D.  Egyptian President Nasser closes the Gulf of Aqabah to Israeli shipping. The Six-Day War, a blitzkrieg attack by Israeli air and ground units, results in Israel capturing the Sinai, the Golan Heights, the West Bank and all of Jerusalem.

1973 A.D.  Surprise attack by Egypt and Syria catches Israel off guard on Yom Kippur, the Jewish day of atonement. Some territory in the Sinai lost; some territory on the Golan Heights expanded.

1979 A.D.  In March of 1979 the Camp David Peace Accord is signed between Egyptian President Anwar Sadat and Israeli Prime Minister Menachem Begin.

In nearly 4,000 years of occupation this land has produced the three great religions of the world but has failed to produce a lasting peace. In 4,000 years the Promised Land has come full cycle and is again occupied by the descendants of Abraham. The Babylonians, Persians, Greeks, Romans, Egyptians, Turks, and others notwithstanding, the promise of God to Abraham in Genesis 13 is as sure today as it was the day the patriarch left Ur in search of a homeland.

As you walk the shadowy streets of Old Jerusalem it is as if you had entered some mysterious time machine and were transported back to the days of Jesus of Nazareth. There you see the blind, the beggar, the destitute. You are jostled about by the crowd and brushed by the overladen donkey being led to the market place. As you stroll over the hills of Samaria you rise to a knoll which was taken in battle by Joshua, and again by David, and again by Judas Maccabaeus, and again by Moshe Dayan. You are in the land of the Bible, a land of living history. In Israel you don't just read about the past; you experience it. You are in the Promised Land, God's Land, Bible Country, the Holy Land.

# CHAPTER 2

# The Hinge Between Europe and Asia

◆

## THE LAND AND THE PEOPLE

*"For the LORD thy God bringeth thee into a good land, a land of brooks of water, of fountains and depths that spring out of valleys and hills; a land of wheat, and barley, and vines, and fig trees, and pomegranates; a land of olive oil, and honey; a land wherein thou shalt eat bread without scarceness, thou shalt not lack any thing in it; a land whose stones are iron, and out of whose hills thou mayest dig brass"* (Deuteronomy 8:7-9).

## THE LAND

Just look at a map and you'll understand why the war-ravaged land of Israel is so important. God cast it geographically as the land bridge between three major continents. Located 6,000 nautical miles from the shores of the United States, the Holy Land acts as a hinge between Europe and Asia, with Africa hanging by a small thread at the Suez Canal. The armies of history past have marched through this land on their way to victory/defeat.

In this jet age the size of the country may seem small. *"From Dan to Beersheba,"* only a distance of 150 miles, and from the Jordan River to the Mediterranean Sea encompasses territory only a bit larger than the state of Connecticut. Still with such diverse terrain as mountains, deserts, lowlands and plateaus, with rivers, lakes, fresh and saltwater seas, keeping one small geographical fact in mind will help you in understanding the Holy Land. Palestine is oriented vertically, that is, north to south, not east to west. This is evident from the five natural regions of the land.

**(Aerial) View from Apollo 7.**

## MAJOR REGIONS

Whether you dock at the port of Haifa or land at Ben Gurion Airport in Lod, your first encounter with the Land of Promise is with the COASTAL PLAIN. This narrow strip of land unfolds from the base of Mount Carmel, where the plain is only a few hundred feet wide, through the luxuriant Plain of Sharon and continues south to the gently rolling hills of Philistia until it vanishes into the desert south of Gaza. Boasting of such cities as Haifa, Tel Aviv, Jaffa, Ashdod, and Ashkelon, nearly two-thirds of modern Israel's population lives along the Mediterranean coastal plain.

The second natural region is the CENTRAL HIGHLANDS, sometimes called the Western Hills. Rising over 6,000 feet in Lebanon, this mountain range averages between 2,000 and 3,000 feet in Israel. In biblical times this rather monotonous mass of mountains was referred to as Upper and Lower Galilee, the Hill Country of Ephraim and the Hill Country of Judah. Safed, Nablus, Jerusalem, and Bethlehem are all located in these mountains.

In striking contrast to the highlands is the JORDAN VALLEY, known as the Rift Valley. It is a deep depression in the ground which begins between the Lebanon and Anti-Lebanon Mountains and continues south through the Sea of Galilee, following the course of the Jordan River to the Dead Sea, and then southward to the Gulf of Aqabah and the Red Sea. Running between two great geological faults, this area contains the lowest spot on earth, the Dead Sea, as well as Jericho, Beth Shean and the cities dotting the shores of the Sea of Galilee.

Again the terrain of Palestine changes abruptly as the Jordan Valley rises on the east to the TRANSJORDAN PLATEAU. Generally belonging to the Hashemite Kingdom of Jordan, these Eastern Hills tower over the Great Rift as the Western Hills do on the opposite side. Drive from Amman, Jordan's capital, to Jerusalem and on the way you'll descend to the floor of the Jordan Valley. Don't be surprised if you think you are driving the switchback trails of a barren and snowless Switzerland. The roads are just as steep, the curves just as hairpinned. Your ears will "pop" as you drop in on the Jordan Valley from the mountains of Moab and Gilead.

The final natural region of the Holy Land is the NEGEV. Situated south of Palestine, this steppe is like an inverted pyramid providing the base for the sculpture we affectionately have come to know as the Holy Land. It is more than 12,500 square miles of sand and barrenness with the desert encroaching upon it. The only inhabitable area is a small strip about 30 miles wide from north to south around Beersheba, the capital of the Negev.

**Haifa climbs the western slope of Mount Carmel and overlooks Israel's most important harbor.**

## FLORA AND FAUNA

Bounded by her Arab neighbors, Lebanon on the north, Syria on the northeast, Jordan on the east and Egypt on the southwest, Israel is the most agricultural country in the Middle East today. More than 1,075,000 cultivated areas blanket the Israeli hills and plains. Much of the blossoming of modern Israel is due to irrigation. In fact, 82 percent of Israel's water supply is used for agriculture. Because of the subtropical climate and the ingenious use of water, Israel's flora is among the richest in the world with 3,000 species of plants. By comparison Great Britain only has 1,700 species. And what's more, tree planting in Israel has almost become a ritual. While the land was heavily wooded in Bible times, this wooded wealth was ravaged through centuries of warfare. Since 1948 a total of 125 million trees have been planted over 100,000 acres of Promised Land soil by both natives and pilgrims.

Like her flora, Israel's fauna abounds with species from all over the world. Some of the animals found roaming the countryside are the leopard, hyena, jackal, porcupine, antelope, wild boar, wolf, coney, ibex, and the list goes on and on. Three hundred and fifty species of birds also are found in the Promised Land and, as in the days of the Old Testament, eagles, ospreys and vultures nest in the crags of the highest mountains.

And just as God promised in Deuteronomy 8:9, the Holy Land abounds in mineral wealth. Mineral deposits in commercial quantity include bromide, potash, copper, phosphates, clay, sulphur, bitumen, and manganese. Is it little wonder that God calls this a "good land"?

## CLIMATE

Although the Holy Land lies roughly about the same latitude as Georgia or Southern California, nonetheless much of her climate is determined by the configuration of her mountains and her proximity to the desert. The Israeli seasons are but two, winter and summer. Israeli winters start with the "early" rains about October initiating the major agricultural season of the year. These rains get heavier during November, December, and January, sometimes turning to snow in higher elevations like Jerusalem. The "latter" rains arrive in March and continue for a month or more until the crop is ripened (cf. Jeremiah 3:3; Amos 4:7). It almost never rains between May and September.

In David's day as in ours, the land drinks water by the rain from heaven (Deuteronomy 11:11). Average rainfall on the coastal plain, at Acco for example, is about 25 inches per year. In Galilee it is much more, 47 inches, about the same as New York City. Jerusalem averages only 20 inches annually, with Beersheba lessened to 8 inches on the average. But don't despair, the lower Jordan Valley only receives one or two inches of rainfall in a year.

Holy Land temperatures are moderate. January and July averages for major cities are:

| City | January | July |
|------|---------|------|
| Jerusalem | 45-57 | 67-83 |
| Tel Aviv | 48-66 | 71-87 |
| Tiberias | 54-69 | 77-98 |
| Eilat | 52-72 | 80-105 |

But be aware that the combination of oppressive humidity and the super activity of the sun make

*Left*, flora of the countryside.

*Right*, the Mount of Beatitudes and the Church of the Loaves and Fishes.

Once famous as the Wailing Wall because the Jews mourned here for their loss of the Temple, it is now called the Western Wall since its restoration to the Jews in the Six-Day War of 1967 and has become a scene of joy and celebration as well as of prayer.

the summer days of Jericho and other cities of the Jordan Valley almost unbearable.

## THE PEOPLE

When the twelve spies were sent on a reconnaissance mission to spy out the Promised Land they reported, *"The Amalekites dwell in the land of the south: and the Hittites, and the Jebusites, and the Amorites, dwell in the mountains: and the Canaanites dwell by the sea, and by the coast of Jordan"* (Numbers 13:29). The 3,750,000 population of Israel today is as diverse as it was in Moses' day. Grouped according to religion (is there any other way in the Holy Land), some Israelis you will meet are:

*THE JEWS.* About 15 different Jewish sects are represented in the nearly 3,150,000 Jews living in Israel. In general the Jews of Israel are rough, outgoing and brash almost to the point of arrogance. But don't let that rough exterior fool you. About half of the Israeli Jews are immigrants; the other half are called "Sabras." These are the sons of the pioneers who were born in Israel. The Sabra is an indigenous fruit of the cactus family which is prickly on the outside but sweet on the inside. So, once you get to know the people of the land, even the Sabras, you come to love them.

*THE SAMARITANS.* Having dwindled to less than 500, the Samaritans of Israel live in Nablus, the capital of the Arab West Bank, and to a lesser amount in a suburb of Tel Aviv called Holon.

These people of mixed ancestry were barred by the Jews from rebuilding Jerusalem after the Babylonian Exile (cf. Ezra 4:1-3; Nehemiah 4:1-8). The Samaritans maintain a synagogue on Mount Gerizim which they hold to be the sacred mountain of God. Samaritans recognize only the Pentateuch, the five books of Moses, as God's Word.

*THE KARAITES.* Founded in Baghdad in A.D. 706 by Anan ben David, the Karaites are a Jewish sect living chiefly in Ramla. Numbering a little more than 10,000, this religious people repudiates the oral tradition of the rabbis. In their nine synagogues they expound only the Old Testament.

*THE MUSLIMS.* Numbering approximately 463,600, the Muslims of Israel are almost entirely Arabs. Since the Six-Day War they live in the occupied territory of the West Bank, Gaza Strip and East Jerusalem. Muslims are followers of the 7th Century A.D. prophet Mohammed and the religion of Islam. Islam teaches that there is but one God, Allah, and that Mohammed was his prophet. In Israel there are 200 Muslim clergymen serving nearly 100 mosques.

*THE DRUZES.* These Arabic speaking people believe that there is but one God who has revealed Himself in successive incarnations, the final and most perfect incarnation being that of Al-Hakim, the sixth Fatimid caliph of Egypt (A.D.

996-1021). They follow the Bible and venerate men from its pages, especially Jethro, father-in-law of Moses. Due to intermarriage with the Romans and Crusaders, many of the Druzes are blond with large swarthy mustaches. Several Druzes serve in the Knesset, Israel's Parliament.

**THE BAHAIS.** Bahaism is an eclectic religion emphasizing the unity of mankind and the commonality of all religions. The forerunner of the movement, Mirza Ali Mohammed, a descendent of the prophet Mohammed, was born and martyred in Iran during the last century. One of his followers, Mirza Husayn Ali was also born in Iran but died in the Holy Land after a 24-year imprisonment in Acre. Most Bahai doctrine came from him. The World Center of the Faith is located on the side of Mount Carmel at Haifa.

**THE CHRISTIANS.** You may be surprised to learn that about 85,500 Christians live in Israel. Most of these are Arabs and fall into four main categories: (1) Protestant (Anglican, Baptist, Lutheran, etc.); (2) Catholic (Roman, Greek, Armenian, etc.); (3) Orthodox (Greek, Romanian, Russian, etc.); and (4) Monophysite (Armenian, Coptic, Ethiopian, etc.). Many Christian sites are maintained in the Holy Land and "Christmas in Bethlehem" is a lifelong dream of many of the faithful.

Another group worth noting, although they are not a religious group, is **THE BEDOUIN.** Living in black-tented camps, there are roughly 27,000 Bedouin in the Negev and 5,000 in the Galilee mountains. These semi-nomadic people usually do not respect traditional land boundaries but take their flocks to graze wherever they find grass. Appearing to barely eke out an existence, one of the most incongruous sights in the modern Holy Land is television aerials scanning the Palestinian skies over Bedouin tents in search of American TV reruns.

Samaritans still worship at Mount Gerizim. Pictured is the Samaritan synagogue at Nablus.

# ISRAEL: OLD AND NEW

While the Bedouin move from hillside to valley and back again, most Israelis (85.5%) have settled in the 104 towns and cities of the land. Today thousands of people live in cities inhabited by their ancestors in Old and New Testament times. For example, the population of Jerusalem is 400,000; Beersheba is 93,400; Ashkelon now has 46,000 inhabitants; and Nazareth numbers 36,400. Some modern cities did not exist as population centers in Bible days. Although the population of Tel Aviv is 343,300, the greater urban complex makes this city founded in 1909 the largest in Israel. Natanya's population numbers 79,500. Established in the mid-1930s, Nahariya now numbers 30,000. Cities old and new, the Holy Land is both.

Those Israelis who do not live in urban centers tend to live on one of two kinds of settlements. The kibbutz is a village in which property is commonly owned by the members. Those who choose to join a kibbutz have all their needs satisfied by the community. Nearly everything is communal, the dining room, classroom, cultural and sports centers, a clinic, etc. Married couples occupy small apartments but children are cared for in a nursery or kindergarten. Kibbutzim are largely agricultural in nature and most invite guests to observe their villages. Today in Israel there are 229 kibbutzim with a membership of 101,600.

The other kind of rural settlement is the moshav, a family-owned cooperative village. The farmsteads are individually owned but there is a unique system of mutual aid, cooperative purchasing and marketing, and collective development. Most of the machinery is owned and operated by the moshavim rather than the individual farmer. Today Israel boasts of 352 moshavim with a population of 134,700.

These cooperative efforts are reminiscent, to some extent, of Joseph's great grain project in Egypt (Genesis 41:34-36, 46-49). A less successful incident of cooperative farming in the Old Testament is that of Jacob and Laban (Genesis 30:30-43). Nonetheless, farming methods old and new, the Holy Land has both.

Israelis are hearty eaters. Breakfast is likely to be the most elaborate meal of the day. A typical Israeli breakfast consists of a buffet of fresh fruits, cheeses, juices, boiled eggs, herring, sardines, and other delicacies. Breakfast also includes cucumbers, radishes, onions, tomatoes and a wide variety of raw and luscious vegetables. As you experience an Israeli breakfast you may hear a faint Israeli voice echo, *"We remember the fish, which we did eat in Egypt freely; the cucumbers, and the melons, and the leeks, and the onions, and the garlick"* (Numbers 11:5-6).

Israel's modern answer to ancient manna is pitta. This is a flat, pancake-shaped Arab bread, usually six inches in diameter and split in the middle. When pitta bread is stuffed with balls of deep-fried ground chick peas, spiced with peppers and other oriental delights, plus salad it makes an unforgettable and unregrettable delight known as felafel. No one can truthfully say he has imbibed the spirit of the Holy Land until he has sampled a felafel from an eager vendor on the streets of Old Jerusalem.

When all of this is eaten with humus, a paste made from ground chick peas and olive oil, or tchina, a similar paste made from ground sesame seeds, neither the experience nor the flavor is soon forgotten. Perhaps this food contributes to the temperament of the Middle East. Exotic foods old and new, the Holy Land has both.

A pilgrimage to the Holy Land, whether in the mind or in the flesh, is a delightful encounter with the past and present, the old and new. The official language of Israel is Hebrew, a tongue which all but disappeared through disuse until the establishment of the State of Israel. Still today all road signs are given in Hebrew, Arabic and English. Neither the buzzing of Israeli jets overhead nor the cosmopolitan nature of the population can diminish the fact that this is ancient land. It exudes history. It provides a constant reminder of God's promises to His people. It is *"A land which the LORD thy God careth for: the eyes of the LORD thy God are always upon it, from the beginning of the year even unto the end of the year"* (Deuteronomy 11:12). Of all the terrestrial acreage created by God, this land alone, old and new, is the Holy Land.

# CHAPTER 3

# Sands of Old-Fields of New

◆

## THE COASTAL PLAIN

*"And the LORD spake unto Moses, saying, Command the children of Israel, and say unto them, When ye come into the land of Canaan; (this is the land that shall fall unto you for an inheritance, even the land of Canaan with the coasts thereof:). . .And as for the western border, ye shall even have the great sea for a border. . ."* (Numbers 34:1-2, 6).

The Coastal or Maritime Plain begins in the southern extremity of the Holy Land at the River of Egypt (Wadi El Arish) and narrows northward to Mount Carmel. The lower half is Philistia; the upper half is divided between the Plain of Sharon and the Plain of Dor. The best place to start our journey in the Holy Land is at one of the real beauty spots of Palestine, the Plain of Sharon. Today the center of Israel's citrus industry, Sharon extends from the serpentine curves of the Yarkon River north to the Plain of Dor and the Carmel range. So beautiful is the fruit of this plain that the *"Rose of Sharon"* (Song of Solomon 2:1) is a figure applied to the Messiah. Though the plain itself is super fertile and very beautiful, don't be shocked when you see sand dunes along the coast. Carried by the sea from the Nile River, sand is washed ashore along the Maritime Plain and blown inland to form dunes, especially in the area around Caesarea. Let's begin our exciting journey.

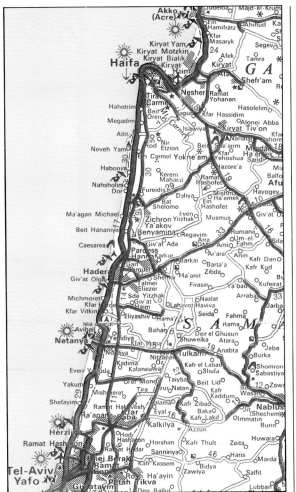

## *The Road North*
### TEL AVIV

The largest all-Jewish community in the world, TEL AVIV is a model product of the 20th century. It is noisy, frantic, crowded, uncoordinated, cosmopolitan and delightful. It is a microcosm of all of Israel. This rapidly growing metropolis is the business, entertainment and cultural center of Israel. It is a city born of necessity.

In 1909, tired of cramped quarters in the Jewish sector of the Arab city of Jaffa, 60 families bought 32 acres of sand dunes on Jaffa's northern outskirts and decided to plant their own town. Led by Meir Dizengoff, these 250 people named their settlement Tel Aviv ("Hill of Spring," cf. Ezekiel 3:15). Dizengoff prophesied that one day their small town would contain as many as 25,000 residents. His estimate was grossly anemic.

During World War I the Turkish general dispossessed the Tel Avivians, but they returned when General Allenby's British Army dispossessed the Turks and the war ended. Perhaps as much as anything the city's motto, "I shall build thee and thou shalt be built," has inspired many Jews who have immigrated to the Promised Land to remain right in Tel Aviv rather than brave the sands of the Negev or the mortar shells of northern Galilee.

The most striking feature of this modern city's skyline is the sparkling white Shalom Tower

(Migdal Shalom). Thirty-four stories make it the tallest building in the Middle East. The glass elevator ride to the observatory on top gives the best view of the city and the Coastal Plain in general. From this vantage point it becomes obvious that the main streets of Tel Aviv look like squiggly strands of spaghetti laid parallel to the coastline.

Like any modern metropolis, Tel Aviv has its share of museums, theaters and parks including the handsome campus of Tel Aviv University. With more than 18,000 students this is the largest university in Israel. The Tel Aviv Zoo, at the end of Ben-Gurion Boulevard, specializes in near-extinct animals. At the zoo can be seen Aldabras tortoises, Swinhoe pheasants, Cyprus wild sheep, and Syrian bears, among a host of other animals.

Given the brief history of Tel Aviv you would not expect any correlation between this bustling city which never sleeps and the biblical period. But in 1955-61, an archaeologist named Kaplan discovered artifacts above the harbor which date back to the 18th century B.C. Here too was discovered a Hyksos citadel with walls 20 feet thick and a city gate inscribed with the name Ramses II of the 13th century B.C. Hence the city of Israel's future is built on the cities of Israel's past.

## JAFFA (JOPPA)

Interlocked with Tel Aviv, one of the world's newest cities, is JAFFA, one of the world's oldest cities. Now part of "greater Tel Aviv-Jaffa," a sprawling complex with a population of 950,000, Jaffa's history dates to biblical days. Tel Aviv and Jaffa are like two candles placed so close together that their flames flicker as one. Whereas Jaffa was the original city, Tel Aviv became her unwanted offspring. Now the old section of Jaffa is but an oriental balcony overlooking the mushrooming metropolis.

The harbor of Jaffa is one of the oldest in the world. Known as Japho in Joshua's time (Joshua 19:46), it became the chief seaport of ancient Israel. Here the famous cedars of Lebanon were brought en route to Jerusalem and Solomon's Temple (II Chronicles 2:16; cf. Ezra 3:7). Joppa was the seaport city from which Jonah embarked to Tarshish in his futile attempt to run from God (Jonah 1:3). This was the home of Tabitha, or Dorcas, who was raised from the dead by Peter (Acts 9:36-43). Here too Peter had the vision of the great sheet by which he learned that God was as interested in the salvation of the Gentiles as He was the salvation of the Jews (Acts 9:43—10:48).

South of lovely Independence Park in Jaffa is the Kikar Atarian Tourist complex and Yacht Marina. High rise hotels line the Mediterranean shore.

A quiet lane in the reconstructed quarter of Jaffa.

But with all this Bible history there is one spot you simply must visit in Jaffa. Let's wind our way up the climbing streets of Old Jaffa. High on the hill above the harbor is the Franciscan Monastery of Saint Peter. Close to the monastery in a narrow alley you will find an old mosque. Dating from 1730, it is the oldest mosque in Jaffa. Face the harbor below and get your camera ready for one of the quaintest scenes in the Holy Land. With the blue-green waters of the Mediterranean as a backdrop, the old mosque is a picturesque reminder of the place where, according to Christian tradition, the house of Simon the tanner stood (Acts 10:5-6, 32) and where Peter had the vision of the great sheet.

Jaffa has been seaport city to the world of antiquity. Solomon, Jonah, Peter, not to mention Richard the Lion-Hearted and Napoleon, have all come by way of Jaffa. The ancient harbor and Crusader fortifications are but a fraction of the historical reminders to a former glory now swallowed up in urban living.

## NETANYA

Let's leave the glamor and glitter of Tel Aviv behind and take the coastal road north toward Haifa. In a very few minutes we arrive at the coastal city of HERZLIZA. The name of this town is synonymous with luxury and expense. With perhaps the most beautiful beaches in all of Israel, the shoreline is studded with palatial villas, diplomats' residences and deluxe hotels. Some dozen miles north of this Mediterranean mecca is NETANYA, the "pearl of Sharon." This beautifully clean and sparkling city, flanked by a flawless beach of pure white sand, is considered to be the capital of the Plain of Sharon.

Established in 1929, the city honors the name of American philanthropist Nathan Strauss. But the golden rays of the sun do not alone make the city sparkle. There are also diamonds. Belgium refugees started a diamond industry here which has today become the center of Israel's diamond cutting and polishing trade. The export of cut and polished diamonds from Netanya grosses over $120 million a year. Shades of the splendor of Solomon.

## CAESAREA

Now we are midway between Tel Aviv and Haifa. Nestled between the banana groves and the sand-skirted sea is the ancient city of CAESAREA. Built on the site of Strato's Tower, a small Phoenician anchorage dating to 250 B.C., Caesarea was the spectacular city of Herod the Great. Named in honor of Caesar Augustus (Luke 2:1), this great city was not only the site of Herod's summer palace but the capital of the Roman government in the Holy Land for nearly 500 years. Here, perhaps better than anywhere in Israel, is the splendor of Rome still evident.

Caesarea is a multiplicity of sites. Originally enclosed by a city wall nearly three miles long on the landward side, today only the ancient city is enclosed by a wall. As you enter Caesarea from the main road your first glimpse of the city sights may be a shocker for on your left you will see Israel's one and only golf course. Over 2,000 overseas members have joined the club, but nonmembers may play the course as well. Scarcely does the course end when the clear outline of a Roman hippodrome begins. Over 1,000 feet long and built to accommodate 20,000 spectators, this hippodrome was once the site of enthusiastic crowds watching spirited horse races. Today it is but a grassy rectangular depression in the ground. Just beyond the hippodrome you will notice, if you look closely, a number of 2nd and 3rd century statues of Roman emperors. A fitting introduction indeed to a marvelous ruin.

The two major sites of Caesarea are dead ahead. First, there is the port of Herod and the Crusader fortress of St. Louis. Enter from the side by the sea. Now, where do we begin? Let's climb the steps on the right to the top of the mound overlooking everything. As you face the Mediterranean you can actually see the lines of Herod's great harbor.

Herod the Great had a penchant for building. One look at Jerusalem, Samaria, Masada and other cities in the Holy Land will convince you of that. Since the Palestinian coast is smooth and quite regular, it did not provide a good harbor. Herod determined to build an artificial harbor at Caesarea and make it the chief seaport. The Jewish historian Josephus records that the king succeeded very well (cf. *Antiq.* XV.9.6; *Wars* I, 23).

The manmade harbor consisted of a sea wall or barrier 50 feet in length, 18 feet wide, built in water 30 fathoms deep. Peer into the green waters below and you will see the sea wall was a semicircle opening at the sea. Originally each end of the semicircular wall was dominated by a tower. Through this seaward opening ships would pass into the harbor to unload their cargo. One of the reasons why you can make out the lines of the harbor so clearly is that it is estimated that some of the stones used in the sea wall were 50 feet in length.

Before you leave the mound take a panoramic view and drink in the beauty of the fertile valley, eerie sand dunes, magnificent ruins and a sea of unmatched beauty. Breathe in that salt air and behold the pageant of God's goodness. Watch the breakers crash into the sea wall and billow up like puffy clouds. What a sight! Now let's retrace our steps to the city below.

With the sea behind you and the ruins before you, concentrate on the dusty debris that was once a sailors' paradise. And now, shut your eyes. Remember with me.

You are standing in the city which was once the home of the Roman procurators, including Pontius Pilate. Here Herod Agrippa died, being *"eaten of worms"* (Acts 12:19-23), because he denied God the glory due Him.

Caesarea was the home of Cornelius, the centurion to whom Peter preached and who believed and was baptized (Acts 10). Here too Peter came after his deliverance from prison (Acts 12:19).

This was the city of Philip the evangelist who preached and lived here (Acts 8:40) and had four daughters who prophesied here (Acts 21:8-9). Philip's house became a haven for the Apostle Paul on his final fateful journey to Jerusalem. It was here that Agabus prophesied that Paul should not go to Jerusalem (Acts 21:10-13). And after being taken into custody in the Holy City, the apostle was escorted to Caesarea by a group of soldiers (Acts 23:23-33). Open your eyes and take a peek for some say that you're looking at Paul's Caesarean prison. Near this prison is where Paul made three outstanding defenses of Christianity before Felix, the governor of Judaea (Acts 24:1-22), two years later before Festus, who succeeded Felix (Acts 25:1-12), and before King Agrippa (Acts 26).

Several years later the massacre of Jews in Caesarea precipitated the great revolt of A.D. 66. This revolt was crushed with the destruction of Jerusalem in A.D. 70. By the end of the first century A.D. the city had a healthy Christian community. In the third century A.D. the Christian scholar Origen founded the School of Caesarea here and the great church historian Eusebius was bishop of Caesarea from A.D. 313 to 340. The Crusader fortifications were built by Louis XIV of France in A.D. 1251.

Leaving our thoughts behind with the ruins of Caesarea, let's begin to make our way to the Crusader fortress gate. From the Roman ruins at the harbor and the Turkish remains in the city, including a minaret, we pass to the Crusader fortress. Originally the fortress was about one-tenth the size of the city itself and comprised some 30 acres. Today only a portion is restored, the main gate which consists of a Gothic gate tower with an adjacent vaulted street. As you walk along the walls of the city your eye will be caught by the granite columns laid horizontally throughout the walls. The Crusaders did this to keep the walls from being undermined from without. In the hall of the main gate can be seen the slit-windows for Crusader archers. Once we cross the bridge over the impressive moat encircling the city, we have left the urban area of ancient Caesarea. This mighty moat is today but a bed for the abundant vegetation growing from its unused walls.

Now let's travel to the south side and visit the magnificent Roman amphitheater. Here the splendor of ancient Rome is graphically dis-

The Crusader fortress on the sea is a favorite place for tourists to roam and view the Mediterranean Sea.

played. Don't go far after you've entered the gate. One of the most significant archaeological discoveries of Caesarea is just to your right. Notice the grayish-white stone just in front of the trees. If you're up on your Latin you'll know that the inscription on this stone bears the names of Emperor Tiberias and Pontius Pilate. Pilate, you'll recall, ruled Judaea as Roman procurator between A.D. 26 and 36 and was the government official who could find no fault with Jesus Christ (Matthew 27:24) but scourged Him nonetheless (John 19:1). This is the only known inscription bearing his name and supplements well the description of the man given by Josephus, the 1st century A.D. Jewish historian, and the New Testament. Although the real stone is now in the Israel National Museum, this exact duplicate is worthy of a picture.

Even more photogenic is something just to your left and behind you. Notice the gigantic white foot placed in the little fenced enclosure. This foot, which sports a remarkably good pedicure, is so large that it would put both Goliath and the Jolly Green Giant to shame. Most visitors to Caesarea get a "kick" out of being photographed in front of the foot.

Now let's make our way across the compound to the amphitheater itself. Reminiscent of a miniature Roman Coliseum, we enter at the back and near the top. This ancient structure has obviously been restored. The numbered seats give evidence of summer theatrical and musical performances during the annual Israel Festival. The first performance in the 100 yard long, sixty yard wide amphitheater in over 1,700 years came in the summer of 1961 when Pablo Casals played

here. But leaving the 20th century trappings behind, this site breathes of ancient tragedy. Almost certainly gladiators fought with lions here to entertain the Roman citizens. It was here that Vespasian was hailed as emperor by his soldiers. Here too Titus celebrated the birthday of Domitian his brother by pitting the beasts of the amphitheater against 2,500 Jews in a classic act of Roman butchery. If the stones and columns you see strewn between the amphitheater and the beach could talk you'd hear a tale of horror.

It is ironic, isn't it, that a city of so much culture and grace, built by a people of so much culture and grace, could also exhibit so much cruelty and debauchery in the name of entertainment. The ruins of this ancient Caesarean amphitheater stand as mute yet mighty testimony of man's innate unacceptability to God. Little had changed in ancient Rome from Noah's day when *"God saw that the wickedness of man was great in the earth, and that every imagination of the thoughts of his heart was only evil continually"* (Genesis 6:5). Little has changed today.

Before we leave Caesarea we have one more stop to make. North of the city are the remains of a Roman aqueduct. Running parallel to the shoreline atop the sand dunes, this extremely picturesque aqueduct was built to carry clear mountain water from the slopes of Mount Carmel some 12 miles north into Caesarea. Today the fine sands around the aqueduct form a favorite beach and picnic site for the Israelis and not a few tourists as well. An excellent picture can be taken from the south, with the Mediterranean to our left. This gives depth to this marvelous feat of engineering.

**Roman aqueduct at Caesarea.**

**Ruins from the times of Herod the Great and Augustus Caesar lie along the shores of the Great Sea.**

# HAIFA—MOUNT CARMEL

We're on the road again heading north toward Mount Carmel. If we take the shoreline branch of the main road about eight miles north of Caesarea we'll pass by the ruins of DOR, in antiquity the chief city of this plain. The king of Dor was among the 31 kings conquered by Joshua (Joshua 11:2, 8; 12:7, 23). It was again captured from the Philistines by David. Solomon awarded the city to Ben-Abinadab, his son-in-law (I Kings 4:7, 11), to be one of the 12 administrative districts organized under Solomon's empire. In antiquity Dor was a center for producing Tyrian purple or "royal purple," a purplish red dye extracted from mollusks which abounded along the Mediterranean coast. Only the rich, the nobility or the Emperor could afford the expense of this purple dye.

North of Dor, and still nine miles south of Haifa, is the ancient Phoenician port of ATLIT. Here are the impressive remains of the Crusader fortress Chateau de Pelerin, the Castle of the Pilgrims. Built in 1217-18 by the Templars it was destroyed by the Baybars in 1291. Most impressive is the high wall of the citadel near the beach. Unfortunately the castle, fort, and cathedral of Atlit have been dismantled over the years to build wall breakwaters and basements throughout the Holy Land.

As we approach HAIFA you can see why the city has been compared to San Francisco and Naples. It is precariously perched on a hill overlooking a sleepy bay. This third largest city in modern Israel is both beautiful and unique. Its orientation is definitely vertical rather than horizontal. Like a club sandwich, Haifa climbs Mount Carmel on three levels. The lowest level is the port area, permeated with the sights, sounds and smells of the sea. The central level is called Hadar Ha Carmel or Hadar for short. This is Haifa's business district. The highest level is the residential district on the mountain's peak.

The origin of Haifa is uncertain. The Crusaders called the site Caife or Cayphe and sometimes even Caiphas. This has led to speculation that the High Priest of Jerusalem in the days of Jesus may have been the originator of the city. Others think the word Haifa may be a contracted form of the Hebrew words "Hof Yafeh" meaning beautiful coast.

Inhabited by ancient Phoenicians, as well as the Greeks and Jews, Haifa was destroyed by the Muslims in the seventh century, conquered by the Crusaders in 1100 and destroyed again in 1761. It wasn't until the 20th century that the city really began to grow. The British began a harbor here in 1929 and turned Haifa into the trading and commercial center of Israel. Custom officials have become callous to the sight of immigrant Jews falling on Haifa's docks and kissing the ground of their newfound Promised Land. More than a million and a half immigrants have disembarked ship here and embarked on a new life in Israel.

*Level one.* The port level of Haifa is pandemonium. As you pass by the bazaar and oriental shops selling shish kebab and pitta you may assume that this section of the city is a complete waste of time, but don't be fooled. Near the docks piled high with crates of oranges, machines, and the like is the Maritime Museum. Here on display are models of ancient Phoenician and Jewish sailing vessels, the kind built by King Hiram of Tyre and King Solomon of Jerusalem. They are fascinating. Also nearby are the huge grain elevators of Haifa, the Dagon Grain Silo and Archaeological Museum which exhibit ancient and modern methods of storing grain. Some samples of grain in the museum are 4,000 years old.

But enough of this nautical nostalgia. Let's climb the Carmel. *Level two.* To get to the Hadar you must negotiate a zillion hairpin turns, a constant stream of pedestrians crossing in front of you, and an army of road-hog truck drivers who delight in taking full advantage of the fact that while you are coming up they are coming down. To avoid this harrowing experience you may take the Carmelit, Israel's only subway, from sea level to 1,000 feet at the top, but it's not nearly as much fun. The Hadar is both business and residential. Here German immigrants settled and built a predictably clean and functional town. But two sites make this area of more than passing interest to us.

To get to the first we turn off Herzl Street, the main thoroughfare, onto Balfour and there is the entrance to Israel's answer to M.I.T., the Israel Institute of Technology or the Technion. This institution enrolls 8,500 students in its departments of aeronautical and agricultural engineering, civil and electrical engineering, mechanical and nuclear engineering and the like. The technology which went into building Solomon's Temple, Hezekiah's tunnel, and Nehemiah's wall lives on in Israel.

The second site is easily seen from the street above it. One of the most impressive structures in the Holy Land, the Baha'i Temple with the Baha'i Shrine and Gardens, mark the world center of the Baha'i religion. Buried in the golden domed temple is Mirza Ali Mohammed, the forerunner of the Baha'i faith. The gardens are as immaculate as they are beautiful. And since this is the world center of the eclectic religion, the Corinthian-styled archives museum houses the historical records of the three million Baha'is in the world. All of this is located on the seaside of Mount Carmel in a thick forest of trees.

And now, to the top. *Level three.* Mount Carmel is roughly triangular in shape. The Carmel range is an outcropping of limestone mountains extending southeasterly some dozen miles inland and averaging 1,500 feet in elevation. The range separates the Plain of Sharon from the Plain of Esdraelon and formed the four corner boundary between the tribes of Asher, Zebulun, Issachar, and Manasseh. Carmel, which means "Vineyard of the Lord," has always been a biblical symbol of beauty and majesty (cf. II Chronicles 26:10; Song of Solomon 7:5; Isaiah 35:2; Jeremiah 46:18; 50:19). Israel's largest national park, 25,000 acres of cypress, eucalyptus, and pine trees, is located here.

Mount Carmel always possessed a sort of religious sanctity. Here stood an ancient altar unto Jehovah (I Kings 18:30). It was on this mountain that the prophet Elijah chose to engage in a contest with the prophets of Baal (I Kings 18:19-39) when he thundered, *"How long halt ye between two opinions? If the LORD be God, follow him: but if Baal, then follow him"* (I Kings 18:21).

The traditional site of this confrontation is now a Carmelite Monastery on the lower Carmel road. When the 450 prophets of Baal were bested by the prophet of God they were taken to the foot of the mountain, to the brook Kishon, and slain (I Kings 18:40). This small, reed-lined stream is quite visible and quite unimpressive, but one day millennia ago it received the blood of pagan prophets who mocked God and His servant.

## ACRE

The road north to ACRE clingingly curves around the bay. About a mile past the Na'aman Bridge is a traffic circle. From this the road to the right approaches the New Town of Acre; we'll take the road to the left, to the Old Town.

Acre, also spelled Acco, Akko, and Accho, is a 4,000 year old Canaanite and Phoenician seaport city with a rather troubled past. Conquered by the Egyptians Thutmose III, Seti I and Ramses II,

The medieval Khan or Caravanserai at Acre is surrounded by homes and shops of varying styles and ages, some dating back to the Crusades. (Left)

The picturesque harbor at Acre.

Fishing on the blue Mediterranean at Acre.

Acre was the chief city of the territory of Asher, although never taken by this tribe (Joshua 19:24-31; Judges 1:31). Incorporated into Israel during the reigns of David and Solomon, it was returned to the Phoenicians as payment to King Hiram for men and materials to build Jerusalem (I Kings 9:11-13; II Chronicles 8:1-2).

After the conquest of Tyre by Alexander the Great, Acre submitted to this world conqueror and its name was changed to Ptolemais. Emperor Claudius (A.D. 52-74) made it a Roman colony. The Crusaders arrived in 1104 making Acre the principle port of the Holy Land. Saladin claimed the city in 1187 but Richard the Lion-Hearted reoccupied four years later. In 1799 Napoleon besieged the city unsuccessfully and this decisive defeat dashed his hopes for an Eastern Empire. Jezzar Pasha, whose cruelty earned him the nickname "the Butcher," strengthened the city's fortifications and built Acre's mosque and luxurious steam baths.

A picturesque city in which tiny minarets are set against a blue Mediterranean sky, we enter Acre along the sea wall. Just opposite the wall is the citadel. The double walls, exceptionally deep moat, and cold feeling that comes over you, make you instinctively know you are in a prison. It became the nation's central prison during the British mandate. After World War II the Citadel held hundreds of Jewish political prisoners. Today you can visit the English hanging-room where many of the Israeli underground were put to death. If you descend to the dungeon make sure you see the names of the Jewish freedom fighters inscribed on the walls. Now named Museum Hagourah, this infamous Citadel is not a prison anymore but a mental institution. What a twist of irony.

Let's continue our way around the sea wall past the lighthouse and enter the main street of the old city. It's like taking a walk back in time. Immediately you see the Khan. This quadrangle and the maze of galleries which lead from it were constructed by the Crusaders. The amazing thing is that they are still inhabited today. Acre is the only "live" Crusader town in the Holy Land. Originally Crusader knights and their horses were housed in the stalls branching from the courtyard. For centuries the rooms of the Khan have been used as overnight quarters for weary travelers. The Israeli government would like to restore this area and accommodate 20th century travelers. In the courtyard, where caravans once stopped and bartering took place, the modern traveler can still browse and barter in shops that once housed Crusader horses and camels.

If you continue through the square on which the Khan is located you come to the Mosque of El Jezzar. Claimed by some to be the largest and most decorative mosque in Israel, it was built in 1781 and named in honor of Jezzar Pasha its builder. The courtyard is surrounded on three sides by a massive wall crowned by more than 40 white domes and gracefully lined with palm trees. Jezzar's tomb, inside the large-domed mosque with a single minaret, is gracefully decorated with oriental carpets and lavishly ornamented with red, white, and black marble. The interior is truly beautiful, after the fashion of the great mosques of Istanbul.

For the Christian, Acre is more than just a splendid site preserving medieval character. As the most important seaport city throughout the centuries it was a natural port of call in the early church. Luke records, "And when we had finished our course from Tyre, we came to Ptolemais, and saluted the brethren, and abode with them one day" (Acts 21:7). A seaport, a stopover, a stronghold of the Christian faith. That's the story of Acre.

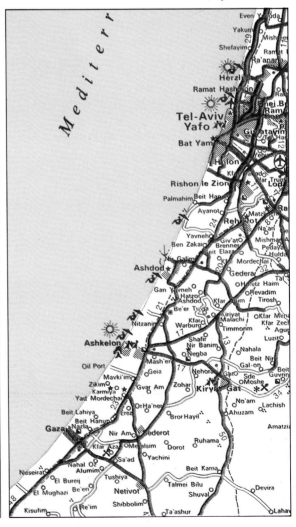

## The Road South
# LOD (LYDDA)

Since many who travel to the Holy Land fly there, and since Israel's largest airport is located here, we cannot forget to mention LOD. Chiefly a Jewish town, the history of Lod leads us into obscurity. Mentioned in Egyptian hieroglyphics 3,500 years ago, Lod was a fortified town in Joshua's day and was built by Shamed, a Benjamite (I Chronicles 8:1, 12; Nehemiah 11:13-35). It was apparently resettled after the Babylonian captivity (Ezra 2:1, 33; Nehemiah 7:6, 37). The Greeks changed the name to Lydda and thus when Peter was used of God to heal Aeneas, who had been bedridden with the palsy for eight years, it is said that the apostle *"came down also to the saints which dwelt at Lydda"* (Acts 9:32-35). During the first Jewish revolt (A.D. 66-70) the city was demolished by the Roman armies on their way to Jerusalem. Later it became a center for Jewish scholarship and the permanent residence of the famed Rabbi Akiva and his academy.

But don't go to Lod looking for some commemoration of Peter or the healing of Aeneas. You won't find any. What you will find is the Saint George Church. Believed to be a native son of Lod, this patron saint of England became a soldier in the Roman army and rebelled against the anti-Christian edicts of the Emperor Diocletian. George was martyred by the Romans and buried here in A.D. 303. The church marks the site.

# ASHDOD

The journey south through the Coastal Plain must most certainly include the cities of the Philistines, at least the three coastal cities. First Samuel repeatedly tells us of the five lords of the Philistines and their pentapolis or five cities. While Ekron and Gath are inland cities and less important (their exact locations are somewhat in dispute), the coastal cities of Ashdod, Ashkelon, and Gaza are very noteworthy.

Destined to be Israel's largest sea gateway, ASHDOD is growing furiously. Highrise condominiums, hotels, apartment buildings, as well as factories and industrial complexes, are springing up almost daily. Adjacent to the city of 70,000 inhabitants, the newer deep-sea harbor makes Ashdod Israel's port of the future. The dust and flying dirt of the Holy Land usually means an archaeological dig nearby. In Ashdod it means new construction.

Ashdod was an ancient Hyksos town which later became a Philistine stronghold. The name itself in Hebrew means "fortress." Little remains today of the biblical city, although the tell or ancient ruins is located three miles south of the mouth of the Lachish River on the Via Maris, a major north-south highway of antiquity. Some excavations finally have begun at the site.

It was here that the Anakim lived, those giants of Joshua's day, and prevented Israel from conquering Gaza, Gath, or Ashdod (Joshua 11:22). Although allotted to Judah, it was not taken (Joshua 13:1-3; 15:46-47). Perhaps Ashdod's greatest claim to fame was that it was the center of the worship of Dagon, half fish and half man. What a thrilling story is recorded in I Samuel 5 when the Philistines captured the ark of the covenant and brought it to Ashdod unto the house of Dagon. So powerful was the presence of Jehovah that every morning the people of Ashdod found Dagon flat on his face before the ark.

The paganism of this city was legend. Nehemiah's indignation was aroused when the Jews intermarried with the Ashdodites (Nehemiah 13:23-24). Both Amos (Amos 1:8) and Zephaniah (Zephaniah 2:4) prophesied against the city. With the coming of the Greeks the city's name was changed to Azotus and in the irony of biblical history this pagan city became the launching pad for a great preaching ministry.

After Philip encountered the Ethiopian eunuch and the black court official of Candace believed and was baptized, Philip took an unexpected journey to Azotus. Acts 8:40 records, *"But Philip was found at Azotus: and passing through he preached in all the cities, till he came to Caesarea."*

# ASHKELON

Halfway between Ashdod and Gaza is the lovely city of ASHKELON. Its history is one of opulence and splendor. It has always stood on the Via Maris and is the only one of the five cities of the Philistine pentapolis to have its own harbor.

One of the oldest known Canaanite cities in the world, as a Philistine city it was rich and beautiful. Still the city inhabitants had a lust for life that brought them to unceasing attempts to gain or hold their freedom. The Tell el'Amarna Letters (14th century B.C.) record Ashkelon to be a rich and rebellious city. Egyptian Pharaoh Ramses II (c. 1280 B.C.), in a bas-relief carved picture at his temple in Karnak in upper Egypt, shows Egyptian troops subjugating the bearded Ashkelon defenders. About the year 1225 B.C. the Egyptian Pharaoh Merneptah made this notation on a stele, a carved pillar: "Carried off is

**A view of modern Ashkelon.**

Ashkelon; seized upon is Gezer . . . Israel is laid waste, his seed is not."

The king of Ashkelon was deported for rebellion against Sennacherib the Assyrian king in 701 B.C. Later the Babylonians conquered the city and deported Ashkelon's king. The Romans gave the city political independence and spruced up the place with many new and beautiful buildings. It is believed that Herod the Great was born here. During the Crusades Ashkelon became an important fortress until it was destroyed in 1270 by Sultan Baybars. This rich and beautiful city thereupon lay dormant until 1953.

Many ruins from this illustrious history have survived. Let's make our way to the Ashkelon Antiquities Park. This is a favorite spot for Jewish picnickers, and why not; it is simply beautiful, one of the most restful spots in the troubled Mid-

dle East. In fact, why don't we join them? Spread a blanket over the grass and lean against a 2,000-year-old Roman column and just relax awhile. From this vantage point look around you and see the wonders of this unique combination of past and present. In the center of the park lie the foundations of several buildings and the remains of an ancient wall protruding from the sand. Three statues of the Goddess of Victory highlight these remains. If you dare brave the Palestinian sun and the aerial hazards of the ubiquitous frisbees, you may take a stroll half a mile away to the beach to see the Philistine Harbor, evidenced by granite pillars and rubble strewn across the mound overlooking the sea.

Old Ashkelon, mentioned by Joshua (Joshua 13:3) and taken by the tribe of Judah (Judges 1:18) was rich and distinguished. New Ashkelon,

30

with its tailored lawns and gardens, is rich and distinguished. Old Ashkelon, where Samson slew 30 men (Judges 14:19) and where the ark was returned with a trespass offering (I Samuel 6:17), was the scene of frequently interrupted tranquility. New Ashkelon, where Israelis from all over the country flock to as a summer resort or a weekend getaway, is the scene of frequently interrupted tranquility. Old Ashkelon, where King David asked that Saul's death not be published (II Samuel 1:20) because of the Philistine inhabitants and a city frequently chastised by Jehovah's prophets (Jeremiah 25:20; 47:6-7; Amos 1:8; Zephaniah 2:4, 7), was an irreligious center of man-oriented activity. Ashkelon is just like the State of Israel as a whole, increasingly restful but increasingly irreligious.

## GAZA

Our southernmost stop in the line of cities which dot Israel's coastal plain is GAZA. On the way a good stop is YAD MORDECHAI, about seven miles south of Ashkelon. This kibbutz was established in 1943 and named in honor of Mordechai Anilevits, the leader of the Warsaw Ghetto revolt against the Nazis during World War II. The town is known for its strong defense against the Egyptian armored divisions encroaching on it in 1948. There is an extremely lifelike battlefield reconstructed there with tanks and men realistically depicting the 1948 battle.

From here we are only two miles from the Gaza Strip border. A word of warning. The Gaza Strip is an Israeli-occupied Arab territory in which 20th century tensions run high. It is unlikely we will be permitted to enter the strip due to "military reasons." Still Gaza is probably the oldest and most important of the five Philistine cities of antiquity. A prominent city in Canaanite times (Genesis 10:19), it lies at the southern tip of the Fertile Crescent. The soil in the region is very productive and abounds in olive orchards. Gaza is the first oasis of any importance after crossing the sandy desert wastes from Suez. As Beersheba is the gateway to the Negev, so Gaza is the gateway to Egypt.

With a somewhat idyllic setting in a hostile environment, you would expect Gaza to be a peaceful island in a belligerent sea. Just the opposite is true. Gaza has seen more than its share of bloodshed. The exploits of Samson make this abundantly clear. To escape being killed by the Philistines God's strongman carried the huge gates of Gaza all the way to Hebron, some 40 miles away (Judges 16:1-3). Still later it was to Gaza that Samson was brought after his seduction by Delilah. Here the Philistines gouged out his eyes and forced him to grind in the prison house (Judges 16:21). Here Samson pulled down the pillars of the house of Dagon and killed more than 3,000 in the process (Judges 16:23-30). It was here that Alexander the Great captured the portal to Egypt in 332 B.C., killing all of Gaza's men and selling the women and children into slavery. Here was the scene of many Christian martyrdoms. Here the British lost 10,000 men in capturing the city from the Turks. And here, in 1967, the Israeli forces saw much bloodshed before they gained control of the city. If we do not get to visit Gaza, we may be better off.

The 441,300 inhabitants of the Gaza Strip occupy an area 25 miles long and 3.6 miles wide. But since it is administered by a military government don't be surprised if our journey on the coastal road south stops at Ashkelon. From Acre to Ashkelon the journey in the Holy Land is inspirational, informative, and intriguing. But above and below the coastal plain the journey becomes dangerous and its only visitors are Israeli soldiers on patrol.

# CHAPTER 4

# Land of the Nations

◆

## UPPER AND LOWER GALILEE

*"And Jesus went about all Galilee, teaching in their synagogues, and preaching the gospel of the kingdom, and healing all manner of sickness and all manner of disease among the people"* (Matthew 4:23).

From the Hebrew word meaning "ring" or "circle," Galilee is used as a designation for a district or region. It is the northernmost region of the Holy Land. The boundaries of this region are not exact nor are they easily defined. In general, Galilee extends from the southern ridges of the Lebanon and Anti-Lebanon Mountains southward through the Esdraelon Valley to the edge of the hill country in central Palestine. The east-west boundaries of Galilee are usually considered to be the Mediterranean Sea on the west and the Sea of Galilee on the east. Roughly then, Galilee is a rectangle more than 50 miles north to south and nearly 30 miles east to west.

Galilee is essentially an upland area bordered on all sides but the north by valleys and plains. The land is naturally divided into two rather well distinguished "steps." Upper Galilee to the north is almost double the altitude of Lower Galilee to the south. Accordingly, the vegetation and climate are somewhat different between the two. Volcanic activity and geological faulting have thrown Upper Galilee into sharper relief than Lower Galilee. The northern "step" is a craggy highrise compared to the southern "step" which is more gently rolling countryside.

Galilee did not come into its own until New Testament times. In fact, it is only mentioned six times in the Old Testament. For the Christian, Galilee's importance arises from being the boyhood home of Jesus. He grew up in these lower hills and during the years of His earthly ministry He made several preaching tours throughout Galilee (Matthew 4:23-25; 9:35—10:15; 11:1-6; etc.). All but one of His disciples were Galileans. It was in Galilee that our Lord prophetically announced His death, burial and resurrection (Matthew 17:22-23) and from these hills He launched His journey to the hill of Calvary (Matthew 19:1). Galilee was the rendezvous point for Jesus and His disciples after His resurrection and here He mandated to the disciples, including each of us, the Great Commission (Matthew 28: 16-20).

Separated from Judaea by Samaria and its variant religious beliefs, and completely surrounded by non-Jewish and frequently hostile populations, it is little wonder that the strict rabbis of Jerusalem distrusted the religious purity of the Galileans. Even Isaiah refers to them as *"Galilee of the nations"* indicating their distant position from the heart of the Jewish faith. Rough people who even more doggedly resisted

the Romans than did the Judaeans, the Galileans were considered uneducated, uncouth and unwieldy. Hence, Nathanael questioned whether any good thing could come out of Nazareth, one of the chief cities of Galilee (John 1:46). Yet, ironically, after the fall of Jerusalem in A.D. 70, it was to Galilee that the rabbinic scholars and pietists flocked in an attempt to maintain the Jewish religion.

Galilee, upper and lower, along with the land around the sea of the same name, is lush and green most of the year. It is a delight, a pageant of beauty, a tribute to God's love for this Holy Land. It is Galilee; the very name strikes a stronger beat in the breast.

## Upper Galilee
## CAESAREA PHILIPPI/BANIAS

The topography of northern Galilee is absolutely dominated by Mount Hermon. This majestic, snow-capped natural wonder rises 9,232 feet above sea level. A sight of breathtaking beauty, its snowy crest is sometimes visible from as far away as Tel Aviv or the lower Jordan Valley. At the base of this mighty mountain is the source of the Jordan River. It is here, at BANIAS, we begin our journey southward through Galilee.

Banias, sometimes spelled Baniyas, is the Arab alteration of the Greek name for this site. The Greeks called it Panias after Pan, the god of forests and flocks. Here is the main of four source streams which form the Jordan.

As we approach the headwaters area I'm sure you'll be impressed with two things. First is the beauty of the spot. It is one of the most gorgeous, most luscious areas of the Middle East. Second, especially if it's summer when you visit, you'll be impressed with the coolness of the spot. In the heat of the summer sun, the thick foliage of the abundant trees provides a pleasantly relaxing atmosphere for rest and refreshment. In fact, it was to this very spot, after many days of strenuous teaching, that Jesus brought His disciples to rest and pray (Luke 9:18).

On an adjacent hill to this Edenic-like paradise, Herod the Great built a temple to the god Pan in 20 B.C. After the death of Herod his son Philip was awarded this region to rule as a tetrarch or provincial governor. At this site Philip erected a shrine to Caesar Augustus and rebuilt a city giving it the combination of Caesar's name and his own. It was called CAESAREA PHILIPPI to distinguish it from Caesarea on the coast. Its association with paganism was well known.

As we approach the headwaters area along a winding path we see before us a gigantic cliff of 100 feet high. This cliff is a part of a steep ridge. At the base of the cliff you will hear and then see the waters gushing forth from a cave. Bubbling over the rock debris at the entrance to the cave, the water soon becomes a peaceful and broad stream. If you really want to be refreshed, don't use the little bridge over the stream to get to the cave; take your shoes off and stone-hop the stream.

As intriguing as these headwaters of the Jordan are, we dare not miss a close inspection of the three niches carved in the face of the cliff just to the right of the cave. The niches resemble tiny apses cut in the rock in an ascending pattern. The one above the cave is the most perfect and presumably held a statue at one time, probably of Pan. That this scenic arena was a pagan worship center in ancient Greece and Rome makes it even more significant that it was here, while resting and praying, that Jesus asked His disciples, *"Whom do men say that I the Son of man am?"* In the place of pagan duties and in full certainty of his answer, Peter gloriously confessed, *"Thou art the Christ, the Son of the living God"* (Matthew 16:13-16; Mark 8:27-30; Luke 9:18-21). No statue or niches for Peter. He was in the presence of the Living God.

## DAN

Four miles west of Banias is a second source stream of the Jordan. Forming a valley of luxuriant vegetation, these copious waters flow from the western base of a volcanic cone known as Tell Kedi. This mound is better known to Jews and Christians alike as DAN (Judges 18:29), the familiar Old Testament city which marked the northern limit of the Promised Land. Who has never heard the expression, *"From Dan to Beersheba"* (Judges 20:1; I Samuel 3:20; etc.)?

First mentioned in Scripture as the place to which Abraham pursued Chedorlaomer and his armies in order to rescue Lot (Genesis 14:13-16), the city was originally a Phoenician town named Laish (Judges 18:27-29), also called Leshem (Joshua 19:47). It appears that the Danites, unsatisfied with their allotted territory in Judaea (Joshua 19:40-47), decided to occupy this unclaimed area far to the north. The Danites found it much as it is today, *" . . . very good . . . a large land . . . a place where there is no want of any thing that is in the earth"* (Judges 18:9-10).

Because of its proximity to the Lebanese border it is sometimes impossible to visit Dan. Whenever Middle East tensions rise, this northern-

Mount Hermon, the snow-capped natural wonder which dominates the topography of northern Galilee, rises 9,232 feet above sea level.

The waterfalls near Banias are on the Hermon River, one of the sources of the Jordan.

most archaeological dig is sometimes abandoned, the diggers scurrying to safer territory. Every student of history will see some parallels to this in the history of the site. Dan was subdued by Benhadad, king of Syria (I Kings 15:20; II Chronicles 16:4), regained by Jeroboam (II Kings 14:25), and conquered again by the Assyrian king Tiglath-pileser, the inhabitants being carried off captives (II Kings 15:29). Being a border town does have its trying moments.

As we view the plentiful Jordan source stream, the lush vegetation and the beauty of the site itself, there is little reason to wonder why King Jeroboam I chose this spot, the northern extremity of his realm (I Kings 12:29; II Kings 10:29), to es-

tablish an unauthorized center of worship. Placing a golden calf here, and another in Bethel, the king of the ten northern tribes unwisely proclaimed to Israel, *"Behold thy gods, O Israel, which brought thee out of the land of Egypt"* (I Kings 12:26-33). As a consequence he is referred to in the Old Testament as *"Jeroboam, the son of Nebat, who made Israel to sin"* (I Kings 22:52; II Kings 3:3; 10:29; etc.).

Thus, both Banias and Dan, two of the four sources of the Jordan, were gorgeous gardens of dense vegetation and sparkling water. And both of them were the sites of pagan religious shrines. Do you begin to see why pious Judaeans looked upon the Galileans as spiritually degenerate (cf. John 1:46)?

## HAZOR

Our journey south to HAZOR will take us through the modern town of KIRYAT SHMONA ("city of eight"). Established only 20 years ago, this settlement is named in honor of eight valiant Jews who withstood an Arab attack at Tel Hai just to the north. The settlement is frequently in the news today for when the PLO shelling of northern Galilee begins Kiryat Shmona is usually first to receive the menacing missiles.

From here the road to Hazor skirts the western edge of the Hula Valley. Until 1950 there was a lake here called Lake Hula. It was fed by the Jordan River, as are the Sea of Galilee and the Dead Sea. A vast marshland teeming with wildlife, water buffalo, wild boar, exotic birds and the like, the lake was also a mosquito-infested swamp. Between 1950 and 1951 the marshland was drained, leaving thousands of acres of very fertile soil, which the modern Israelis turned into the patchwork of farmland you see on your left.

At the southeastern end of Hula Valley the highway runs just left of a very huge mound of dirt. This is not a natural mound but a tell. "Tell" (*Tel* in Hebrew) is Arabic for an artificial mound where successive levels of occupation, much like the layers of a cake, are evidenced. It's like one mud pie piled on another mud pie, piled on another, etc. The highway winds around the tell very close to its base.

On this 25 acre rectangular plateau archaeologists have identified 21 levels of occupation. What remains at the site, left by Professor Yigal Yadin and his 1955-58 archaeological team, is interesting and very photogenic, especially the Hazor column rows, but if you want to see any artifacts or finds from Hazor you'll have to go to the museum of Kibbutz Ayelet Hashahar, near the base of the mound. The view of the Hula Valley, however, makes the climb to the top of Hazor worthwhile, even if you aren't an archaeology buff.

Hazor has been inhabited for 4,500 years and was once the largest city in Israel, with a population of over 40,000. Its strategic location, in a position to command the traffic moving through the Hula Valley, contributed to its importance and made it, in Joshua's words, *"the head of all those kingdoms"* (Joshua 11:10). Joshua knew he had to capture Jabin, king of Hazor, and his stronghold if his northern campaign to establish Israel in the land was to be successful. He took the city and burned it to the ground (Joshua 11:1-14). The charred remains discovered by archaeologists in the area north of the tell witness to this fact. Later a different king of Hazor named Jabin, who possessed an army having 900 iron chariots, held dominion over Israel for 20 years. At the urging of Deborah, Barak and the armies of Israel defeated Sisera and the armies of Hazor in the Esdraelon Valley. We can read this amazing story in Judges 4.

Although Solomon rebuilt Hazor as his own chariot city, along with Megiddo, Gezer and others (I Kings 9:15), and although, like Megiddo, Hazor has a phenomenal water tunnel measuring 82 feet long, 13 feet high and 13 feet wide, dating back to the days of King Ahab (732 B.C.), we'll wait until we get to Megiddo to go through such a tunnel. Therefore, let's drink in some archaeological history, some fresh Galilean air, and a final spectacular view of the fertile Hula Valley, and move on to the south to Safed.

## SAFED

At an elevation of 2,790 feet, SAFED is Israel's highest town, perched atop the Mount Jermak range, Israel's highest mountain range (3,962 feet). As you approach the mountain range from any direction, you will be able to identify Safed; it will be that city up, way up.

A Jewish stronghold in the war against the Romans, Safed slept until the 16th century. When the Sephardic (Spanish) Jews fled the Spanish Inquisition, these persecuted people came to the Holy Land and established a learning center for Jewish intellectuals. They were known as Cabalists, after their complex and intricate system of applying a mystical interpretation to every sentence, word, and letter of the Old Testament. Their influence can still be felt if you choose to visit one of the six synagogues found on the tiny street sloping left off the main street just beyond the Hotel Herzlia. Don't let the labyrinth of streets and alleys deter you from locating one or more of the synagogues. Their exterior may be plain, but their interior is dazzling and displays intricate design.

Not interested in synagogues or Cabalists? Try this reason for making the effort to climb the heights of Safed. Here you will find a touch of medieval living in the 20th century. The charm of the old windy cobblestone streets, the ancient

The recently excavated Tell of Dan is close to the Lebanon border and sometimes unavailable to tourists.

buildings, the chant of prayers, and the Crusader castle situated on the crown of the city is sure to earn a well-deserved gasp of breath. The Crusader castle, built in the 12th century A.D., is situated on the site of the 1st century Galilean citadel. As if this isn't enough to earn Safed the "charm city" of Israel nomination, it has now become the center of an artists' colony. Just after you pass under a stone bridge on main street, walk down the street to the right that takes you to the canvas cabala. Here is the Israeli Montmartre, home of sculptors, ceramicists and painters. It is old world charm in an ancient/modern country.

Frankly, most Christians prefer simply to look up at Safed rather than drive up to it. With all its Cabalistic history, with all its medieval charm, still Safed is an all-Jewish city and is not even mentioned in the Bible. However, when Jesus was concluding His beatitudes, delivered from the Mount of Beatitudes nearby, He said to His followers, *"Ye are the light of the world. A city that is set on a hill cannot be hid"* (Matthew 5:14). This He said that the light of our Christian faith might shine before a watching world and *"that they may see your good works, and glorify your Father which is in heaven"* (Matthew 5:16). Most people believe that it was the ancient site of Safed which Jesus used as an illustration of this truth. So if you don't enjoy the superb view of Galilee from Safed, enjoy the superb view of Safed from Galilee.

*Lower Galilee*

## CANA

Nestled on the side of a lower Galilean mountain ridge is the city of CANA. As you approach the town you are immediately dazzled by the brightness of the white buildings against the darker hillside. Cana is perhaps the most picturesque village in Galilee.

Although there is still some debate as to whether or not this is the Cana of the New Testament, nonetheless this village tucked in the folds of the hills four miles north of Nazareth is commemorated as that city.

As we enter this sleepy village from the north we must be mindful that it was on this road, the road from Nazareth to Tiberias and Capernaum, that a bereaved nobleman met his servants with the most exciting news of his life. The nobleman had heard that Jesus was in Galilee and left a gravely ill son in Capernaum to seek out Jesus, hoping the Master would come to Capernaum and heal him. Instead Jesus spoke the miracle of healing and sent the nobleman on his way back to Capernaum. Meeting him on this road, the servants announced that the man's son was alive, the deadly fever leaving him the same hour Jesus spoke in Cana (John 4:46-54).

On the north side of town we pass a small chapel honoring Nathanael. The Saint Nathanael Church of the Franciscans is built on the site of the traditional birthplace of Nathanael, one of Jesus' disciples (John 21:2). Near this church is the red-domed Catholic Franciscan Church built over the remains of what was believed to be the house where Jesus' first miracle occurred. Here Jesus attended a wedding feast and changed the water into wine (John 2:1-11). Make sure you see the stone waterpots on display at the church. They are similar to those used in Jesus' day. Today the village well bubbles from the same source as that 1st century well at which Jesus commanded, *"Draw out now"* (John 2:8) and the water miraculously became wine.

## NAZARETH

So unimportant and unimpressive was the boyhood home of Jesus, clinging to the side of the lower Galilee hills like the tiered strings of tinsel on a Christmas tree, that the city is scarcely mentioned in historical works or even recorded on ancient maps. NAZARETH's name never graces the pages of the Old Testament. The city's importance is inextricably linked to the life of Jesus Christ.

Anyone with average imagination can envision how in Nazareth *"Jesus increased in wisdom and stature, and in favour with God and man"* (Luke 2:51-52). On these surrounding hills the boy Jesus must have romped and played with His friends. From the peaks above the town He could look southward and see the trade caravans on their way to Egypt. He would observe *"the lilies of the field,"* watch the new mown grass wither in the hot August sun, and follow the rhythm of the men as they sowed or winnowed grain. Do you recall Him mentioning these things in His ministry? *"One shall be taken, and the other left"* (Matthew 24:41) was probably furnished by memories of the Nazarene ladies grinding meal at the circular stone mill.

A short walk from Nazareth northwest would bring Jesus to the neighboring town of SEPPHORIS (Diocasarea), the Roman administrative center of Galilee. Here He could mingle with the rich and the poor, the proud and the humble, the pious and the profane. Though a tiny hamlet midway between the Mediterranean and the Sea of Galilee, perched above the broad valley below, nevertheless Nazareth and environs would provide the developing young Nazarene with a myriad of sights and sounds from which later He would draw anecdotes and parables in His earthly ministry.

The hairpin turns on the road approaching Nazareth provide a delightful opportunity to view the city from a variety of interesting angles. Today Nazareth is really two cities rather than two levels of the same city. The lower city, the biblical town in which Jesus grew up, is the largest Arab community in Israel, apart from the Arab quarters of Jerusalem. Here some 40,000 Arabs live, about half of them Christian. With over 40 convents, monasteries, orphanages, churches, and private schools located there, Nazareth is the undisputed headquarters of the Christian mission movement in Israel. In 1957 the Upper Nazareth suburb of Kiryat Natsrat was established by Jewish immigrants from Eastern Europe. A settlement of about 30,000, the New City is almost exclusively Jewish.

Our interest is in the Old City. It is a maze of interesting Christian sites, mostly housed in white buildings under brown/orange roofs.

Wander down any one of the narrow, crowded, cobblestone streets of Old Nazareth and absorb some local Arab color.

Without question the most important church in Nazareth is the Church of the Annunciation. You can't miss it. The large polygonal tower, which slopes at a steep pitch upward, rises impressively above a buff-white masonry church. The tower strikingly resembles an Apollo space vehicle of a decade ago, perched atop a stubby Saturn rocket. The best angle for a picture of this basilica is from the road above the church.

Located on Casa Nova Street, the Latin Church of the Annunciation stands on the spot where, according to tradition, the angel Gabriel appeared to the Virgin Mary and announced that she had been chosen by God to bear the Christ child (Luke 1:26). Completed in the 1960s the church was built on the site of an earlier Franciscan church erected in 1730, which in turn was built over a Crusader church. At one end of the church you will see a grotto which is held as the sacred site where the angel appeared unto Mary. The local guide will explain that the two granite pillars in the cave, the column of Gabriel and the column of Mary, mark the spots where the angel and the virgin stood at the annunciation.

At the opposite end of the Latin church and adjacent to the Franciscan Convent between the two, is the Church of St. Joseph. The two caves under this church are said to have housed the carpenter's shop and the storage room of Joseph. Although you will see no carpenter's tools here now, it is delightful that in the area nearby your nose will be treated to the smell of woodshavings and sawdust from the modern carpenter's workbench as he fashions wooden ploughs and tools for the Arab farmers who work the neighboring fields.

Whatever you do, don't leave the area until you have absorbed some local Arab color. Wander down any one of the narrow, crowded, cobblestone streets that sprout from Casa Nova like the legs from a centipede and you are in for a real treat. If you want to, let your nose be your guide in the highly aromatic (and I use the word in the worst possible sense) market place. You will have to sidestep donkeys, waterpot-bearing women, and large piles of garbage as you snake your way through the streets, but the adventure is well worth the adversity. Steer clear of the two-foot wide trench running down the center of the street as this is the city's sewage system and is usually a "busy" place, and not just with the winter rainfall.

Lining the narrow streets are tin-roofed shops which add new meaning to the concept of "cramped" quarters. Here you will find luscious fruit in stalls lining the streets and inside hard-ware, leather goods, ancient coins, glassware, clothes, rope, and just about anything else your heart desires. Side by side hang trash and treasures. In one smelly opening you'll see plastic buckets and sponges hanging from the roof; in the next smelly opening you'll see authentic archaeological artifacts on sale at inflated prices. Remember, the deeper you venture into the Arab market the smaller the shops become, but the smaller the prices become as well.

On the road toward Tiberias is the Greek Orthodox Church of the Annunciation or Gabriel's Church. This is rival to the newer Latin Church of the Annunciation toward the center of the city. Originally built in the days of Constantine, this dark and gloomy Greek church is presently over 300 years old, the oldest church in Nazareth. Inside the Orthodox priest will show us a spring which bubbles out of the hillside below the floor. Steps lead down to the original well. It is believed that here Mary came to draw water, perhaps accompanied by the boy Jesus. Since this is the only spring-fed fountain in Nazareth, and since springs rarely change in Palestine, there is a good chance this is the same stream which provided cooling refreshment for the Lord Jesus.

Outside the church, by the side of the road, is the round-faced masonry well known as Mary's Well or the Virgin's Fountain. This is an outlet for the spring which originates below the church and before the water was piped to the residences of town, Nazarene women would come here daily for their families' water. You may yet see a woman carrying water home in four-gallon jars or shiny square tin containers, just like Mary did for Joseph and Jesus.

While you're in Nazareth you may want to visit the old synagogue in the western part of town on Market Lane. According to tradition, this ancient synagogue is where Jesus *"went into the synagogue on the sabbath day, and stood up for to read"* (Luke 4:16), astounding those present. Also interesting is a drive by the Hill of the Precipice ("Leap of the Lord") southeast of the city. This sharp, tree-dotted hill is thought to be the cliff over which the enraged townspeople of Nazareth plotted to throw our Lord (Luke 4:28-30). The most impressive view of this steep hill is from the road running parallel to it when you catch the craggy cliff against the clear blue of the Palestinian sky.

As we leave the city of Jesus' youth, the words of Nathaniel still ring in our ears: *"Can any good thing come out of Nazareth?"* (John 1:46). Jesus proved that adage wrong, and now so have you.

## VALLEY OF ARMAGEDDON

Below Nazareth, the crown jewel of the Galilee hills, spreads the Plain of Esdraelon. Commonly called the Emek, this Jezreel Valley is known to Christians as the VALLEY OF ARMAGEDDON. The largest and most fertile valley in Israel, the Esdraelon lies between the Galilee hills on the north and the hills of Samaria on the south. On the west is Mount Carmel; on the east Mount Gilboa. Until the early 1920s this was a mosquito-ridden, malarial swampland but the Jewish National Fund inaugurated its largest land reclamation project ever and transformed it into the most beautiful valley in the world. Its patchwork of greens and golds soothes the eyes and stirs the soul.

If we take the main road west through the valley in ten minutes we pass the turnoff to NAHALAL. Among the earliest of Israeli settlements, Nahalal is the most photographed moshav or individually owned cooperative community. From the air the moshav appears as a wagon wheel with farms at the hub and quaint white houses at the rim. Rows and rows of trees and country lanes spoke between the two with tailored fields flaring out from the houses. It is here that the late Israeli soldier-statesman Moshe Dayan is buried.

A few miles farther west to the left of the highway lie the magnificent ruins of BEIT SHEARIM. Everyone familiar with the New Testament is acquainted with the Sanhedrin, as well as the compiler of the Mishna, Rabbi Yehuda Ha'Nasi. The excavation and restoration of these ruins, which remained untouched until a quarter of a century ago, has brought fresh insight into the development of the Jewish religion after the destruction of the Jerusalem Temple in A.D. 70. Not only do you see the ruins of a large synagogue here, but nearby in a grove of olive and cypress trees are extensive catacombs in which many learned and famous Jews are buried.

If you care to, you may enter the burial caves through the rock-hewn doors under one of three arches at the back of the courtyard. Inside these cool refuges from the hot sun are found sarcophagi beautifully carved with menorahs, rams' horns, the Ark, lions, shells, etc. Many of the 200 important sarcophagi have been looted by grave robbers over the years. Of special interest in this necropolis is the entrance to one of the inner burial chambers flanked by a carving of a menorah, the Jewish seven-stemmed candelabrum. You'll see it high on the wall. The broad hallways of this city of the dead are much more

The Valley of Jezreel (Armageddon) viewed from Megiddo.

easily traversed than their counterparts in the Roman Catacombs.

Another road from Nazareth strikes out due south across the Plain of Esdraelon toward AFULA. As you look to your left you will spy a bowl-shaped mountain with a concentration of trees near the top. This quite symmetrical mount is Mount Tabor, the boundary between Issachar and Zebulun (Joshua 19:22-23). It was here that Deborah and Barak rendezvoused in preparation to defeat Sisera (Judges 4:6-17). Here too Zebah and Zalmunna slew Gideon's brothers (Judges 8:18-21). As early as the 4th century A.D. the tradition that this rounded mountain was the site of Jesus' transfiguration had become established. But many Christians who study their Bible believe that the description of the Mount of Transfiguration as *"an high mountain"* (Matthew 17:1; Mark 9:2—cf. 8:27; Luke 9:28) more naturally fits Mount Hermon than Mount Tabor.

We are now driving across the heart of the Valley of Armageddon. The modern town of Afula is dead ahead eight miles. As you look left and right you see the lush Jezreel Valley, the "breadbasket" of Israel. Brilliant flowers, golden grain, green vegetables and rich black dirt are visible on all sides. The rapidly developing market town of Afula is where these crops are brought for distribution. Almost in the center of the valley, Afula serves as the administrative headquarters of Jezreel as well. Although the site of a Crusader fortress and one of Napoleon's victories, Afula is a fairly recent town. Pioneered in 1925, mostly by American Jews, the chief importance of the town for the Christian pilgrim is as a connector to the road leading to Megiddo to the southwest.

As we make our way through the palm-lined streets of Afula, around the flowered park in the center of the town and out the other side, let's not forget the importance of the valley we are crossing. This is Esdraelon. This is Jezreel. This is the Valley of Armageddon. Here Gideon was victorious with his 300 men (Judges 7). Here King Josiah was mortally wounded in battle (II Chronicles 35:20-24). Down this valley some 20 miles Elijah ran from Mount Carmel before the chariot of King Ahab (I Kings 18:46). Through these prosperous fields have tramped the armies of the Egyptians, Philistines, Assyrians, Persians, Greeks, Romans, Crusaders, Turks, and British. And the armies keep coming. A young Israeli paratrooper once told me he parachuted into this valley on a training mission only to land rather messily in a watermelon patch. But the Apostle John records in the Book of Revelation that the greatest battle ever to take place in this valley is yet to come—the Battle of Armageddon (Revelation 16:13-16). As we view the tiny agricultural towns and settlements glistening in the Esdraelon sun, and the fruitful fields of grain waving in the breeze, it is difficult to imagine these as ghost towns and blood-soaked fields, but the Word of God standeth sure. To get some sense of this battle let's climb the mound of Megiddo and view the Valley of Armageddon from there.

## MEGIDDO

A royal city of the Canaanites on the extreme southern edge of the Jezreel Valley, MEGIDDO is the Gibralter of Palestine. Strategically located at the pass through the Carmel Mountain range leading from the Plain of Sharon on the coast to the Plain of Esdraelon, Megiddo guarded one of the most important highways of the Ancient Near East—the road between Egypt and Asia. Pharaoh Thutmose III conquered Megiddo overpowering the Canaanite kings in 1468 B.C. His escapades are recorded on the walls of his palace in Karnak, Egypt. Pharaoh Necho's armies once marched through the pass at Megiddo and were challenged by Judah's young King Josiah. The young monarch's death in the ensuing battle was a crushing blow to the kingdom of Judah (II Kings 23:29-30). Alexander the Great came this way in pursuit of the world. Vespasian's armies marched here. Napoleon led his army north from Egypt through this pass to an embarrassing defeat at Acre. Allenby came through here in 1917 and Jewish tanks rumbled by Megiddo on June 6, 1967. It isn't over yet.

We arrive at the beautifully manicured gardens outside of the Megiddo museum by driving up a curling road. The site is developed and maintained by Israel's National Parks Authority. Once inside there is not only relief from the heat of the day but refreshment for the parched tongue. Also, some of the most useful souvenirs from the Holy Land can be purchased here. Of special interest are the brass menorahs, Torah scrolls, bottle openers, etc.

It is best to enter the door at the right corner and absorb the museum before you attack the mound. Don't hurry by the oversized photos of the Megiddo excavations hung on the walls. They tell the real story of the pains and pleasures of participating in an archaeological dig. In the far room of the miniscule museum is a model of the Megiddo mound. This mound shows the more than 20 successive levels of occupation on this site. Take careful note of the shape of the

A model of the old fortress at Megiddo can be studied in the nearby museum.

mound, the steep entranceway on the far side and the intricate gate system. In just a few moments you'll be conquering that entranceway yourself. Periodically, since 1903, Megiddo has fallen under the archaeologist's spade and the results of that scientific investigation have provided outstanding validation of the Old Testament.

Now back through the snack shop for one final sip of Coke or lemonade before climbing the Megiddo mound. At the top of the ascent we make a sharp left turn. You may remember it from the museum model. It is part of the gate system which was unable to be negotiated by charging chariots. This simple architectural maneuver added significantly to Megiddo's security.

Stay on the stone-lined path and we soon come to a right hand turn. Here you will see a perfect example of a stone manger and watering trough, one square and one round. These would have been similar to those of Solomon's day. During the great king's reign this city was one of the most fortified defense posts in Solomon's vast empire. First Kings 10:26 indicates that Solomon gave whole cities over to the stabling of horses from his cavalry and Megiddo is mentioned as one of them. Ahead, where the path forks to the right, is an area where archaeologists have uncovered stables large enough to house 450 horses and 150 chariots. There too you'll see mangers and watering troughs. Although more

recently archaeologists have identified these visible stable remains as those of King Ahab (874-853 B.C.), nonetheless Solomon's stables would have been similar if indeed these are not his.

Let's take the path that leads to the edge of the mound overlooking the Jezreel Valley. Behind us is a crater in the mound revealing a large circular Canaanite altar at the center. This is perhaps our best view of the actual archaeological excavations at Megiddo. Now approach the mound's ridge and treat your eyes to a spine-tingling sight—the Valley of Armageddon.

As you peer out over this vast valley, the scene of so many conflicts in the past, it's hard to believe that the quilted field below will be the scene of history's final and bloodiest battle. Yet, five reliable authors record this great battle on the sacred pages of the Bible. They are David, Isaiah, Joel, Zechariah, and John. Read Psalm 2:1-5, 9; Isaiah 34:1-6; 63:3-6; Joel 3:2, 9-16; Zechariah 12:2; 14:2-3, 12; and Revelation 14:14-20; 16:16; 19:11-21. In the valley before you, God will gather the nations together in a battle which will extend from here to the Valley of Jehoshaphat at Jerusalem and all the way to Moab. *"And he gathered them together into a place called in the Hebrew tongue Armageddon"* (Revelation 16:16), the name meaning "the mound of Megiddo." This judgment of God on the nations of the world results from the godlessness of the last days, but God will be victorious. He always is.

41

To leave the mound of Megiddo you may retrace your steps down the steep entranceway or you may exit through an ancient marvel of engineering—the Megiddo water tunnel. I suggest the latter. On the far side of the mound is a circular depression in the ground. Except for the faint traces of long-unused steps clinging to the side, you would think this depression is but a mysterious sink hole. Yet this is the opening to the Megiddo water system which dates back 2,800 years. As we enter the cave-like mouth of the earth again we descend, this time on a system of metal steps. Our minds turn from the heat of the outdoor sun to the echo of the shaft. Down we go, down, down. In fact, once we reach the base of the shaft we will be 120 feet below the surface. There we see an ingeniously carved tunnel 215 feet long which connects with a spring outside the city. Our feet will remain dry as we walk on the four-foot wide wooden boardwalk which leads to the opposite end, soon ascending metal stairs and out of the back side of the mound. The short walk down to the road gives us time to reflect on the wonders we have just seen as we bid a fond farewell to the fortress of Megiddo.

## Around the Sea of Galilee

Much of the ministry of our Lord Jesus transpired on and around the Sea of Galilee. Some of Galilee's most important towns are located on its shores. We will visit those towns from north to south, as the reversing hands of a clock. Let's pretend that the sea is the clock and Bethsaida is at high noon. In a counterclockwise fashion we will travel southward from where the Jordan River empties into the Sea of Galilee near Bethsaida to Degania at 6 o'clock, where the Sea of Galilee empties into the Jordan River. But first, let's explore the sea itself.

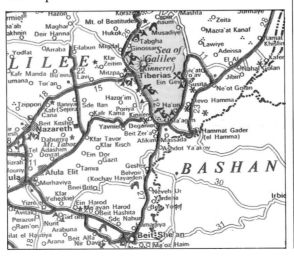

## SEA OF GALILEE

Of the five main roads which lead to the Sea of Galilee, the most impressive view is given by the road from Nazareth. As you roller coaster over the Galilean hills toward the sea you descend into a dip in the road, up the other side, and suddenly there it is. The Sea of Galilee breathtakingly spreads below you.

This sea fills a depression between the hills of Galilee and the heights of Golan. Thus, it is nearly 700 feet below sea level and averages between 130-157 feet deep. From the point where the Jordan River flows into Galilee unto the point where it flows out again is a little more than 13 miles with a width of half that size. Its area is about 64 square miles and thus the sea cuddles approximately 141 billion cubic feet of water.

Don't be at all surprised if you see this body of water listed under a variety of names on the map. In olden days the Arab poets called it The Bride, the Silver Woman, and the Handmaiden of the Hills. In the King James Version of the Bible it is known as Chinnereth (Numbers 34:11; Joshua 12:3; 13:27). The modern spelling of that is Kinneret which is taken from the Hebrew word "Kinnor" meaning lute or harp. The sea is roughly harp-shaped. In the New Testament it is dubbed Gennesaret (Luke 5:1) but usually called Tiberias after Herod Antipas built the city by that name on its western shore and made it his capital (John 6:1, 23; 21:1). But it was also affectionately known as the Sea of Galilee (Matthew 4:18; 15:29; Mark 1:16; 7:31; John 6:1).

Israel today only has two large inland bodies of water (since Lake Hula was drained). One is fresh water; one is salt water. One is the Sea of Galilee; one is the Dead Sea. You can guess which one is fresh water. In Galilee fish are abundant. Here are caught sardine, mullet, catfish, carp, and the combfish. There are the same fish once caught by Jesus' disciples when they cast their nets into the sea much as is done today. The only difference is that today's fishing boats are usually diesel powered. Haven't you ever wondered why a relatively small body of fresh water is called a sea? The answer is the configuration of the mountains around the sea. With the high mountains on either side, the tunneling wind whistles down across the surface of the water churning a placid lake into a howling sea. The incident in Mark 6:45-52, where a sudden and violent storm arose and just as quickly was calmed at the Master's command, is a classic example of this natural phenomenon.

Along the shores of this sea the tribe of Gad

settled after the conquest of the land (Deuteronomy 3:17; Joshua 13:27-28). Down the eastern cliffs which rise above the sea a herd of swine rushed into the water after Jesus cast the demons out of the demoniac (Matthew 8:28-34). On the northern shores of Galilee Jesus called Peter, Andrew, James, and John to leave their fishing business, follow Him and become fishers of men (Luke 5:1-11). Multitudes were healed (Luke 9:1-6), multitudes were fed (Luke 9:10-17), and multitudes were taught (Luke 9:23-27; 37-62) along these shores.

One of the great thrills of being in the Holy Land is a boat ride on the Sea of Galilee. Usually the trip begins at the docks of Tiberias and the boat carries us across to Capernaum on the north. As the boat backs away from the dock, we wave to the army of little children who have gathered on the shore. Once we set out across the water we get a perfect view of the now infamous GOLAN HEIGHTS on our right. This tableland east and north of the Sea of Galilee was assigned to the tribe of Manasseh (Deuteronomy 4:41-43; Joshua 20:8). At the end of World War I these

The Sea of Galilee, near the place where Jesus preached the Sermon on the Mount.

Modern-day fishermen on the Sea of Galilee.

mountains were awarded to Syria. It was the Syrian bombardment of EIN GEV on the eastern lakefront from the Golan Heights that precipitated the Six Day War in 1967.

As we cross the sea you can almost hear Jesus say to Peter, *"Launch out into the deep, and let down your nets for a draught"* (Luke 5:4). Fish do not abound alone in the depths of this sea. Tiny shells, conical in shape, abound as well. The captain of our boat and his crew will undoubtedly have a supply of these shells crafted into beautiful pins and brooches. Dozens of these tiny shells symmetrically arranged on a pin make a delightful and inexpensive gift.

When we have completed about half our crossing, to our left are clearly visible the famous Horns of Hattin. The odd configuration of this ridge seven and one-half miles west of Tiberias, at a natural pass in the range, resembles the horns of an animal. Hence the name. During the period of the Crusades the Muslims had overrun Palestine. The conflict between the Christian Crusaders and the Muslims came down to one final battle. Here, at the Horns of Hattin, the Crusaders suffered their final devastating defeat at the hands of Saladin in 1187 and the Crusades were over.

Before we dock at Capernaum be sure to look ahead and a bit to the right at the huge mountain range towering to the clouds. This is the Anti-Lebanon Mountain range and the snowcapped peak we see is Mount Hermon. Nearly 20 miles long north to south and about 9,200 feet high, Mount Hermon is the highest and most spectacular mountain in the Middle East. This was the northern limit of the territory of Israel (Deuteronomy 4:47-48; Joshua 11:1-3; 12:1-5; 13:5). Its snowy crown is white year round.

In just a few minutes we'll dock at Capernaum. The 45 minutes we've been on the Sea of Galilee have taken us back in time to the days when Jesus conducted His ministry on the shores of this sea. Having viewed these sites from the sea, let's retrace His steps on land.

## CAPERNAUM

CAPERNAUM is located about two and one-half miles west of where the Jordan River feeds the Sea of Galilee. If we were to set out overland, cross the Jordan and travel east another mile and a half, we would come to the ruins of Tel Beit Zaida. Situated 100 feet above the elevation of the sea, this site is believed to be the biblical BETHSAIDA. This city was the birthplace of Peter, Andrew, James, and John (John 1:44). On the grassy fields between the city and the sea the feeding of the 5,000 took place (Matthew 14:13-21; John 6:1-14). Also Jesus took the blind man out of the city and healed him (Mark 8:22-26). Perhaps the Master did this because of the unbelief of the people (Matthew 11:21-22). At any rate, because Bethsaida failed to repent of its sin

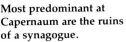
Most predominant at Capernaum are the ruins of a synagogue.

and believe the message of the Savior, it was cursed by Him (Luke 10:13-14). The adjacent cities of Capernaum and Chorazin were cursed as well and all three of them lie in ruins today. On the other hand, Tiberias was not cursed by the Lord and it thrives today.

CHORAZIN is about two miles north of Capernaum. A Jewish center of the 2nd century A.D., all that remains is an old 3rd or 4th century synagogue. The site is quite overgrown with briars and brush now and is a haven for lizards. It stands as mute testimony to the judgment of God.

Capernaum features by far the most impressive ruins of the three cursed cities. Still, as we enter the city, either from the dock or up the highway which hugs the shore from Tiberias, we see but a clump of trees, a partially-excavated ruin and a huge black basalt building (the Franciscan Monastery) at the entrance of Capernaum. Entering from the highway we pass through the iron gate entrance on a beautiful mosaic path and see before us a square hedged by a gravel path. From the dock we arrive at the square on our right. Let's take the path around the south side of the square, the side closest to the sea.

Notice as we walk along, in the coolness provided by the trees, that on both sides of the path stonework from ancient Capernaum is on display. These pieces of stone are sometimes beautifully and intricately carved depicting rosettes, fruit, candelabra, and even a star of David can be seen. The variety of things carved in stone is fascinating. But there is one carving we absolutely must see. Look on the lake side less than halfway down the path leading to the excavations and you will see a very detailed replica of the ark of the covenant sculptured in stone. This bas-relief shows a pillared chest mounted on six-spoked wheels, looking not unlike an ornate conestoga wagon or stage coach of early America. Don't miss it for it's one of the very few representations of the ark known today.

As we reach the end of the path we run headlong into the excavations of the city and a fence prohibiting us from entering them. These diggings are not particularly impressive except for the synagogue to our left. Let's follow the path and climb the three steps to the synagogue area.

The present structure is one of the finest limestone synagogues in the Middle East. It bears the telltale design of Roman architecture. When the Franciscan fathers began to reconstruct the site in the last century, only the lower three or four courses of the walls, the column bases, and the

paved floor were in place. All else was repositioned and restored. If you're up on your Latin you may want to take a crack at the Roman inscriptions on some of the four columns still standing.

Probably a 4th or 5th century A.D. edifice, it was likely constructed on the site of the 1st century Jewish center of worship. It was here that Jesus taught (Mark 1:21; Luke 4:31-33). This city became *"his own city"* (Matthew 4:13-17) after Jesus withdrew from Nazareth. It became the headquarters for His Galilean ministry and this ancient synagogue the central focus of that ministry. Here He healed the man with an unclean spirit and nearby healed Peter's mother-in-law (Luke 4:31-41). It was in this town He healed the centurion's servant (Luke 7:1-10) and the palsied man let down through the roof (Mark 2:1-12). Here too He healed the woman who had an issue of blood (Luke 8:43-48), the blind and dumb demoniac (Matthew 9:27-35), the withered hand (Luke 6:6-11), and the nobleman's son (John 4:46-54). In fact, great multitudes were brought to Jesus and healed in this town (Matthew 8:16-17; 9:36-38). As we look around us we must

Stonework lines the path, such as this capital displaying the Menorah.

45

wonder what stories the stones beneath this synagogue floor must have to tell.

But the sun is hot and beating down on our heads and since the synagogue is built outside of the Capernaum clump of trees, we need to seek shelter. As we walk the northern path back to the iron gate entrance and our waiting transportation, let's take note of one more astounding site in the Holy Land. At the northeastern corner of the path, in a small fenced area, there is a perfectly preserved olive press. Made of the same black basalt stone the blocks of the Franciscan monastery are made of, a volcanic stone native to the shores of Galilee, the millstone of this press is tipped on its side to give us a better angle at it. It is a photographer's dream, a huge black stone against a light sand background. Once we get a glimpse at the size of that stone, more than two feet in diameter, and more than a foot thick, we will gain a better appreciation of Jesus' statement that rather than offend a little child it might be better for the offender *"that a millstone were hanged about his neck, and that he were drowned in the depth of the sea"* (Matthew 18:6). Jesus said this at Capernaum. Could this be the same millstone?

As we leave the city that for 18-20 months was the headquarters of Jesus' healing and teaching ministry, perhaps an ice cream bar at the little cold drink hut outside the city would be in order. It's a long walk to the parking lot. Well, even if it isn't, that ice cream sure would hit the spot.

## MOUNT OF THE BEATITUDES

As we leave Capernaum behind we travel less than two miles along the lake road. Suddenly there is a branch of this road that sharply slices back to our right, away from the sea. This road climbs steeply and in two or three miles we would see the spur leading to Chorazin. But we will take the road less than a mile to visit the spot where Jesus delivered the Sermon on the Mount.

Again we are confronted with a forestlike, extremely restful spot. As we approach the site, to our left is a large Italian convent and hospice, the Hospice of the Beatitudes, operated by an Italian missionary society. It was a personal project of Mussolini in 1937. A right turn (toward the sea) takes us through an abundance of palm trees to the beautiful and picturesque Chapel of the Beatitudes. Again partially built of the dark black basalt rock so prevalent in the area, the chapel has a black dome built over a square pavilion with arched colonnades trimmed in white. The interior decor of the chapel depicts symbols of the seven virtues: charity, justice, providence, faith, hope, fortitude, and temperance (cf. Galatians 5:2), very reminiscent of the Sermon on the Mount. As quaint as the interior is, the colonnaded walkway around the exterior of the chapel is as big as all outdoors. There are many terrific views of the Sea of Galilee, but none is better than this. The panorama afforded by this delightful chapel takes your breath away. It is indescribable.

While visiting this site I have always found it spiritually revitalizing to slip off by myself under one of the multitude of trees and read Matthew 5—7, the Sermon on the Mount. It can be done in only a few minutes. As I read I always find it difficult to keep my eyes on the pages of my Bible. They want to drift to the beautiful scenery surrounding me. So many of the things the Lord mentions in that sermon can still be seen around this mountain today.

## TABGHA

As we descend the Mount of Beatitudes and rejoin the main road where the Galilean hills gently edge the highway toward the sea, the village of TABGHA lies before us. Here we enter the very bland-looking Church of the Multiplication. This church stands on the site where tradition says Jesus fed the 5,000. However, the Bible places this miracle near Bethsaida, east of the Jordan River (Luke 9:10). Nonetheless, this is a significant stop in any Holy Land itinerary as the church boasts one of the best preserved mosaics in Palestine.

We enter the church through the rear. On either side of the center aisleway a mosaic floor of an older church dating back to the 4th century A.D. is clearly visible. Discovered in 1932, these mosaic tiles are magnificent. The designs are of wildlife and flowers. For example, as we study the floor we can discern a dove on a lotus flower, a bird attacking a snake, a goose with an oleander bush, as well as swans, cranes, wild geese, storks, etc. How well this testifies to the lush nature of the Holy Land during those centuries.

Now, don't spend all of your time looking at the mosaics on either side of the present floor. There is something else we want to see in this church. Let's go to the front where there is a splendid Byzantine mosaic, one of the most beautiful I've seen, depicting a basket of loaves with an upright fish on either side. This is an almost perfect mosaic and appears as if it were done only yesterday. It is a fitting commemoration of Jesus' great miracle.

A view from the chapel on the Mount of Beatitudes.

Just next door, along the seashore, is Saint Peter's Church or the Mensa Christi ("Table of Christ"). This little basalt church was erected by the Franciscans in 1943 on the ruins of an earlier church. Both were built over a massive rock called the "Table of Christ" as it was believed that here Jesus prepared the breakfast of fish and bread for His disciples at a post-resurrection rendezvous in Galilee (John 21:9-14). The invitation of the Lord Jesus to them is His invitation to all who experience physical or spiritual hunger, *"Come and dine"* (cf. John 4:13-14; 6:47-51). It was also here, after they had eaten, that three times Jesus commanded Peter to *"Feed my sheep"* (John 21:15, 16, 17). Responsibility always follows refreshment.

## MAGDALA

Leaving Tabgha we cross the Plain of Gennesaret which extends westward from the sea of Galilee. The highway never strays far from the shoreline, however, as we soon pass the famous Kinneret Pumping Station on our left. Israel exploits 93 percent of its scanty water potential and of that amount 82 percent is used for agriculture. Unfortunately, while the rainfall is abundant in the Galilee, it is almost nil in the Negev. In 1964 a project was completed to alleviate the water scarcity in the south.

Nestled behind a hill on the northwest shore of the Sea of Galilee is the large Kinneret Pumping Station. Here water is pumped out of the sea and by means of giant pipes (nearly ten feet in diameter) is brought to an installation on the Yarkon River near Antipatris and from there through open canals, aqueducts, tunnels, and dams it flows to the Negev. In all the water travels through 81 miles of pipes and aqueducts to give just a little foretaste of what the land shall be like in that day when *"the desert shall rejoice, and blossom as the rose"* (Isaiah 35:1-2; cf. Ezekiel 36:33-36; Amos 9:14-15).

Just before we arrive at Magdala we pass a fine example of an Israeli phenomenon—the kibbutz. Kibbutzim are remarkable experiments in voluntary socialism. Everything is owned in common and all the services of the community are provided in common. The kibbutz to our left is NOF GINOSSAR Guest House. Only minutes from downtown Tiberias, Nof Ginossar is a popular guest facility for it is rated four-star and is situated right on the sea with private beaches and gardens. One hundred and six rooms with all the modern conveniences await weary travelers. The view of the Galilee from the second story kosher dining room is fantastic. If you're interested in learning more about life on a kibbutz, a regular series of lectures and slides is provided by the resident kibbutzniks. It is a delightfully restful stop.

We have now arrived at MAGDALA, believed to be the home of Mary Magdalene (Mark 16:9; Luke 8:2). It was here that our Lord came after the feeding of the 4,000 (Matthew 15:39). On this occasion Jesus apparently looked out over the Sea of Galilee to remind the belligerent Pharisees and Sadducees of an ancient meterological lesson. When asked by His antagonists for a sign from heaven He responded, *"When it is evening, ye say, It will be fair weather: for the sky is red. And in the morning, It will be foul weather today: for the sky is red and lowering. O ye hypocrites, ye can discern the face of the sky; but can ye not discern the signs of the times?"* (Matthew 16:2-3). As we look out over the Plain of Gennesaret to the west and the Sea of Galilee to the east we can easily conjure up sunrises and sunsets which would give Jesus occasion to rebuke these hypocrites for their inability to accept His teaching.

The name Magdala itself means "tower," the adjacent modern Jewish village taking the name Migdal meaning the same. A city of some significance in the Greco-Roman Empire, because of its position at the juncture of two main highways, Magdala was apparently the most important town on the lake before Tiberias was built. The 1st-century A.D. Jewish historian Josephus notes that the city had a population of 40,000 in his day (*Wars* II.21.4). When the city fell to the Roman general Titus in the Jewish struggle for independence, 6,700 Jews were killed; 6,000 were sent to Nero to dig the Corinthian Canal in Greece; and 30,400 were auctioned off as slaves. This occurred just decades after Jesus' death and resurrection. Although the community was rebuilt, it has been but a ruins for centuries.

## TIBERIAS

We now leave the general tranquility of the rustic, almost idyllic, northwest shores of the Sea of Galilee for the hustle and bustle of the sea's largest city. As we enter this city of contrasts a glance to the left reveals fishing nets drying in the Galilean sun and a glance to the right, up on the hillsides above us, reveals a chorus of highrise hotels. The new and the old, both are here.

Built sometime within the first two decades of the Christian era, TIBERIAS was the pride of Herod Antipas, son of Herod the Great. Apparently he built it over the ruins of Rakkath, an ancient town of Naphtali, and named it in honor of the Roman Emperor Tiberias. It became the capital of Galilee under Agrippa I and the Roman procurators. After the fall of Jerusalem in A.D. 70, when the Temple was destroyed, Tiberias became the great center of Judaism in the Holy Land. It was here that Rabbi Yehuda Ha'Nasi and his colleagues codified the traditional civil and ritual laws of the Jews and compiled them in the Mishnah (A.D. 200). Here too the Jerusalem Talmud was compiled (A.D. 400) and a system of pointing (adding vowels and punctuation to Hebrew consonants) was introduced into the Hebrew language. The great and learned men of Judaism once gathered to live in Tiberias. But that was yesterday, and yesterday's gone.

Today's Tiberias is somewhat of a resort town with crowded beaches and fun-loving frolickers. Galilee Street, the main thoroughfare of the town (and about the only one), is typical of the contrasts in this town. It runs outside of the old city wall where you can still see the remains of the old rampart that encased the city, but is filled with buses, cars, jeeps, and a variety of other forms of locomotion. Street urchins mix with

**The Plaza Tiberias, a modern tourist hotel.**

tourists who mix with bathers who mix with the bearded townspeople. On the right is a small park which is fairly unkempt. Sitting on the benches may be relaxing but the pigeons have been there before you. At the water's edge, down from a number of artists' galleries, you will find the Tiberias teenagers leaping into the lake from the ancient sea wall and returning for repeated leaps.

The only mention of Tiberias in the Bible is in John 6:23 where it is said that many came from Tiberias across the sea to Capernaum, near the scene of the feeding of the 5,000. Still the city abounds in reminders of the New Testament era.

On the southern edge of town are the world famous hot springs of Tiberias. These thermal baths have been drawing the sick and infirmed to the shores of Galilee for over 3,000 years. The hot springs contain high amounts of calcium and sulphuric salts and for centuries have been reported to cure rheumatism, arthritis and similar ailments. Perhaps the earliest known such thermal baths in the world, it may well be that they are the reason for a large concentration of people around the Sea of Galilee who needed the healing power of Christ Jesus.

Today these hot springs range from the sublime to the ridiculous. Some resemble Turkish baths and are housed in ancient basalt buildings complete with vaulted ceilings, domes and the mystique of the Middle Ages. Others are found in modern, sanitized clinics that resemble the spic and span hospitals of the United States. In fact, frequently visitors to the Holy Land eat lunch at restaurants which feature such hot baths and I usually skip lunch for a dip in the bath. The water is incredibly warm and soothing. In the modern baths, which look just like a swimming pool, it's such a relaxing feeling to stand in front of the jets which propel the water into the bath directly from the underground bubbling springs. The experience is worth the small expense.

But if you prefer lunch to hot baths, don't leave Tiberias until you've had Saint Peter's fish. This local delicacy will make your mouth water and give you no rest until you return to Tiberias for more. This white fish is a bit boney but the succulent flavor of the fish is more than a match for an occasional bone. When it arrives at your table, try not to think of the fact that it's the whole fish, head, tail, and all. Just lay a sprig of parsley over the fish's eye to keep him from watching you as you enjoy a truly Galilean feast.

Very nearby the hot springs, opposite the bus station, is the tomb of Rabbi Moses Ben Maimon, better known as Maimonides. This greatest Jewish theologian of the Middle Ages was also a humanist physician, astronomer, scientist, and Aristotelian philosopher. A white tomb surrounded by piles of rubble now mark the burial site of the Sephardic Jew who died in A.D. 1204. Nearby is the tomb of Rabbi Yohanan Ben Zakkai, founder of the Yavne (Yeshiva) Academy, Israel's ancient and earliest center of learning, and Rabbi Akiva, the Jewish scholar who compiled many commentaries of the Mishna before the Romans tortured and killed him at Caesarea in A.D. 150. Located in a white building on the hill nearly a mile south of the hot springs it is the holiest of Tiberias' tombs. It is the tomb of Rabbi Meir known in Jewish tradition as the "Miracle Worker." Not only are these tombs a constant reminder of the importance the Jews attached to this Roman-built city, but a Jewish school of rabbinic theology has operated here for a long, long time as well.

A city of remarkable contrasts, Tiberias is a city with a serious past and a fun-filled present. During the winter months Israelis flock to this resort city because it offers one of the country's most pleasant winter climates. However, during the summer months, the heat is oppressive and most Israelis flock to the Mediterranean coast. A popular Israeli story is that Tiberias, down at the lake, and Safed, on top of the mountains, have the same population. Tiberias' 25,000 inhabitants live in the coolness of Safed all summer and return to Tiberias for the winter. However, not many residents of Tiberias could afford such a practice.

Just a 15-minute drive south of Tiberias brings us to "six" on our Sea of Galilee clock. Here is where the Jordan River empties out of the Sea of Galilee and meanders southward toward the Dead Sea. Just east of the Jordan is DEGANIA, Israel's oldest kibbutz. Begun in 1909 by ten men and two women, all immigrants from the Russian town of Romni, this one-time swamp is now a showcase in modern Israel. Surrounded by plenteous orchards and gardens, green fields of vegetables and rows of golden corn, Degania is the result of determined effort and hard labor. At the entrance to the kibbutz is a Renault tank, today a memorial to Degania's farmers who stopped an advancing Syrian column with Molotav cocktails in 1948. Degania is a fitting conclusion to an excursion around the Galilee, Israel's lushest natural region.

# CHAPTER 5

# In the Heart of the Holy Land

◆

## THE WEST BANK

*"And the children of Joseph said, The hill is not enough for us. . . And Joshua spake unto the house of Joseph, even to Ephraim and to Manasseh, saying, Thou art a great people, and hast great power: thou shalt not have one lot only: but the mountain shall be thine; for it is a wood, and thou shalt cut it down: and the outgoings of it shall be thine . . ."*
(Joshua 17:16-18).

Although the hill country of the Holy Land's Central Highlands extends from Mount Hermon to the Negev, the territory through which we now travel is but the hill country of Ephraim and Manasseh. This is the mountainous land bordered by the coastal plain and the Jordan Valley, from the southern edge of Esdraelon to about ten miles north of Jerusalem. Roughly speaking, the

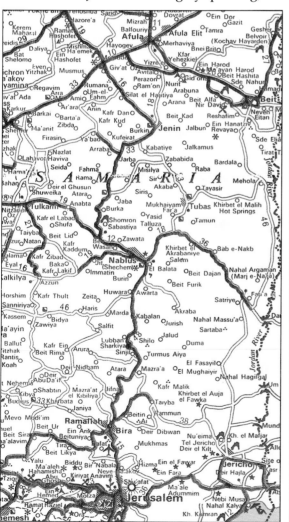

territorial allotment to the sons of Joseph coincides with what we have come to know generally as Samaria. It is the West Bank. It is the heart of the Holy Land.

In the northern sector of this hill country, comprising all of Manasseh's and most of Ephraim's territory, the mountains are opened by valleys running north, south and west. Thus, rain is brought to these valleys by the Mediterranean winds making the Valleys of Dothan, Lebonah and others far more productive than the mountainous areas to the south. But the valleys also allowed freer access to Samaria which ultimately meant the introduction of new ideas political and religious to the very center of the country.

Occasionally Christian travelers to the Holy Land must skirt these mountain roads and passes. As political tensions rise, prudent travelers lower, lower themselves, that is, to the coastal roads or the valley road paralleling the Jordan River. But usually the direct route from Galilee to Jerusalem is the best and it will take us right through the Central Highlands.

### JENIN

Situated on the imaginary border line between Galilee and Samaria is JENIN (En-gannim). This border is marked by the Carmel and Gilboa mountain ranges. That this is a border town between the hill country to the south and the Valley of Esdraelon to the north is even evidenced in the meaning of Jenin ("guarded spring"). The Jewish historian Josephus calls the town Ginea and reports that it is located between Galilee and Samaria. He also mentions that here a large number of Galileans were killed by Samaritans as they were passing through on their way to Jerusalem (*Antiq.* XX.6.1).

Thus there should be no doubt that we are passing from one territory to another, one people to another, one heritage to another. You will notice a world of difference between the Jews of Afula and the Arabs of Jenin. In fact, there have been frequent occasions since the Six-Day War of 1967 where Christian pilgrims like us have not been permitted to go through Jenin to the hill country. The reason is clear. At Jenin we enter the notorious West Bank. This is an area originally part of Jordan but now under military occupation by Israel. Its inhabitants are mostly Arabs. Its peace keeping forces are mostly Jews. To the Arabs it is known as "the occupied territory." To the Jews it is known as Samaria.

On the western outskirts of Jenin, a very oriental town, is a hill which is dominated by a tower and a sacred tree. It is known as Khirbet Belame. Since it is unimportant to the Christian we will bypass it to enter the town. Jenin is mentioned in the Old Testament as En-Gannim in Joshua 15:34; 19:21; 21:29). It was at least partially in the tribe of Issachar. But its greatest biblical importance lies in the New Testament. It is believed, according to tradition, that this was the city where Jesus healed the ten lepers, as *"he passed through the midst of Samaria and Galilee"* (Luke 17:11-19). As you recall, only one of those healed, a Samaritan, returned to thank the Lord for His act of mercy and kindness.

As we pass through Jenin, on the road from Afula, we take a right at the square in the middle of the town and proceed south through our first valley in the hill country, the Valley of Dothan.

## DOTHAN

It is immediately obvious to us, as we enter the

Tucked between the Carmel Mountains and the Gilboa Mountains lies the Dothan Plain where Joseph sought his brothers.

Dothan Plain, that this is a broad and fertile valley. It is tucked away between the Carmel Mountains and the Gilboa Mountains. Just one mile southwest of Jenin we pass the ruins of the ancient fortress of IBLEAM. The name of this ancient town means "place of victory" and there could be no more fitting name.

Given to the tribe of Manasseh (Joshua 17:11), the Canaanites successfully prohibited the men of Manasseh from securing the city (Joshua 17:12; Judges 1:27). Frequently the scene of bloody battles, it was near here that Jehu assassinated King Ahaziah (II Kings 9:27) and that Shallum killed Israel's King Zechariah (II Kings 15:8-10). However, as a Levitical city, Ibleam was a more peaceful town known as Bileam (I Chronicles 6:70).

As we begin to cross the Valley of Dothan we see all about us the rich red dirt of the plowed fields, a striking contrast to the chalky color of the hills. TELL DOTHAN is spread over the northeastern head of the valley, just a half mile east of the highway. This site is vibrant with biblical history. It was here that Joseph's brothers tended their flocks. You can almost see them across the valley today. This was the scene of the infamous sale of Joseph by Jacob's sons (Genesis 37:13-28) to Ishmaelites journeying to Egypt. Joseph's coat of many colors was torn here by his brothers and dipped in blood to masquerade their sin before their father (Genesis 37:31-32).

Some twelve miles north of Samaria, Tell Dothan is an extremely impressive mound owned and excavated by the late Joseph P. Free of Wheaton College. The surface of the mound covers a full ten acres and rises 175 feet above the plain. It is a "must see" for archaeology buffs, especially if they are photo fanatics as well. On the southern slope of the tell is a small Arab village. Most of the villagers tend sheep, just like Joseph's brothers did hundreds of years ago. Not much has changed in these fields over the years. They are still among the best grazing fields of Israel and shepherds and their flocks abound everywhere.

Dothan is also important as the home of the prophet Elisha (II Kings 6). It was here the prophet lived when he warned the king of Israel about the troop movements of the king of Syria. When the Syrian king sent *"horses, and chariots, and a great host"* (II Kings 6:14) to surround Dothan and Elisha, the prophet's servant became frightened until Elisha calmed him saying, *"They that be with us are more than they that be with them"* (II Kings 6:16). What follows is a fascinating story of God's grace and mercy.

## SAMARIA

As we leave Tell Dothan behind, also the scene of Judith's triumph over Holofernes in apocryphal history (Judith 3:9; 4:6; 7:3), the fertile plain begins to rise somewhat to the high country of the central Holy Land. This is the hill country of Manasseh, still with considerably less altitude than the hill country of Ephraim to the south. Ahead of us, on the left, is a mammoth mound of some 300 feet high. Obviously, you can't miss it. This mound is a unique combination of ancient and modern, high/low civilization. It is the hill of SAMARIA, the capital of the northern kingdom of Israel. Ancient Samaria shares the mound with the present village of SEBASTE.

The hill of Samaria is a round mound of history covering an unbelievable 50 acres at its summit. As we turn off the main road climbing the hill, keep a close eye out for the niches in the hillside. Discovered when the modern road was built, they are burial caves complete with ancient sarcophagi dating back to 800 B.C. As we approach the south side of the hill we enter the modern (using the term loosely) Samaritan village of Sebaste. Here the stones of ages past have been used to build the houses of the present. These winding, narrow streets sit atop ruins of winding, narrow streets. It's a living tradition in the Holy Land. The houses are small, the people poor, the lifestyle simple.

Inside the village is a small mosque curiously built within an old Crusader cathedral. Dating back to the 12th century, the minaret of the mosque (the tall, slender tower from which Muslims are called five times a day to prayer) is an easy mark of identification to locate the site. In a subterranean area beneath the courtyard of the mosque is a cave. The natives claim that the prophets Elisha and Obadiah are buried there. Also, there is a tradition that a dungeon at this site was where John the Baptist was imprisoned. Although Machaerus, east of the Dead Sea, is a rival claimant for this dubious honor, nonetheless the tradition persists that at the very least the head of John the Baptist was brought here by Herod Antipas at the request of Salome (Matthew 14:1-14).

Originally settled by the tribes of Ephraim and Manasseh, the children of Joseph, when the division of the Israelite kingdom came after the death of Solomon, Samaria became the capital city of the ten tribes of the north. Here was both the residence and the burial place of Israel's kings Omri, Ahab, Jehu, Jehoahaz, Joash, and Jehoash.

The site owes to Omri most of its importance. He bought this imposing hill with a valley encircling it from Shemer and began to build a beautiful palace on it. Only six years later he died and son Ahab continued the building project. Dur-

**Replete with history of the patriarchs, biblical Shechem is the site of Jacob's Well, housed within this roofless shell of a church.**

ing the continuing archaeological excavations of the site numerous pieces of furniture with ivory overlays were found validating the Bible's reference to the palace of Ahab as an *"ivory house"* (I Kings 22:30; Amos 3:15). But Ahab married the infamous Jezebel who brought to the house of Israel's king the worship of pagan idols. Is it any wonder that the prophet Amos warned, *"Woe to them . . . that trust in the mountain of Samaria . . . that lie upon beds of ivory . . ."* (Amos 6:1, 4)? Jezebel induced her husband to build a temple to Baal in the city of Samaria (I Kings 16:31-33) and although Ahab's son put away the image of Baal (II Kings 3:2) and later Jehu destroyed Baal worship and killed the priests of Baal (II Kings 10:17-28), nonetheless, the damage was done. Samaria was eventually captured and overthrown by Sargon, king of Assyria. The inhabitants were carried off into bondage in 721 B.C. (II Kings 17; 18:9-12).

But Samaria was not to be denied future existence. Later this mound was occupied by the Babylonians, Persians, Greeks, and Romans. Alexander the Great besieged the city in 331 B.C. and later, in 120 B.C., John Hyrcanus destroyed it. But the Roman general Pompey rebuilt the site in 27 B.C. and when Caesar Augustus gave Samaria to Herod the Great, Herod carried out large scale renovation of the city. Most of what we see before us is from the Roman era. The absolutely fantastic colonnaded street by which we entered the city to the columns and ruins of the public basilica are clearly Roman. In fact, climb to the summit of the hill to view a temple built there honoring Augustus. Samaria is one of Israel's finest exhibits of the Roman presence in a Jewish land. The forum, theater, gateway, hippodrome, and street of columns give you the feeling that you are taking a stroll in ancient Rome, now crumbled and dusty. If Rome, the city of seven hills, were to have an eighth hill, certainly Samaria would be it.

Throughout history many men of God have found themselves preaching or prophesying in Samaria. Here Elijah destroyed the messengers of King Ahaziah and prophesied the king's death (II Kings 1). Naaman, the leper from Syria, came to Samaria to be healed by Elisha. Prophecies concerning Samaria's sin and doom frequent the pages of the Old Testament (cf. Isaiah 8:4; 9:8-21; 36:19; Jeremiah 23:13; Ezekiel 23:1-4; Hosea 7; 13:16; Amos 3:12; Micah 1:6).

Still, Samaria had its brighter history as well. Acts 8:5, 8 records, *"Then Philip went down to the city of Samaria, and preached Christ unto them . . . and there was great joy in that city."* The Old Testament prophets had the right method—prophecy, and the right message—doom without repentance. The New Testament preachers had the right method—preaching, and the right message—Christ died for our sins. Peter and John joined Philip at Samaria, *"And they, when they had testified and preached the word of the Lord, returned to Jerusalem, and preached the gospel in many villages of the Samaritans"* (Acts 8:25). Today Samaria is left without such a witness to Christ's power to save men from sin. As we view the ruins before us we must remember that the tragedy of Samaria is not its tumble from the heights of glory but its turning away from the heralds of God.

## NABLUS

The villages of Nablus, Shechem and Sychar are like three peas in a time-warped pod, the sides of that pod being Mount Ebal and Mount Gerizim. The road from the north passes through (or by) these three villages in that order, but the villages were not simultaneously inhabited.

Today NABLUS is the largest town on the West Bank with a population of 45,000 inhabitants. Its reputation for turbulence, both political and physical, is world-renowned. Since 1967 Nablus has spawned most of the Arab resistance and PLO agitation within the territorial boundaries of Israel. Therefore, we will not delay as we pass through the town quickly.

The white houses of Nablus, piled on the hillsides like sugar cubes, appear restful and serene. The town itself is buzzing with activity. Here is the West Bank commercial center. A large soap manufacturing plant is located here. But if the Christian traveler knows anything about business in Nablus, he knows that here is where the sweetest, stickiest baklava pastries in the Holy Land are made.

Founded by the Roman general Titus and named Flavia Neopolis in honor of his father, Flavius Vespasian, the town went by the name Neopolis in the Greco-Roman period of history. Nablus is but an Arabic contraction of Neopolis. Just before we enter the town a road forks back to our right toward Netanya. We stay on the main road toward town. Passing through a succession of smaller villages, and a number of modern-looking villas, we arrive at the north sector of Nablus. Off to our right is the Casbah, the older quarter of the town and charming but unsafe for visitors. Within this quarter is an old mosque and on the hillside above it, opposite the Muslim cemetery, the Samaritan quarter. Here black-veiled women and white-robed men, unshaven with long hair and hats covered with red cloth, walk the streets. Approximately 240 Samaritans live here; another 160 reside in Holon, a suburb of Tel Aviv. As we continue through Nablus, notice the beautiful stained-glass windows and blue-green dome on the mosque ahead. It is the largest mosque in this Arab town. And on our left, just before we leave the town for another villa-studded suburb, is the large old Arab-British prison, still in use.

On either side of the city the landscape is dominated by mountains. On the northeast of Nablus is Mount Ebal; on the southwest is Mount Gerizim. Ebal, the higher of the two at 3,077 feet, is easily recognized as the bald mountain. Gerizim, rising 2,848 feet, partially sports a fuzzy cover of trees. It was here that Israel renewed her covenants with God. Mount Ebal was the *"Mount of Cursing"* while Mount Gerizim was the *"Mount of Blessing"* (Deuteronomy 11:29-30; 27:11-26; Joshua 8:30-34). With the priests, Levites and the ark of the covenant in the valley between, Joshua stationed half the tribes on Ebal and the other half on Gerizim. The people rehearsed what God's blessings would be if they were faithful and what curses would be theirs if they were not.

It was on Mount Ebal that Joshua built an altar and *"wrote there upon the stones a copy of the law of Moses"* (Joshua 8:30, 32). And from Mount Gerizim Jotham heralded his parable to the people of Shechem below (Judges 9:7). But the great continuing importance of this mountain is for the Samaritans.

Remnants of the ten tribes, the Samaritans are those people who were not carried off into captivity when Samaria was captured by the Assyrians in 721 B.C. (II Kings 17:6, 23). These Jews intermarried with colonists imported to Samaria by the Assyrians (II Kings 17:24). As a result they were a mixed race and, in their zeal for racial purity, Ezra and Nehemiah rejected Samaritan assistance in rebuilding the Temple of Jerusalem (Ezra 4:1-3). The Samaritans never forgot this rebuff and thus the woman at the well was right when she said to Jesus, *"The Jews have no dealings with the Samaritans"* (John 4:9). In fact, the Samaritans erected a rival temple to that of Jerusalem and established a temple priesthood on Mount Gerizim. Again in her conversation with Jesus the Samaritan woman at the well noted, *"Our fathers worshipped in this mountain* [Mount Gerizim]; *and ye say, that in Jerusalem is the place where men ought to worship"* (John 4:20).

This Samaritan temple was destroyed by the Maccabean leader John Hyrcanus in 128 B.C. However, the Samaritans continue to worship on this spot today. For a week before the Passover the whole Samaritan community removes itself from Nablus and camps out on top of Mount Gerizim near where the old temple stood. The entire Passover service is followed to a "T" (Exodus 12), including the roasting of a lamb.

The Samaritans even claim they have preserved altars built by both Adam and Noah on the top of the mountain. Also, in the wall of the Justinian Castle built in A.D. 583 on Gerizim's summit, the Samaritans say are preserved the twelve stones that the Israelites removed from the bed of the Jordan River as they made their miracle crossing (Joshua 4:1-9).

The few visitors who take the time to enter the Samaritan synagogue of upper Nablus are shown a magnificent scroll of the Pentateuch. Since this sect only accepts the writings of Moses as divine revelation, their Pentateuch scrolls are some of the best preserved anywhere. The cylindrical, engraved case, carved with figures of the ark of the covenant, the menorah, the temple altar, etc., consists of three parts about 18 inches high and encases the treasured Torah scroll with a green inscribed protective wrapping. It is truly well preserved. All of this is part of the worship mystique of a dying people who have staunchly maintained their uniqueness and who will be remembered by Christians as the people who gave the world the *"good Samaritan"* (Luke 10:33).

## SHECHEM

On the main road just south of Nablus, nestled between Ebal and Gerizim, is biblical SHECHEM. The mound is clearly visible off to the left. It is known as Tell Balata and has been the site of archaeological activity off and on since 1903.

When Abraham made his famous journey from Ur of the Chaldees to Canaan, his first stopover was Shechem. Here he built an altar to his God (Genesis 12:6-7). Sometime later, after his 20-year hiatus to Haran, Jacob returned to Shechem and purchased a plot of Promised Land from the sons of Hamor (Genesis 33:18-20). The rape of his daughter Dinah took place here. Still later his son Joseph came here in search of his brethren tending flocks, only to find them in Dothan (Genesis 37:12-14). And it was here that the Israelites carried the bones of Joseph from Egypt for burial (Genesis 50:25; 33:18-19; Joshua 24:32). In a little white-domed house about 100 yards north of Jacob's Well is the traditional site of Joseph's tomb. This, along with the Jerusalem Temple and the Patriarch's Tomb in Hebron, is claimed by orthodox Jews to be the three parcels of Promised Land which documentation proves to be theirs (Joshua 24:32).

Shechem was also the scene of Joshua's farewell address to Israel when he made that famous declaration, *"As for me and my house, we will serve the LORD"* (Joshua 24:15). One of the six Cities of Refuge (Joshua 20:7; 21:21), it was at Shechem that Abimelech, the son of Gideon, attempted to establish himself as king over all of Israel (Judges 9). He slew his 70 brothers, only one escaping, and ruled in Shechem three years before God brought judgment upon him.

Eventually Shechem did become the site of an authorized coronation. It was here that Rehoboam, son of Solomon, chose to be crowned and so *"all Israel was come to Shechem to make him king"* (I Kings 12:1). But Rehoboam foolishly failed to heed the advice of his father's counselors and increased the financial burden of the Israelites which precipitated the tax revolt led by Jeroboam and the ten northern tribes. *"To your tents, O Israel!"* (I Kings 12:16) has since become the rallying cry of free men everywhere.

Shechem pops up again in the pages of the New Testament. On one of His early junkets from Judaea to Galilee, Jesus came *"to a city of Samaria, which is called Sychar, near to the parcel of ground that Jacob gave to his son, Joseph. Now Jacob's well was there. . ."* (John 4:5-6). Very near Tell Balata, at the fork in the road, is that parcel of ground and the well which Jews, Samaritans, Muslims and Christians associate with Jacob's Well. You'll spot the Convent of Jacob's Well easily. Just look for the walled area to the left with beautiful greenery growing inside the compound. If you don't spot this, the two bright blue metal doors to the compound are a dead giveaway.

Once we are admitted by the Greek Orthodox monk, we enter a peaceful garden setting with beautiful flowers and well-trimmed trees and hedges. We proceed straight ahead through the two pillars on a path that takes us to a huge unfinished church. Begun in 1912, the Russian Orthodox Church wanted to erect a basilica which would be fitting for such a sacred spot, but unfortunately, World War I interfered. Today this roofless church is but a shell under which is located Jacob's Well.

Near the back of this partially weed covered basilica are two small structures that resemble the little building at the end of the path in pre-plumbing days. Actually, these two enclosures are the entranceways to the 18-step passages leading down to the chapel and well. We'll enter the left one as the stairs are steep and narrow and traffic is one way. Floored with painted tiles and walled with paintings and icons, your eyes will first be caught, not by the well, but by the many shiny incense burners hanging from the ceiling.

The well is in the center of the room. One hundred and fifteen feet deep, the lone, gracious monk will lower a metal pail into the well to get us a drink. The pail travels 90 feet before it reaches the water. Although you can't see the water level, it's fun to lean over the center of the seven and one-half foot wide, three foot high well covering and peer down the shaft. When the monk reels back the pail filled with water, he will offer us a drink in a tin cup provided for that purpose. Although the water is crystal clear, great tasting and frosty cold, remember that every pilgrim along this well-traveled route today drank out of that same tin cup. You may want to have your own collapsible cup ready just in case.

Back above ground and outside of the compound there is a delightful bit of local color kitty-cornered across the street. This establishment is a combination general store, parlor, dining room, antique shop and flea market. Although the owner may not be as friendly as most Arab shopkeepers (in fact, he threw me out of his shop one time for bargaining too tenaciously), nonetheless you will be amazed at the diversity of items for sale in such a tiny shop. To the left and behind the door are shelves of "authentic" artifacts discovered in and around Shechem. But the prices are exorbitant and the artifacts are unregistered and therefore unattested as authentic. You will probably want to wait to get to Old Jerusalem for shopping anyway.

## SHILOH

As we head south on the main hill country road to Jerusalem we are still in the territory of Manasseh. In about 15 minutes we will pass biblical OPHRAH on our left. This Benjamite town (Joshua 18:21-22) is where the angel of the LORD appeared unto Gideon and called him to service for God. After the angel proved he was indeed the messenger of Jehovah, Gideon exclaimed, *"I have seen an angel of the LORD face to face"* (Judges 6:22). Here he built an altar unto the Lord calling it Jehovah-shalom, *"The Lord our Peace"* (verse 23). Gideon was buried here in Ophrah (Judges 8:32).

In a few more minutes we pass the village of LUBBAN and leave the beautiful Lebonah Valley. In biblical days this area was famous for myrrh and other incense. Today myrrh is still grown in the valley, along with a more modern commodity, tobacco. This area also marks the traditional frontier between Samaria and Judaea.

But we must keep an eye out for up ahead, as we climb out of the valley to higher terrain, we will be able to see two stone watchtowers on our left. They are worth stopping for a picture. These two nearly perfect watchtowers are circular with a wide bottom tapering slightly toward the top and made entirely of stones gleaned from the fields round about. Just tall enough to get a shepherd out of the reach of hungry animals, the watchtowers would also guard the road against intruders. Watchtowers are prominently featured in the Bible (cf. Isaiah 5:2; Matthew 21:33-44).

Soon we will see a five-foot stone pillar pointing to SHILOH. The ruins are located on the spur road to the left, cutting back toward Ophrah. Today the only remains of Shiloh are a group of ancient tombs cut in the rock, small piles of stones and two blazing white but unfinished and roofless churches begun in the 1930s on the site of ruined Byzantine churches. But Shiloh was once the pride of Israel and her first capital for 300 years prior to the conquest of Jerusalem.

It was at Shiloh the tribes assembled to receive their allotments of the Promised Land (Joshua 18—22). Here the ark of the covenant found a home and here the tabernacle was erected (Joshua 18:1; Judges 18:31). This was the center of Israel's religion and so here Eli judged and Hannah came to pray that God would give her a son (I Samuel 1:1-10). When Samuel was born to Elkanah and Hannah she brought him to Eli the High Priest to raise in the service of the Lord (I Samuel 2:12-26). And it was at Shiloh that Eli died (I Samuel 4) and Samuel judged Israel in his place (I Samuel 7:16-17).

About the year 1050 B.C. Shiloh was destroyed by the Philistines. They took possession of the ark of the covenant and the once sacred city was left in ruins. Since that time Shiloh's ruins have been a point of reference and comparison in God's repeated warnings to His people (Psalm 78:59-61). The prophet Jeremiah uses Shiloh as an example of the destruction God would bring on Jerusalem if Israel did not repent (Jeremiah 7:12-15; 26:6-7). Israel refused to repent and centuries later Jerusalem experienced a similar destruction to that of Shiloh (II Kings 25:8-11). God always provides opportunity for repentance but when repentance is not made, God always keeps His word.

## BETHEL

Leaving Shiloh the road twists and turns south through the hills blanketed with olive groves. We have now passed into the hill country of Ephraim and the inclines become steeper. Only 11 miles north of Jerusalem, we arrive at biblical BETHEL. About a mile and a half off the main road to the east is BEITIN, the Arab village adjacent to the site of Bethel.

Originally called Luz (Genesis 28:19), this was the site where Abraham built his second altar upon arriving from Ur of the Chaldees (Genesis 12:8). After returning from Egypt to escape the Canaanite famine (Genesis 13:3-4), Abraham again migrated here and then strife between Lot's herdsmen and his forced a painful separation (Genesis 13:5-12).

The real prominence of Bethel, however, came with Abraham's grandson. After fleeing from the wrath of his duped brother Esau, Jacob spent the night at Bethel (Genesis 28:11-22) and saw the vision of a ladder with angels ascending and descending from heaven. Jacob's waking response to this dream was, *"How dreadful is this place! This is none other but the house of God, and this is the gate of heaven"* (Genesis 28:17). Hence, the name Luz was changed to Bethel ("House of God"). Jacob revisited Bethel after he returned from his sojourn in Haran (Genesis 35:1-8).

After Israel captured this royal Canaanite city (Joshua 12:16; Judges 1:22-26), Bethel became a major religious center in Israelite life. The city was on Samuel's circuit as prophet and judge (I Samuel 7:16). When the ten northern tribes seceded from Judah, Jeroboam set up two golden-calf worship centers in the north to keep the tribes from making the pilgrimage to Jerusalem to worship. Dan was the northernmost site; Bethel the southernmost. Later when King Jeroboam presumed to burn incense at Bethel he was denounced by an unnamed prophet (I Kings 12:33—13:2). The prophet predicted that one named Josiah would offer the bones of the priests on that altar. During King Josiah's reforms of the 6th century, he removed bones from nearby tombs and burned them on the altar fulfilling exactly this mysterious prophecy (II Kings 23:15-19).

Because he foretold King Jeroboam's death, the prophet Amos was forbidden to prophesy in

Bethel and was expelled from it. This religious center was frequently the subject of Amos' prophecies (Amos 3:14; 4:4; 5:5; 7:10, 13), as well as Jeremiah's (Jeremiah 48:13). Bethel fell with Samaria in 721 B.C. when the Assyrians swept through the land.

As we visit the ancient site of Bethel we are in much less awe than Jacob was on his first visit there. Although several seasons of archaeological excavations have been undertaken, still the finds have not shaken the scientific community and the excavations have been partially restored to use by the residents of Beitin. But still the air on this hill is vibrant with history and stones beneath our feet, and there are millions of them, are rounded by the feet of ancient Israelite worshipers at the site that once was the "House of God."

## RAMALLAH

The road to RAMALLAH winds through a rustic landscape, vineyards, vegetable fields and numerous small villages. Just eight miles north of Jerusalem, Ramallah is one of the most popular resorts in the Holy Land. The name in Arabic means "the Heights of the Lord." The town's elevation, at 2,930 feet above sea level, brings it cool weather when much of Israel is warm and sultry. Actually, Ramallah is 300 feet higher than Jerusalem. As part of the West Bank occupied territory, until the June War of 1967 Ramallah was the best summer resort in Jordan. It was popularly called the "Switzerland of Jordan."

Now the largest village between Jerusalem and Nablus, Ramallah boasts of a population of 50,000 people of which, surprisingly, 25 percent are U.S. citizens. But don't let this fool you. Although an educational and commercial center, Ramallah is decidedly an Arab town. There is much local color here from the veiled women to the water-pipe smoking men. About 95 percent of the population are Christian Arabs.

Since no biblical significance is attached to Ramallah, most Christian crusaders to the Holy Land in this century drive right by this neat and clean city with the simple passing notation, "Oh, over there is Ramallah." But should you take the time to zip up to Ramallah from Jerusalem, you'll enjoy the green hillsides, the plush villas and the town's beautiful park. Also, the former palace of King Hussein is located here, but don't expect to see an opulent wonder for it is plain and unostentatious.

Perhaps the best reason to visit Ramallah is the Arab pastries. Here you can treat your sweet tooth to baklava and other goodies as thin as can be and covered with honey, coconut or pistachio nuts. It's a taste delight you'll never forget from the hill country of the Holy Land.

# CHAPTER 6

# An Intriguing River

## THE JORDAN VALLEY

*"And it came to pass in those days, that Jesus came from Nazareth of Galilee, and was baptized of John in Jordan. And straightway coming up out of the water, he saw the heavens opened, and the Spirit like a dove descending upon him: and there came a voice from heaven, saying, Thou art my beloved Son, in whom I am well pleased. And immediately the Spirit driveth him into the wilderness"* (Mark 1:9-12).

The Jordan Valley is much more than a valley; it is a deep depression in the ground. The valley is referred to as the Rift because it is located between two great geological faults. This rift begins far in the north between the Lebanon and Anti-Lebanon Mountains and cuts a path south deepening steadily into the Dead Sea and then rising slightly until it reaches the Gulf of Aqabah and the Red Sea.

This great valley is divided naturally into three parts: the upper Jordan or Hula basin; the middle Jordan or Tiberias district; and the lower Jordan affectionately known to the Arabs as the Ghor. The floor of the lower valley features these same natural divisions. The land closest to the mountains on either side of the river is developed and filled with fields of bananas and lush vegetables. The subtropic climate contributes to the valley's abundant ability to produce juicy fruits and gigantic vegetables. Closer to the river itself nothing grows. You will see the barren mounds of sand blown there over the years. Then, just before the water's edge is another mini-rift, another depression in the ground known as the Zor. Down in this trench is the Jordan River. The banks of the Jordan are dark green with trees

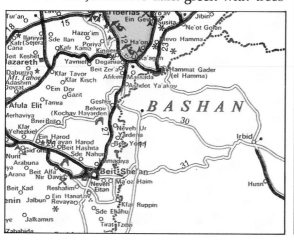

and brush, a striking contrast to the brown barren sand just a few feet away.

The only river in the world which flows predominantly below sea level, the Jordan springs from the foothills of Mount Hermon and flows down to the Hula Valley, through the Sea of Galilee and down the Jordan Valley to the Dead Sea. The largest of Israel's seven permanent rivers, and the only one which does not flow into the Mediterranean, Jordan's headlong drop from its source has given it the name Yarden, the downrusher or descender. Along its 158 mile course from north to south the Jordan descends over 2,300 feet. Still the path of the river is an uncertain one. It meanders over much of the Ghor winding about 200 miles from the Sea of Galilee to the Dead Sea, a distance of only 65 miles. The river swells overflowing its banks during the rainy season, but for most of the year the Jordan is just a small muddy stream with a swift current.

While it doesn't compare with the width of the Amazon or the length of the Nile, or even the might of the Mississippi, still the Jordan has figured prominently in history. No less than three times have its waters been stopped by the miraculous power of God. The first was when the Israelites entered the Promised Land while the river was in its flood stage (Joshua 3:13-17; 4:18). The second was when Elijah struck the waters to allow Elisha and him to cross over the river (II Kings 2:6-8). The third was when Elisha returned to Canaan after Elijah's translation (II Kings 2:12-15). It was on these same waters that Elisha caused the axe head to float (II Kings 6:4-7).

The floor of the Rift Valley is dominated by the winding river, but there are several very important cities in that valley as well. And when we add the cities along the western shore of the Dead Sea it makes for an exciting adventure indeed. So let's begin.

Israelis find the fishing profitable where the Jordan River empties out of the Sea of Galilee.

## BETH SHEAN

There are two main roads that lead to the Jordan Valley from the north. One stretches almost due south from the tip of the Sea of Galilee at DEGANIA toward Beth Shean. Nine miles south of the sea the road passes BELVOIR on our right. A National Parks Authority site, Belvoir's location, as the name indicates, gives an excellent view of the Jordan Valley. The remains of a 12th century French Crusader fortress can be seen here as well. The second road to the valley approaches from the northwest. It begins at Afula in the Jezreel Valley and ends at Beth Shean. Today our route will take us along this highway.

As we leave Afula and cross the valley we soon pass the Kibbutz JEZREEL or Yizreel. Although a recent settlement, founded in 1949, nearby is the ancient site of Jezreel. It was to this city, 20 miles distant from Mount Carmel, that Elijah ran before the chariots of Ahab after defeating the prophets of Baal (I Kings 18:42-46). Here King Ahab built one of his famous palaces. Here too an innocent man named Naboth had a vineyard *"hard by the palace of Ahab king of Samaria"* (I Kings 21:1). Jezebel, Ahab's wicked queen, arranged the murder of Naboth which did not go

unnoticed by God. Elijah prophesied that Jezebel would be eaten by dogs and Ahab's blood would be licked up by dogs. Both prophecies were fulfilled (I Kings 21:17-25; 22:37-38; II Kings 9:30-37). Jehu's judgments on the house of Ahab occurred in and about Jezreel (II Kings 9:14-37; 10:6-11; etc.).

Near Kibbutz Jezreel and just off the main road is EIN HAROD, a copious spring which emerges from the foot of Mount Gilboa. This was Gideon's camp where God reduced the army to 300 by bringing them to the water's edge and instructing Gideon, *"Every one that lappeth of the water with his tongue, as a dog lappeth, him shalt thou set by himself . . . And the LORD said unto Gideon, By the three hundred men that lappeth will I save you . . ."* (Judges 7:5-7). Today this same site is under the administration of the National Parks Authority and includes a modern youth hostel, a culture hall, an amphitheater, as well as a developed community of 2,000 settlers.

Just a short distance beyond Ein Harod on the road to the Jordan Valley is a highway sign for BEIT ALPHA. This communal settlement is off the main road but boasts a most interesting archaeological discovery. Settled by Polish pioneers in 1922, during the process of draining a nearby swamp, these workers discovered the remnant of an old synagogue. Most amazing is the mosaic floor. Divided into three panels the mosaic depicts Abraham's sacrifice of Isaac (Genesis 22:3-13), a Zodiac wheel, and finally, a number of religious emblems such as the ark, the menorah, etc. The synagogue is dated to the 6th century A.D. by an Aramaic inscription refering to Emperor Justinus (A.D. 518-527) as the ruler when the mosaic was laid.

Next stop, BETH SHEAN. The valley beneath us has been steadily descending but now that we have passed under sea level the floor of the valley plummets. We have left the Esdraelon Valley and are now nearing the eastern end of the Jezreel Valley (technically they are not the same, although few draw the distinction). Jezreel rapidly drops to meet the Jordan Valley. They merge at Beth Shean.

Also spelled Beit She'an and Bethshan, this site bears remarkable similarities to Megiddo. Both are situated at a strategic pass, one on each end of Israel's only east-west valley. Both have witnessed a continual parade of armies marching to and from battle through antiquity until now. Both are fine archaeological specimens featuring multiple levels of occupation. Both housed garrisons for Solomon's mighty armies (I Kings 4:12). Other similarities abound.

You have probably already noticed the rise in temperature which accompanies our drop in elevation. We have reached the Jordan Valley, the great Rift Valley. Here at Beth Shean we're already 300 feet below sea level. The fields around us are quite productive even though this area of the Holy Land only receives 12 inches of rainfall annually. To the east of the modern city lay fertile fields fed by streams flowing down from Mount Gilboa. We can easily recognize the crops growing here; there are acres and acres of wheat, cotton fields, and banana groves, not to mention a wide variety of vegetables.

Aside from the strategic and fertile location of Beth Shean, the ancient mound is one of the most important archaeological tells in Israel. Of the myriads of mounds in the Holy Land, this one may exhibit what archaeology is all about.

Between 1921 and 1933 Beth Shean was excavated by a team from the University of Pennsylvania. No less than 18 strata of civilization have been identified going back to 3000 B.C. Because of its ideal location, fertile fields and abundant streams, when one level of occupation was destroyed subsequent settlers would simply repopulate the site rather than locate a new site. Consequently, the city is like an 18 layer cake; the lower the layer, the older the occupation.

For archaeology buffs, levels nine through seven coincide with the Egyptian occupation of the site. Egyptian artifacts abound at these levels, including sarcophagi, scarabs and a stele of Pharaoh Seti I (1303 B.C.). Strata four and five, the Israelite level, contained many interesting Hebrew ceramics, characteristic of King Saul's day. Closer to the top evidence of the Greek era (when the city was renamed Scythopolis), Roman era and the Byzantine era were also discovered. The uppermost level revealed jugs and farm implements from the Arab and Turkish settlers on the site. Something for everyone, a living lesson in archaeology. That's Beth Shean.

If you have the stamina, you may want to climb the mound to the top. It is an impressive site, and climbing it is an impressive feat. While the top of the tell is flat, the sides slope upward at a 45 degree angle. All along the way you will spot pieces of broken pottery, ceramics, jug chips, etc., but they are from the last decades and are not extremely ancient. The real artifacts of Beth Shean are viewed in the Rockefeller Museum in Jerusalem, the University of Pennsylvania Museum in Philadelphia, and the small Beth Shean Museum near the mound.

Although part of the inheritance of Manasseh (Joshua 17:11), this tribe was never able to expel the Canaanites from Beth Shean (Judges 1:27) because of the Canaanite chariots of iron (Joshua 17:16). Perhaps the city's greatest claim to fame is its association with the death of King Saul. Nearby, at Mount Gilboa, Israel's first king and his sons were killed by the Philistines. As was the custom of these "Sea Peoples," the Philistines carried the bodies of Saul and his sons and fastened them to the city wall of Beth Shean. There they would have remained in disgrace had not the brave men of Jabesh-gilead retrieved the bodies by night and buried them (I Samuel 31:8-13). Later David exhumed the bodies and reburied them in the hill country of Benjamin (II Samuel 21:12-14).

Near the Tell Beth-Shean is Palestine's most perfectly preserved Roman theater. Strikingly similar to the Roman theater at Caesarea, this marvel consists of 15 white limestone tiers in near perfect condition with several additional tiers of black basalt in deteriorating condition. The upper gallery, with its nine exit tunnels, makes the Beth Shean theater resemble the Los Angeles Coliseum. Built in A.D. 200, it is estimated that this theater once seated 8,000 spectators.

There are few sites in the Holy Land which

dominate the surrounding countryside like Beth Shean. Few sites preserve the archaeological integrity of a mound like Beth Shean. Few sites have been a fortress for the Canaanites, Egyptians, Philistines, Israelites, Greeks, Maccabeans, Romans, Byzantines, Turks, British, and Israelis like Beth Shean. With its 15,000 inhabitants, the modern Beth Shean must quietly reside in the clamor of the ancient mound next to it.

## THE JERICHO ROAD

Now we begin the long journey south through the Jordan Valley to Jericho. As we drive keep an eye on the black-green vegetation to our left. Although you can't see the water, as long as you see that black-green strip wiggling alongside you know that the Jordan River is there. To our right is the sandy barrenness of the upper Jordan Valley and beyond that the green of its hills.

We are approaching Jericho from the north.

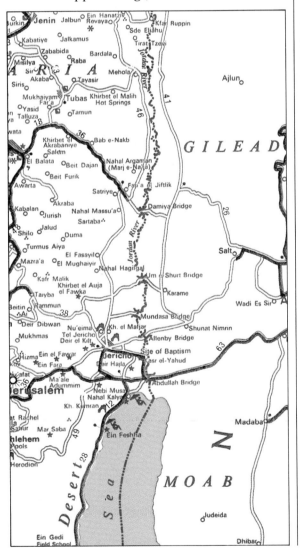

Actually there are four approaches to this desert oasis, one from each corner of the earth. From the south the road twists and turns north then west then north again from the Dead Sea. From the east the road is straight. It arrives from the Jordan River and the single crossing point from Jordan into Israel, the Allenby Bridge. The five and one-half mile trip is usually a relief for those travelers who have just come into Israel from Amman, Jordan's capital. Crossing the Allenby Bridge we are at best a political pawn in the hands of the two governments. Delays of up to six hours have been my experience on three separate occasions. Nonetheless, near this bridge the Israelites crossed the river at flood stage and entered the Promised Land for the first time. For those ancient Israelites the knowledge that Jericho was dead ahead brought little comfort. For today's traveler crossing the Allenby that same knowledge may be the only source of comfort after demoralizing detainment and delays.

By far the most famous approach to Jericho is the legendary Jericho Road. Actually, three such roads have existed crossing from the northern end of the Dead Sea and ascending to the northern boundary of Judaea. One road was built by the Romans and was traveled by our Lord Jesus many times. A second road was built during the British Mandate (1918-1948) and curved around the hills of this eastern wilderness. The present road was built in the early 1960s and is a very good highway, well paved and wide (for a road in the Middle East). It is well contoured to the wild and rugged terrain, occasionally carving passes in the mountains, exposing the crusty stone and revealing a variety of pastel colors when in the shadows and orange and rose colors when struck by the mountain sun. Alongside this highway we can still see the traces of the British road and even on occasion the old Roman road.

This is the famous road that goes from Jerusalem *down* to Jericho. If you glance at a map of the Holy Land you might think the word *down* was ill chosen as Jericho is actually 17 miles to the northeast of Jerusalem. Ordinarily we would describe that as going *up* to Jericho. But here's where our knowledge of the topography of the Holy Land (chapter two) comes in handy.

Jerusalem is approximately 2,700 feet above sea level. The floor of the Jordan Valley at the Dead Sea is 1,300 feet below sea level with Jericho itself being 850 feet below sea level. Hence the 45-minute drive from Jerusalem to Jericho means a drop in elevation of nearly 3,600 feet. As

you will learn, it's an ear-popping experience and the road is definitely *down* to Jericho.

Shortly after leaving Jerusalem, and bypassing Bethany, the Jericho Road rumbles over a knoll exposing the great wilderness of Judaea before us. Most people think the word "wilderness" implies a forest but now we know different. It refers to absolute desolation, similar to the badlands of South Dakota. Far less inhabitable than the sands of the Negev, this wilderness is virtually rainless and therefore vegetationless. It is a place of solitude, a place of refuge as witnessed to by David, Herod and Jesus. It looks like a lifeless moonscape, but we should not confuse the absence of civilization with the absence of life. These wilderness hills sporadically show signs of life. Most prominent is the Bedouin shepherd. As we descend to Jericho we will pass the black-clad Bedouin women, the friendly, waving children and the tiny herds of sheep. Rarely are the men seen but their black tent houses erected on stakes stand out in bold contrast to the chalky sands of the wilderness. Usually they can be seen away from the highway on distant hills or nestled in ravines.

One of the most incongruous things about these Bedouins is their simple lifestyle in floorless black tents with dirt-covered faces and dilapidated shoes decades old, and the subtle evidences of 20th century technology. Frequently, if you look closely, you will see a tractor or a car, usually a Mercedes Benz, behind the black tent. And wonder of wonders, what's that I see sneaking up above the tent? It is! It's a television antenna. With probably the "Days of Our Lives" beamed to be shown during the Arabian nights.

A Bedouin tent with a mast for a TV antenna.

At about the halfway point in our journey from Jerusalem down to Jericho stands an old khan or caravansary, an ancient stopover where travelers could find accommodations for their camels and themselves. This is the traditional INN OF THE GOOD SAMARITAN. As we look around us at the millions of crags and crannies in which robbers could hide to prey on unsuspecting travelers, we can see the appropriateness of the Lord's story about the Good Samaritan and the man who *"went down from Jerusalem to Jericho, and fell among thieves . . ."* (Luke 10:30). The present inn was built by the Turks nearly 400 years ago and is a stark building with a large entranceway which goes through the rectangular building and opens onto a large central courtyard. On either side of the entranceway are huge rooms with arched windows. Although it is impossible to determine whether or not it was at this spot the "neighbor" lay robbed and bleeding, nonetheless this has historically been an important landmark in this wilderness. Prior to the June War of 1967 the Jordanian police used this ancient building as a patrol station from which they monitored the activities of the wilderness. Today it is but a brief stop to and from Jericho to Jerusalem.

A bit farther "down" the road we pass a highway marker on our right. It is the five-foot tall masonry monument indicating in Arabic, Hebrew and English that we have passed below sea level. At this point both Arab and Jewish guides usually quip, "Oh, you'd better roll up your windows or you'll get wet" and we respond with a polite chuckle. Don't encourage them; the jokes get much worse.

Just before we enter Jericho from the west we pass the still visible ruins of HEROD'S WINTER PALACE. Herod built this winter playground near the mouth of the Wadi Kelt, a rainy season stream, and it was here he died in 4 B.C. Off to our right is an abandoned Arab refugee camp. When you spot it, look to the left of the Jericho Road, west and a bit north of the refugee camp to see the ruins of Herod's palace.

## JERICHO

But let's come back to our trip down the Jordan Valley. Just north of Jericho, on the valley road from Beth Shean, we pass CALIPH HISHAM'S PALACE on the left. Not many Christians visit this palace for it was a winter resort for the Omayyad caliphs whose capital was in Damascus, Syria. Hisham's palace was nonetheless beautiful rivaling or exceeding the beauty of Herod's winter palace. It was destroyed by an earthquake in A.D. 724 but still preserved are intricate heating systems, bath houses, saunas, pools, etc. The elegant buildings are now part of the National Parks Authority with many of the palace's artifacts now removed to the Palestine Archaeological Museum in Jerusalem. Still intact, however, is a magnificent bath mosaic floor with beautiful wilderness scenes like gazelles feeding under a pomegranate tree. If time permits, it's really worth the stop.

Making reference to JERICHO can become a bit confusing as there are actually three "Jerichos." The first is Old Jericho, the Old Testament Jericho (Tell el Sultan) near Elisha's Fountain. The second is New Jericho, the modern city sifted by palm trees. And the third is New Testament Jericho, to the south and west of the other sites, near the Wadi Kelt and Herod's winter palace.

As we approach the city from Beth Shean and the north our first stop is Old Jericho, Tell el Sultan. You know we are close when we pass what looks to be flat-roofed adobe huts abandoned by a fleeing tribe of North American Indians. Actually, this ghost town is one of two (the other south of town) refugee camps, the largest such camps built in Jordan (now occupied territory) at the time of the 1948 war. When the Israeli armies moved into this sector in 1967 the refugees fled and the houses now stand in eerie silence.

In just about a minute we arrive at the Old Testament Jericho. This large mound, 1,200 feet long and 50 feet high, is surrounded by a security fence. We enter near Elisha's Fountain and immediately begin to climb up and to our right. A succession of archaeological seasons was undertaken here by John Garstang and later by Kathleen Kenyon. Of interest is the circular stone tower, ancient walls and gates with arches. We have to look down into the mound to see them. Be careful not to snag your coatsleeves on the barbed wire surrounding the "hole" in the mound.

Perhaps Old Jericho will be a disappointment to you. The mound is large but archaeologically unimpressive. That's because you don't see the fabled walls of Jericho and many seasons of excavation have disturbed the site. Besides, the feet of millions of tourists have pounded the mound into submission. But never forget the importance of the 23 different levels of occupation upon which you stand.

This walled city (Joshua 2:2-3) was once the front-line of defense for the ancient Canaanites. If Israel was to claim her promised possession, Jericho must fall. Joshua sent in the spies to survey the city's strength (Joshua 2:1-15). His greatest fears were confirmed. Jericho was impregnable. It was only by the power of Jehovah, the Lord God of Israel, that the walls came tumbling down and the city was subdued (Joshua 6:13-17).

Joshua pronounced a curse on anyone who would attempt to rebuild Jericho (Joshua 6:26), *"Cursed be the man before the LORD, that riseth up and buildeth this city Jericho: he shall lay the foundation thereof in his firstborn, and in his youngest son shall he set up the gates of it."* In spite of this curse, Hiel the Bethelite rebuilt the city and I Kings 16:34 records, *"In his days did Hiel the Bethelite build Jericho: he laid the foundation thereof in Abiram his firstborn, and set up the gates thereof in his youngest son Segub, according to the words of the LORD, which he spake by Joshua the son of Nun."* God always keeps His word.

From the top of this mound we get a perfect view of the MOUNT OF TEMPTATION. With your back to Jericho, look toward the ridge of mountains across the valley. Near the top of this ridge you will notice a line of buildings similar in appearance to the cliff dwellings at Mesa Verde in the American West. This is the GREEK MONASTERY OF THE FORTY DAYS, believed to be the site of the middle of Jesus' three temptations by Satan. After fasting for forty days and being tempted all the while, the devil took Jesus *"up into an high mountain"* (Luke 4:1-13). These are also the mountains where the Israelite spies hid for three days while the king of Jericho pursued them toward the Jordan River.

As we make our way down off the mound of Jericho, being careful of the slippery steps, we deserve a stop across the street at the OLD JERICHO REST HOUSE. It's hot at Jericho about ten months a year and at the rest house we can buy a cold soft drink, stand in front of the huge fan, or purchase some luscious Jericho fruit in order to cool off. Bananas, oranges, dates, pistachio nuts, and a variety of melons await us. It's even possible to purchase some souvenirs or a candy bar. Let's sit at one of the tables and chat with the friendly employees of the rest house.

Okay, enough rest. You don't fly 6,000 miles or more to Israel just to rest. Let's go up the street to our right a few hundred feet to see ELISHA'S FOUNTAIN. The spring originates under the mound of Old Jericho and waters the entire area. Jericho is known as the *"city of palm trees"* in the Old Testament (Deuteronomy 34:3). It's the same today. The streets of the present town are lined with date palms and flamboyant-red flowering Poinciana trees. You would not expect

to see such abundant flora or such a beautiful oasis in such an arid valley. But the secret of Jericho's green in a sea of brown is Elisha's abundant stream. The water is crystal clear, pure and plentiful.

But it wasn't always so. Elijah and Elisha and the *"sons of the prophets"* were at Jericho (II Kings 2:4-18) and after the two great prophets miraculously crossed the Jordan and the mantle was transferred from Elijah to Elisha, Elisha returned to Jericho. Here he found this stream to be polluted and of no value to the city. Elisha cast a handful of salt into the water and by the power of the LORD healed the stream, purifying it until

At the Old Testament Jericho site a series of archaeological endeavors have left interesting ruins like this ancient wall and circular stone tower.

this day (verses 19-22). Now the copious fountain is the lifestream of the city. We can dip our hands into the water flowing through the narrow ground channel and feel the swiftness of the current as well as taste the goodness of the water.

Somehow we always seem to arrive in Jericho in time for lunch. I think it's planned that way for lunching in Jericho is an unforgettable experience. Around the town square, which is lined with shops selling fresh fruits and vegetables, soaps, sacks of dried tobacco and just about everything else, we can pick up a snack. But the real atmosphere of a lunch in Jericho is only savored by eating in one of the city's garden restaurants.

On Ein El Sultan Street, for example, there are a number of such restaurants. The food is very good and inexpensive. The most popular dish is chicken served with carrots and peas and of course pitta bread with several bowls of various pastes into which you dip your pitta. The flavors of these pastes or sauces are indescribable (and most people don't care to anyway) but you owe it to yourself to try them all.

One word of caution. Every lunch in Jericho is accompanied by an army of flies. I think they followed the Israelites from Egypt. These restaurants ought to be called "Shew and Chew." Oh, yes, one other thing. Don't be shocked to see one of many cats climb right up on the table which hasn't been cleared and eat what patrons have left behind. This is socially acceptable in Jericho and, in fact, in most Arab cities. But the cats will wait their turn so let's enjoy lunch. Bon appetite.

One of the oldest, if not the oldest, cities in the world, Jericho has played a major role in the history of the Holy Land. Not only was the great battle fought here, but also at Jericho the messengers of King David tarried until the indignities they received at the hands of the princes of Ammon were removed (cf. II Samuel 10:1-5). It was near Jericho that King Zedekiah was captured by the Chaldeans (II Kings 25:5-7; Jeremiah 39:5-7; 52:8-11). In the New Testament era Jericho was also prominent. It was here that miniscule Zacchaeus climbed a sycamore tree to see Jesus (Luke 19:1-10). Such trees can still be seen along Jericho's streets today. Great multitudes followed Jesus from Jericho on His way to the triumphal entry into Jerusalem. It was on this occasion that blind Bartimaeus was healed (Mark 10:46-52).

Now that we are aware that there was more than one town of Jericho, an Old Testament site and a New Tetament site (as well as New Jericho today), maybe that will clear up some confusion about an alleged discrepancy in the Bible. Matthew records that this blind man was healed, *"as they departed from Jericho"* (Matthew 20:29). Luke records that the healing took place *"as he was come nigh unto Jericho"* (Luke 18:35). The simple explanation for this is that both writers were right. The healing of Bartimaeus probably took place on the road leaving one Jericho and coming near the other. The Bible stands.

Now, sad to say, it's time to leave the lush oasis of Jericho and wander out into the wilderness again. We leave behind a city repeatedly ruined and rebuilt. We leave behind an authentic legend. We leave behind the oldest continually inhabited city in the world. But we carry with us some fond memories. We carry with us a sack filled with fruit 25 percent larger than we are used to. And, oh yes, we carry with us a few Jericho flies to be released in the heat of the desert wilderness.

As we make our way south to the Dead Sea, we wind around until just before we get to the very edge of the sea once again visible is the black-green streak which identifies the plant growth of the Zor, the lowest trench through which the Jordan flows. Although it is impossible to approach the river at this point as it is a military zone, it was near here at BETHABARA that John the Baptist baptized Jesus (Mark 1:1-11). Perhaps you can make out the Abyssinian-styled MONASTERY OF JOHN THE BAPTIST built on this spot.

At the very northern tip of the Dead Sea is a complex of buildings known as the LIDO. Built years ago before this territory fell into Israeli hands, this site is a local combination swim and snack retreat. Most tourists do not stop here but if you do you will be able to get a small snack, change into your bathing suit and take a quick dip in the Dead Sea.

The first time I visited this place I went for a midnight swim. It was indescribable. It was incredible. The concentration of salt in the Dead Sea, also known as the Salt Sea (Genesis 14:3; Numbers 34:3, 12; Joshua 15:2, 5), fluctuates between 24 percent and 26 percent. That's five times saltier than the ocean. I had been in the Great Salt Lake in Utah before, but even it can't hold a candle to this. The waters are so dense, so buoyant, that it's impossible to sink. Literally, you can sit up in the water as if you were in a chair. You don't have to be a Mark Spitz to swim here. You can't fail. But if you should swim in the Dead Sea, do not open your eyes or mouth. In fact, every little cut or shaving nick will smart from the salt in the water, but it will heal more rapidly.

Once you leave the sea it is mandatory that you shower and wash out your suit in fresh water. If you don't the oily salt on your skin will dry to a hardness that can be scraped off with a knife. Perhaps it would be best as a pilgrim to stop along the western shore of the sea and simply dip your feet and fingers in the water just to get a "taste" of the Dead Sea.

## THE DEAD SEA

Before we drive south along the western shore of the DEAD SEA, perhaps a word about the sea itself would be in order. Over the centuries this body of water, containing an acrid witches' brew, has been known by a variety of names. The Hebrews called it the Salt Sea (Genesis 14:3; etc.); the Greeks preferred the name Asphalt Sea because of its chemical properties; beginning with Saint Jerome the Latins called it the Dead Sea be-cause it will not support marine life; and the Arabs simply refer to it as the Sea of Lot because of the association of Abraham's nephew with the area (Genesis 13:10-13).

Now let's get really low down—on the earth, that is. The great geological fault or crack in the earth we have been following down the Jordan Valley now reaches its lowest point. We have ar-rived at the Dead Sea, approximately 1,300 feet below sea level—the lowest spot on earth. Some places on the bottom of the sea are as far beneath the surface as the surface is beneath sea level. It is known that there are spots on the floor of the Dead Sea approximately 2,600 feet below sea level. Now, that's low down.

Not a big sea, only 47 miles long and about ten miles wide, the Dead Sea covers 394 square miles in area. Each day about seven million tons of water flow into the sea, mainly from the Jordan River. Since there is no outlet to the sea you might expect that the water level would be constantly rising, but it isn't. Because of the in-

**The Dead Sea viewed from Masada. Visitors from all over the world come to bathe in its mineral-rich waters.**

tense heat and dryness of the Jordan Valley the daily evaporation of the water about equals the daily intake. This means that the water, which remains less than constant in the Dead Sea, is increasingly impregnated with those minerals left behind in the evaporation process.

In addition to being about 25 percent salt, the Dead Sea also contains approximately 45 billion tons of sulphur, potassium chloride, magnesium bromide, sodium chloride, magnesium chloride and calcium chloride. In fact, so rich in mineral content is the Dead Sea that it has enough potassium chloride to supply the world's need for potash fertilizer for 3,000 years. This is not only the lowest spot on earth, it is also the richest. Hence, nasty and noxious or not, the Dead sea is worth incalculable billions of dollars and all of these minerals are slated for extraction from the sea by the Israeli government.

In my own estimation, the Dead Sea appears to resemble a fetal mouse heading south with the Jordan River as a long, squiggly tail. This is because there is a peninsula jutting out from the eastern shore into the sea a third of the way from the bottom. This is called the Lisan Peninsula or "The Tongue." Because of increased irrigation projects by both Israel and Jordan and because the water for these projects comes from the River Jordan, the water flowing into the Dead Sea has not quite equaled the evaporation rate over the past couple of decades. You know what that means. The water level of the Dead Sea is steadily dropping and now the tongue actually extends all the way to the west bank of the sea dividing it in two, creating a deep northern sea and a shallow southern sea. It is possible to walk from one shore to the other on dry land, about 15 miles from the southern tip of the sea. But don't try it. Remember, one shore is Israel and the other is Jordan.

Many Israelis and others feel that while the irrigation projects are necessary for the modern agricultural economies of Israel and Jordan, to destroy a unique sea as old as time itself is unthinkable. Several proposals have been made to save the Dead Sea. The one receiving the most current attention is the Med-Dead Canal. First proposed in 1944 by the American geographysicist, Walter C. Lowdermilk, this plan calls for a canal to be dug from the Mediterranean Sea to the Dead Sea. The flow of the salty ocean water to the salty sea water would be controlled and, due to the tremendous 1,300 foot drop from the Mediterranean to the Dead Sea, eight times the fall at Niagara, an astounding amount of electric-ity could be generated in the process. Environmentalists, sentimentalists, tourists and pilgrims all pray that the Dead Sea will be saved.

## QUMRAN

Who hasn't heard of the Dead Sea Scrolls? No one, right, but do you know where they were discovered? Just about ten miles south of Jericho, as we drive along the northwest shore of the Dead Sea, we'll notice that the sharpness of the sandy-brown mountains changes to a reddish-brown hue and the mountains become a marly plateau. It is here that the Dead Sea Scrolls were discovered. We'll enter the gate, pass the little guard house on our right and drive up the long hill to Qumran.

Now for a fascinating story. In the early spring of 1947 a young Bedouin boy made a startling discovery in one of the more than 250 caves which riddle these hills. In an attempt to retrieve a lost sheep, he wandered into a lonely cave and discovered the seven most famous scrolls in the world, the first of many finds which make up the Dead Sea Scrolls. Unaware of the importance of these manuscripts, the lad took them later to a Bethlehem merchant and antique dealer named Kando. From this dealer four of the scrolls were purchased by the Archbishop Metropolitan Samuel of the Syrian Othodox Church in Jerusalem and three of the scrolls were purchased by the Israeli archaeologist Dr. E. L. Sukenik. Subsequently the Dead Sea Scrolls became known as "the greatest archaeological discovery of the 20th century."

But why are the scrolls so important? The reason is they are dated between 200 B.C. and A.D. 100. The manuscripts from which our Old Testament is translated date to about A.D. 1000 because they are careful copies of earlier manuscripts. But the Dead Sea Scrolls are about 1,000 years earlier than these and are almost identical, wonderfully validating the accuracy of the Bible. That makes these scrolls immensely important. In fact, a special museum at the Hebrew University was built just to house these scrolls. It is known as THE SHRINE OF THE BOOK.

Adjacent to the hills in which the scrolls were found, and just to our left as we ascend the hill from the seashore, are the ruins of ancient QUMRAN. Here lived a monastic community of Jews known as the Essenes. This highly disciplined sect moved from the city life of Jerusalem to the loneliness of the Judaean wilderness in order to lead a more devout and holy life. It was the Essenes who painstakingly copied the Dead Sea Scrolls.

Believed to be one of the *"towers in the desert"* built by King Uzziah in the 8th-7th century B.C. (II Chronicles 26:10), the site of Qumran has been occupied sporadically over the centuries. The major settlement was initiated during the days of the Maccabees, but the site was abandoned after an earthquake in 31 B.C. If we look at one of the larger square cisterns on the sea side of the site we will see a huge crack in the stairway leading down to the bottom of the cistern. This is certain evidence of this great earthquake. Your best picture of this is from the north side of the cistern, with the sea to your left. Qumran was again occupied around the time of Herod the Great's death in 4 B.C. and the Essenes fled from it before the advance of Vespasian and the Roman armies in A.D. 68. Its final occupation by the Jewish zealots of Bar Kochba was in A.D. 132-135.

Today the abandoned ruins are like an outdoor, walkthrough museum. A guide will escort us through the Qumran village, but anyone with a plan of the city and a knowledge of its history can do just as well. We enter to the right of a tower at the north edge of the ruins. If you climb the tower you will get a good view of the village layout. The climb isn't bad, only a dozen or so steps. Let's do it.

One of the most striking features of this community is the evident lines of the aqueduct system which brought treasured water from the western hills to be stored in the village's many cisterns. You can easily trace it through the city. Also, from our perspective above the partially excavated and restored ruins, we can see that the village today somewhat resembles a maze. Cutting left and right through the ill-defined passageways we will discover a bakery, potter's kiln, the community dining hall, a storehouse, workshops, kitchen, a pantry and numerous cisterns. One of the most interesting rooms is the long and narrow scriptorium with stone benches on either side. It was here that the Dead Sea Scrolls were copied.

The community was built on the edge of a marly cliff. Let's walk through the ruins and south about a hundred feet to the very edge of that cliff. Across a deep ravine, which has been cut into the plateau by the restless waters of an adjacent wadi, we can see a cave cut into the side of a neighboring cliff. This is the famous Cave 4 where hundreds of thousands of bits and fragments of scrolls were discovered by archaeologists. Imagine yourself trying to piece together a gigantic puzzle with more than 100,000 pieces. And what's worse, imagine that these pieces were from hundreds of different puzzles, all dumped together in a cave. Well, that's the task which Israeli archaeologists are still undertaking in order to reconstruct the many manuscripts of the Dead Sea Scrolls.

The scrolls were apparently hurriedly hid in this cave when the armies of Rome's Tenth

**The author visits the caves where the Dead Sea Scrolls were found.**

Legion came into view. Over the centuries they have been deteriorating. Unfortunately we cannot climb down into the cave. The marly cliff is steep and slippery. There are no handrails or stairs. The drop to the bottom of the ravine, should we unfortunately slip, would be deadly. Besides, I climbed down into Cave 4 several years ago and all the parchment and pottery fragments have long since been removed from the cave.

As we make our way back to the parking lot and the large sunshelters (where you can buy a cold? drink), don't fail to look off to the distant hills north of Qumran. There, with a little help from the guide or the soda salesman, you can spot Cave 1 where the Bedouin shepherd first discovered the famous Dead Sea Scrolls. Now out of the demon sun and desert surroundings to a far more pleasant environment.

## EIN FASHKHA—EIN GEDI

About three miles south of Qumran is a pleasant oasis called EIN FASHKHA. This island of cool in a sea of sun will quickly refresh us from our visit to the shadeless city of the Essenes. There is a clinic nearby specifically for those who become ill from overexposure to the rays of the sun. But a few minutes in Ein Fashkha will be all the medicine we need.

This beautiful spot is a favorite of the Israelis today. On the weekends, in fact, it's so crowded that it's almost impossible to move among the people. It features a circular pool about 30 feet in diameter filled with fresh water flowing from the mountains behind. Also there are now three pools just for the children. Not only do these pools provide restoration from the hot sun, but the modern dressing rooms and restrooms provide a place to shower and change after a dip in the nearby Dead Sea. Centuries ago the Qumran Essenes used this oasis area to grow food for their ascetic brotherhood. Can you imagine the chagrin on the faces of these pietists to see their nature preserve used by the fun-frolickers of the Dead Sea?

Approximately halfway south on the highway which hugs the western shore of the Dead Sea we arrive at another and more important oasis. This is EIN GEDI, also spelled En Gedi. Just about ten miles south of Ein Fashkha, we are astounded to find another lush area in an otherwise arid region. Here are delightful waterfalls, freshwater pools, palm trees and high grass. But unlike Ein Fashkha, Ein Gedi is a more serious settlement today. Between the spring of Ein Gedi and the Dead Sea is a new kibbutz called Ein Gedi. Here vegetables and other vegetation grow in profusion adjacent to the near wastelands of sand and the wastewaters of the Dead Sea. How is this possible? The answer to the fertility of this kibbutz is DAVID'S FOUNTAIN.

In the days of the Old Testament this area was known as Hazazontamar (II Chronicles 20:2). It was in the territory of Judah (Joshua 15:62). Here is where the mountains meet the sea and the cliffs rise above the sand nearly 2,000 feet. These sharp and flat-faced cliffs are peppered with caves and dens. It was in such a cave, one of these we can still see, that David and his men took refuge from King Saul. It was at Ein Gedi that David spared Saul's life after he cut off a piece of his garment while the king slept (I Samuel 24).

The great fertility of the area arises from a stream and springs which flow in abundance from the limestone cliffs to the west. Because of the importance of the area in the early life of David, the stream has come to be known as David's Fountain. The fruitful vineyards and luxuriant growth of the area are praised in the Song of Solomon 1:14.

To get to the waterfalls we must go to the back of the parking lot and follow the signs of the nature trail, slinking through both palms and pines. Back we go into the desert hills, through rock formations that are absolutely otherworldly. After about 15 minutes of steady climbing we arrive at the fabulous Ein Gedi waterfalls. Here in a canyon of green vegetation the water breathtakingly tumbles from a height of 300 feet. In this oasis from sun and sand we won't easily be pried away but eventually we must leave the Ein David Gorge behind and follow the reed-studded trail back to the parking lot.

There is an ironic similarity between modern Ein Gedi and ancient Qumran. Of course in this land of contrasts that is nothing new. But have you noticed that here in the Ein Gedi Kibbutz there is a community which has abandoned city ways to live in a brotherhood by the sea? Wasn't this true of Qumran? In the Ein Gedi Kibbutz there is a spirit of defiance, defiance of the arid land, the nearby adversaries and the acceptable lifestyle. Wasn't this true of Qumran? History has a strange way of repeating itself. In fact, many modern Israelis consider the Essene community at Qumran to be "the world's oldest Kibbutz."

## MASADA

Continuing to drive south on the Salt Sea-skirting road, we next come to MASADA. This

National Parks Authority site is one of the most significant landmarks in all of Israel. Masada is to the Israeli what the Alamo or Pearl Harbor is to the American. It is a symbol of dynamic leadership and a stalwart defense in the face of insurmountable odds and certain death. Here the oath of allegiance is taken by all the cadet graduates of Israel's military academy. "Masada shall not fall again" is not just a cadet slogan; it is Israel's national determination.

Masada is an immense flat-topped plateau which from a distance resembles a gigantic thumb pushing its way up through the earth's crust. Masada is an enormous aneurysm on the geological depression we call the Jordan Valley. Located some two and one-half miles from the western shore of the Dead Sea, exactly opposite The Tongue, Masada is a half mile long and 220 yards wide. It is a rock fortress the top of which

rises to about sea level, while the valley 1,300 feet below it remains the lowest spot on earth.

It is possible that Masada, also spelled Massada, is mentioned in the Bible. When David fled from the threats of the jealous King Saul, I Samuel 24:22 records, *"David and his men got them up into the hold"* (cf. I Chronicles 12:8). The word translated "hold" is the Hebrew word *metsade*, the equivalent of Masada. Be that as it may, the importance of this sandy brown crag was not really established until the days of Herod the Great.

Herod (37-4 B.C.), the prolific builder of Caesarea, Samaria and Jericho, also established a winter palace at Masada. This combination fortress/palace was considered to be Herod's strongest. Around the perimeter of the plateau's top he erected an 18-foot high wall with 38 towers, each being 75 feet high. Not only was

**Masada is an immense flat-topped plateau near the Dead Sea's western shore. Herod built a fortress/palace on three tiers at the north end.**

the site nearly inaccessible, it was nearly impregnable as well.

Today there are three ways we can ascend to the top of this rectangular rock. Usually only two of these are used by tourists as the third, the ramp path known as The Battery, is on the west side of Masada and approachable only by a road from Arad. The second method, if you are a hearty soul (or think you are) is to climb Masada from the east. Here you will find a two mile long serpentine path, the Snake Path, which is steep, filled with hairpin curves and places an unusual strain on body muscles which have remained dormant since the last time you tried a fool thing like this. You need to allow about two hours for the climb. As for me and my house, we'll take the cable car. This third method affords a breathtaking ride and deposits us just 75 short steps from the summit.

In order to support his summer palace, Herod the Great had to develop an ingenious system of aqueducts and cisterns in order to catch and retain every precious drop of water which fell on this arid area. A series of pools, baths and cisterns are evident as we make our way around the perimeter of Masada's heights. One of the cisterns is estimated to have held 80,000 gallons of water. Also on the top of Masada we will distinguish the royal family's residence, officers' quarters, an administration building in addition to a synagogue (the world's oldest), Zealot quarters and a Byzantine church. Either at the shop on the ground or at the entranceway on the top of Masada you can buy a plan of the site very inexpensively.

There are two things we dare not miss at Masada. The first is the Roman bath adjacent to the partially restored storehouses at the northern end of the rock. A squiggly line of black paint on the storehouse walls divides the original remains from the reconstructed part. The second is the northern palace itself.

The luxurious bath house was built by Herod the Great according to the customary Roman pattern. We enter through the large courtyard facing the northern palace. Originally this area was surrounded on three sides by pillars, the floor being a red, white and black mosaic. The first room we enter is the dressing room (apoditerium) complete with frescoes on the walls. Through the doorway we enter the three chambers of the bath house. To our right is the cold-water bath (frigidarium), ahead the water-warm bath (tepidarium) and to our left, the steam room for hot-water baths (caldarium). This is the most interesting room at Masada.

As we stand on the walkway overlooking the floor we need to reconstruct the room in our minds. What we see on the floor are over 200 tiny pillars each approximately two feet high and six to eight inches in diameter made of round clay bricks. These pillars originally supported a suspended mosaic floor. Adjacent to the caldarium was an oven with pipes connecting the two. From the oven hot air would flow into the space beneath the suspended floor. Since the room was nearly airtight the floor would quickly warm heating the entire room. When water was poured on the heated floor it turned the hot room into a steam bath. Herod had all the comforts of home at his winter residence.

The Northern Palace of King Herod, described in glowing terms by the Jewish historian Josephus, was actually built on three levels. The three terraces, level two being 40 feet below level one and level three 110 feet below, housed the palace which was apparently Herod's private villa, opposed to the Western Palace which was the official residence.

We enter the upper terrace from the side near the Dead Sea. Here was Herod's living room. The walls were highly decorated with colorful frescoes of which, unfortunately, almost nothing remains. The floor was a black and white

A section of the ruins at Masada. The squiggly line of paint on the walls divides the original remains from the reconstruction.

mosaic. The fact that this entire residential area is so small must mean that it was intended for Herod alone, or perhaps for one of his nine wives and him. Let's walk to the very northern edge of the upper terrace. Here we find a rounded balcony, the pride of the palace. Imagine you are the Idumaean king himself. From this semi-circular porch you would get an absolutely breathtaking view to the north, east and west. You can see Ein Gedi and beyond. In fact, on a clear day you could see all the way to Jericho and your palace there.

The descent to the middle and lower terrace levels is on the southwest side of the upper level, away from the sea. On this level we encounter a circular structure which originally had been two concentric walls. These walls served as bases for some sort of a columned structure. Apparently this was Herod's leisure or relaxation center, his family room. On the west side of the bungalow-sized level is a perfectly preserved staircase leading to the upper terrace.

The lower terrace consists of a rectangular area about the same size as the middle terrace. It has, however, perhaps the best preserved remains. On the southern wall we see plastered columns with Corinthian capitals on the facade of the lime rock. The walls are painted with red and green frescoes about three feet high and designed to give the appearance of paneled marble facing. On the east side steps lead down to a small but elaborate private bath with a frigidarium, tepidarium and a caldarium. Here too when the site was excavated were discovered the skeletons of a man, woman and child which recalled in the archaeologists' minds the chilling story of the last tragic night of Masada.

By now everyone is familiar with the drama of Masada. Every school child in Israel has made the climb to the stronghold's summit to hear the story. The events which bring fame and tourists to Masada are both heroic and tragic.

Herod's magnificent palace eventually became occupied by a small Roman garrison. However, during the Jewish revolt of A.D. 66, a band of zealots surprised the soldiers in a sneak attack and overpowered them. From this elevated sanctuary they waged a guerrilla war against the Romans. They had no fear of reprisal for Masada was easily defended and the surface of the plateau yielded enough grain and vegetables to keep the vast storerooms well stocked. The army of Jewish freedom fighters could continue to harass the hated Roman invaders as long as they wished.

But the power and pride of Rome was not to be denied. The emperor knew that even though Jerusalem had been destroyed in A.D. 70, as long as these outlaw Jews continued to occupy Masada a spark of hope beat in every Hebrew heart. The zealots of Masada had become folk heroes and they must be defeated.

This seemingly impossible task fell to the Roman general Flavius Silva. After a three-year siege from A.D. 70-73 Silva was unsuccessful at driving the zealots from the fortress. The Romans used every device they had: rock bombardments, battering rams, flaming torches, siege machines, etc. Nothing worked. Then the long and arduous task of building an earthen ramp from the floor of the valley to the western crest of Masada was undertaken. The ramp attaches itself to Masada just below the western palace. If we stand at the western wall or the northern palace outlook we will easily discern the remains of the ramp. It is truly an amazing feat given the tons and tons of earth the Romans had to move in order to build such a ramp.

With the ramp completed and the Romans literally at the door, it was only a matter of time for the zealots. Their leader, Eliezer Ben Yair, delivered an impassioned appeal to his fortress followers that it would be far more honorable for Masada's doomed defenders to die by their own hands than be tortured and sold into slavery by the Romans. All agreed. When the final Roman assault came the next morning it was met with no resistance, only a deafening silence. Suddenly the horrible truth was evident. One of history's largest mass suicides had transpired during the night. The bodies of 960 men, women and children were lying side by side, in families, the victims of being too small in number and too large in pride. "Masada shall not fall again."

Before we leave the top of this remarkable rock, let's take one final panoramic view of the lower Jordan Valley. From the western edge we clearly see the southernmost ridges of the Central Highlands, the hills of Judaea and Idumaea. These dark and forboding mountains soon level to the uplands of the Negev, visible from the southern tip of Masada. Standing at the eastern lookout, we get a perfect view of the Dead Sea, the Lisan Peninsula, "The Tongue" and the mountains of Moab. Notice how placid the sea appears, how shallow the southern extremity is and how the Valley of Salt flattens out from the lower tip of the sea. From our vantage point we can see the mountains east and west of us and begin to appreciate just how deep the Jordan

Valley and Dead Sea really are. To the north we can see the valley stretch along the sea and wonder what the Jewish zealots must have felt as they saw the Roman armies approaching their stronghold.

Perhaps as we leave this hallowed site we will be treated to one more demonstration of determination. Frequently the mighty Israeli air force flies these skies on training missions. I have never seen Israeli jets streak above the heights of Masada but what they tipped their wings in customary tribute to their respect for the meaning of Masada.

At last we "fly" the cable car back to the reception center/restaurant at ground level and bid farewell to one of the Holy Land's most tragic sites. In a land filled with tragedy, this is a place we will never forget. Ironically, the date of Masada's suicide was April 15th, A.D. 73, income tax day in the United States.

## SODOM

Just south of Masada the road along the western shore of the Dead Sea forks to the right. This highway winds west to ARAD and finally joins the main road of the Negev joining Beersheba with Jerusalem. Our journey down the Jordan Valley will forsake this last opportunity to return to modern civilization and we will continue on the Dead Sea road to the south.

Ten minutes along the road we pass another oasis named EIN BOKEK. Here is a guest house, health resort and beach. It is fed by the hot springs of HAMEI-ZOHAR to the south. Above the resort we can spy the ruins of the Bokek Fort, built to defend the freshwater spring. Two miles south at Hamei-Zohar are additional bath houses and a clinic. The hot mineral springs of this area, frequented by David and Solomon, are busy today providing comfort to all sorts of ailments. Doctors at the clinic claim particular success in curing diseases of the joints, allergies and disorders of the skin. Just south of Zohar the road branches back to the right toward Arad. Like Lot, however, we have set our sights on Sodom and will continue south along the sea.

It is important to remember that a visit to SODOM is not a visit to a city or even a ruins. The wicked city of Sodom is no more. Once five cities dotted this plain: Sodom, Gomorrah, Admah, Bela (Zoar), and Zeboiim (Genesis 14:2-11). It was in this region of the Plain of Jordan that Lot *"pitched his tent toward Sodom"* (Genesis 13:12). But the Bible pointedly says that *"the men of Sodom were wicked and sinners before the LORD exceedingly"* (Genesis 13:12). The sins of the men of Sodom have always been despicable to God and condemned by Him. Thus the Almighty *"destroyed the cities of the plain"* by raining brimstone and fire down from heaven so that *"the smoke of the country went up as the smoke of a furnace"* (Genesis 19:24-29). Since that day Sodom has been used as a symbol of judgment by God and as a warning by Moses (Deuteronomy 29:23; 32:32); by Isaiah (1:1-10; 13:19); by Jeremiah (23:14; 49:18; 50:40); by Amos (4:11); by Zephaniah (2:9); by Jude (4, 7); and even by Jesus Christ (Matthew 10:15; 11:24). You would think that with God's proven distaste for Sodom's sons and the repeated warnings of God's prophets, no intelligent nation on the face of the earth, for its own safety and well being, would ever again tolerate the practice of these sins. That's what you'd think.

Today archaeologists believe the remains of the ruined city lie somewhere beneath the shallow end of the Dead Sea. Hence the drive to Sodom doesn't produce the same kind of results that the drive to other biblical sites does. What we do see as we approach the area are some of the world's most bizarre shapes, desolate deserts, tortured mountains and salt encrusted seashores. Rising from the shallow waters of the Dead Sea are rocks and driftwoods salt-sealed with centuries of saline solutions. Many of them look like agonizing albino octopuses gasping for breath as they struggle to be loosed from the bottom of the sea.

The noxious smell of sulphur fills the air and our nostrils as we see the potash and bromide plants which now make up the only semblance of civilized life here. This is part of Israel's $50 million program to mine the country's most valuable natural resource—the Dead Sea.

A couple of miles north back along the main road are seen numerous salt mines and the famous CAVE OF SODOM. Now closed for safety reasons, the cave is a labyrinth of salt-studded passageways and acrid stalactites. Above the cave is a natural outcropping of stone which has been pointed out to travelers as the stony remains of Lot's curious wife (Genesis 19:26). Even with a vivid imagination the stone pillar doesn't even resemble a feminine figure.

Also along this road, for those who care, is a post office. Travelers go out of their way (about the only reason to drive this far south) to have their letters postmarked here. The post office stamp says, "Lowest Point on Earth." In fact, that is an apt description for the southern end of the Great Rift, the most unique of all the Holy Land's natural regions—the Jordan Valley.

# CHAPTER 7

# The Wild, Wild South

### CITIES OF THE NEGEV

*"And afterward the children of Judah went down to fight against the Canaanites, that dwelt in the mountain, and in the south, and in the valley. And Judah went against the Canaanites that dwelt in Hebron . . ." (Judges 1:9-10).*

According to the Talmudic scholars, the word Negev means "dry" but Old Testament scholars disagree. The Bible refers to the Negev as the "south" (cf. Genesis 12:9). Regardless, both are true. The Negev is the dry south (Deuteronomy 1:7; 34:3; Joshua 15:19; Judges 1:15). But if you're expecting to see unending dunes of monotonous sand, you'll be disappointed.

The Negev is wild and raging, a varying landscape of saw-toothed mountains, wind-sculptured valleys, eroded gorges and a formidable wilderness. Here we will see huge boulders of black volcanic rock, craggy mounds of sandstone and jagged limestone jutting out of the sand like the jaws of a shark piercing through the surface of the ocean. The whole region is a rainbow of yellows, browns, red and blacks.

Some years ago the Negev encroached upon the cities of the south. But today adventurous Israeli settlers have pummeled the Negev into submission and rolled back the encroaching sands like the lid on a tin of sardines. Beyond the modern settlements, however, the Negev is still the wild, wild south. These wilderness crags are the home of some 27,000 Bedouins who roam the Negev much like Abraham did millennia ago (Genesis 12:9; 13:1). With temperatures ranging from 125 degrees during the day to 50 degrees during cold winter nights, the region is as inhospitable today as it was when Hagar was ministered to by an angel after fleeing the jealousy of Sarah (Genesis 16:7-16).

Our excursion to the Negev will actually take us only to the northern fringe of the desert. We are primarily interested in the cities of the Bible and thus we will confine our travels to the area south of Jerusalem to Beersheba, the area of Judaea.

**A timeless scene in the Negev Desert.**

## HERODION

As we leave Jerusalem and head south for Bethlehem, a secondary road just north of the City of David takes us east and then south through barren hills to HERODION. You can't miss Herodion; it's the cone-shaped mountain that gives every resemblance of being a volcano. It's clearly visible from Jerusalem, Bethlehem and just about everywhere else in this part of the Judaean Mountains.

Actually, Herodion (also spelled Herodium) is a manmade mountain. It is the product of that prolific builder Herod the Great. In a colossal earth-moving project, Herod heightened a mound by piling tons of dirt on it and forming Herodion. At the foot of the conical creation were originally palaces, pools and beautifully terraced gardens. Like Masada, Hyrcanus and others, Herodion was built by Herod as a retreat/fortress. With typical Herodian extravagance it must have been a sight to behold.

As we approach Herodion we must park in the elevated parking lot at the base of the manufactured mountain. A path winds clockwise up the side of the mound. Past the entrance house on the path is a series of some 200 white marble steps leading to the citadel on the top. Once we enter the citadel we see four gigantic towers at the corners, three semicircular and one round. The courtyard between these towers is surrounded by Corinthians columns, now of varying heights. As in others of Herod's palaces there are numerous baths and reservoirs. Even a synagogue is recognized in the Herodion dining room.

The outer diameter of this cone is 180 feet and

if we climb to the cap of Herodion we can walk around the perimeter of the mound. This enables us to see the courtyard in detail but even better, the view from here is absolutely incredible. Look toward the east and you will see a gap between the near wilderness of Judaea and the far mountains of Moab. Do you know what it is? It's the Jordan Valley and while you cannot actually see the valley because it is too low, you can definitely detect that it's out there. To the south is sheer wilderness and desert. The north and west display rolling hills with Jerusalem off in the distance. The climb to the top of the Herodian is well worth it, if only for the spectacular view.

Although Herod died at his palace in Jericho, it is here, to Herodion, that his body was brought 15 days later for burial. Ironic, isn't it, that King Herod, himself a half-Jew, ordered the slaughter of innocent children to kill the King of the Jews (Matthew 2:16) and is himself buried just four miles southeast of Bethlehem, the city of Jesus' birth. While few travelers each year come to the city of Herod's burial, millions journey each year to the city of Christ's birth.

**Visitors can climb the conical manmade mountain, Herodion, to see the ruins of Herod's palace on the top.**

**From his palace on the very top of the Herodion, Herod could see as far away as Bethlehem and even Jerusalem and be warned if enemies approached.**

## TEKOA

As we continue on the secondary road south from Herodion we quickly come to the site of ancient TEKOA. Not much is to be seen here today but some simple ruins covering about five acres. Located approximately equidistant between Jerusalem and Hebron, Tekoa is some 2,800 feet above sea level. It is situated on the very edge of the rugged and desolate wilderness to the east. Here the landscape is so difficult that it is barely passable. You can almost picture the prophet Amos tending his sheep in these mountainous crags before he was called of God (Amos 1:1; 7:14).

It was to Tekoa that Joab sent for a woman to feign being a mourner in order to get David to reconcile with his estranged son Absalom (II Samuel 14). Later, Rehoboam fortified this town (II Chronicles 11:6) and when King Jehoshaphat was confronted with a multitude of Moabites and Ammonites, after the prophet Jahaziel assured Jehoshaphat that *"the battle is not yours, but God's"* (II Chronicles 19:14-16), the armies of Israel and he *"rose early in the morning, and went forth into the wilderness of Tekoa"* singing and praising the Lord in the face of the enemy (verse 20). It appears that the wilderness of Tekoa hasn't changed much since Jehoshaphat's day.

Our road winds through the village of SEIR where tradition says Esau is buried. In about three minutes we pass through HALHUL or Halhool. This Canaanite town, which became the possession of Judah (Joshua 15:1, 58), is the highest village in the country. Along the road we see some roadside vegetable and fruit stands. Traffic gets heavier. We can tell we are coming closer to the main highway.

Soon our secondary road joins the main road from Jerusalem just north of Hebron. We have arrived in the famous VALLEY OF ESHCOL. Eschol, which means "cluster of grapes," was the valley from which the men carried back a cluster of grapes after they were sent by Moses to spy out the Promised Land (Numbers 13:23-24). Today, all around the Holy Land, we can see the black silhouette of two pointy-bearded men bearing an enormous cluster of grapes on poles between them. This has become the official tourist emblem of Israel. It is especially prominent on the sides of automobiles. Strangely enough, grapes are still grown in abundance here today. This Valley of Eshcol is an abrupt topographical change from the wilderness of Tekoa just a few miles back the road.

## MAMRE

Just before we arrive at Hebron there is a tiny road which forks back to the left toward the eastern wilderness. The highway sign guides us to Ramat Al Khaled which is Arabic for "the high place of the friend," a reference to Abraham. Here we will see an enclosure marking the traditional site of the OAK OF MAMRE or Abraham's Oak.

The Book of Genesis records that when Abraham returned from his sojourn in Egypt he *"removed his tent, and came and dwelt in the plain of Mamre, which is in Hebron, and built there an altar unto the LORD"* (Genesis 13:18). Later, after his separation from Lot, Abraham was in Mamre resting under an oak tree when three angels approached him and appraised the patriarch of the imminent destruction of Sodom and Gomorrah (Genesis 18).

This site is protected by a vast 150 × 200 foot enclosure which includes walls constructed by Herod the Great. Destroyed by Vespasian in A.D. 68, their enclosure was rebuilt by the Roman Emperor Hadrian in the 2nd century A.D. and made a pagan cult center. Constantine removed Hadrian's altar and built a basilica on the site. We can still see traces of the ruins of this church. In the southwest corner is the WELL OF ABRAHAM, a place where shepherds for centuries have watered their sheep. But of greatest interest by far is a huge, twisted oak tree which is itself ancient. That this oak is the one under which

In Mamre, an ancient twisted oak tree commemorates the place where the three angels visited Abraham.

Abraham rested is highly unlikely for it doesn't appear to be as old as the patriarchs, but it does commemorate well the site and provides a worthy photo by which to remember Mamre, if you don't mind the iron fence around it.

Back on the main road, ahead of us the highway splits. The right fork is the express road to Beersheba. The left road enters Hebron. Let's go left and take a step back in time.

## HEBRON

The city of HEBRON is so biblically important that Old Testament references to it defy space to include them in one small section of our guidebook. In Hebron Ishmael was born (Genesis 16) and here all three of the patriarchs dwelt (Genesis 35:27; 37:1). Joseph left Hebron in search of his brethren, whom he eventually found in Dothan (Genesis 37:14-17). It was from here that Jacob and his sons went to Egypt (Genesis 46) and to here four centuries later Moses sent spies to survey the land (Numbers 13:17-25). Hebron and its king, Hoham, were captured by Joshua (Joshua 10) and given as an inheritance to Caleb (Joshua 15). It was duly made both a Levitical city of Judah (Joshua 15:54) and a city of refuge (Joshua 20:7).

Hebron was an important city in the period of the Patriarchs and the Conquest. Is it possible it could have maintained its importance during the Israelite monarchy? Well, remember this. David was anointed king over Judah, and then all Israel, not at Jerusalem, but at Hebron. Hebron became David's first capital city (II Samuel 2:1-4, 10-11; 5:1-5; I Kings 2:11). At the gate of Hebron, Abner was treacherously killed by Joab preparing the way for David's ascendancy to the throne (II Samuel 3:27-29). It was here David slew Ishbosheth's murderers (II Samuel 4:5-12). In Hebron Absalom organized his revolt against his father, David (II Samuel 15:7-12). Need I go on?

Hebron has been a violent city nearly all of its existence. During the first Jewish revolt the Roman general Titus destroyed Hebron as well as Jerusalem. In the years since the city has been under the domination of one faction after another. A city of mixed Jewish and Arab population, in 1929 a bloody slaughter occurred which decimated the Jewish population. Since that time the city has been almost exclusively Arab. Today the Israelis call the Hebronites citizens of the West Bank; the Jordanians claim them as citizens of the Hashemite Kingdom of Jordan. But if you ask a Bedouin of Hebron who he is he will say he is a Palestinian. In the maelstrom of politics, religion and war, the simple people of Hebron are struggling with exactly where they fit in the mysterious puzzle we call the Middle East.

As we enter Hebron we pass some beautiful homes, villas really, and a few local shops. The real shopping at Hebron, however, is dead ahead. Hebron is known for its manufacturing of glass. Up ahead on the left we see a glass blowing factory next to a pottery factory and a woodworking factory. Here is Hebron's haven for happy shoppers. The little glass-blown items are especially interesting.

The Hebron market is the center of activity, not only for Hebron but for the entire Negev hinterland. Here you will see black-clad Bedouins sitting around, smoking waterpipes, swapping tales and bartering for goods. It has all the sights, sounds and especially the smells of a sheepherders' market. The marketing of goatskins for water carriers and sheepskin vests and jackets is big business in Hebron.

Since Hebron played no role in New Testament history, you might ask why a Christian would be interested in the town. The reason is father Abraham. Here, in Hebron, is Abraham's tomb. Passing through Hebron's shopping areas we follow the streets left to the final earthly resting place of the man who *"looked for a city which hath foundations, whose builder and maker is God"* (Hebrews 11:10).

Genesis 23 relates that *"Sarah died in Kirjatharba; the same is Hebron in the land of Canaan . . . And Abraham . . . spake unto the sons of Heth, saying, . . . give me a possession of a buryingplace . . . give me the cave of Machpelah . . . And after this, Abraham buried Sarah his wife in the cave of the field of Machpelah before Mamre: the same is Hebron in the land of Canaan"* (23:2-4, 9, 19).

The CAVE OF MACHPELAH, being within its limits, brings to Hebron the designation and distinction of being one of Israel's four "Holy Cities" (the others being Jerusalem, Tiberias and Safed). To visit the cave today is to visit a fortresslike mosque of huge proportions. Built originally by our friend Herod the Great, and later added to by the Mamelukes, the windowless hulk measures 193 feet by 112 feet. The walls of this mosque are 40 to 60 feet high.

The Cave of Machpelah is itself inaccessible. But if we climb the steps leading to the mosque and enter the steel-grey building we will see a series of cenotaphs. A cenotaph is a commemorative monument erected in honor of a person buried elsewhere. These cenotaphs are reported to be located over the actual graves of the patriarchs. Though no one may enter the cave, we can get a brief glimpse of it near the cenotaphs of Isaac and Rebekah, under a pillared dome.

The inside of the mosque is beautifully decorated with inlaid wood and intricate mosaic walls, but it takes some orientation. The cenotaphs of Isaac and Rebekah are located in the main section of the mosque, the large room to the south. In an adjoining open courtyard, behind a silver grating, we see the cenotaphs of Abraham and Sarah. They are covered with gold-embroidered velvet. Opposite, in the northernmost room, are the cenotaphs of Jacob and Leah, the room featuring a 700-year old stained-glass window. Just next door to the west is a cenotaph for Joseph, although most agree that the body of Joseph is buried at Nablus.

The city of Hebron is the southernmost city of the hill country of Judaea and the Central Highlands. From here the land drops off rapidly to the east but only gradually to the west and south. The road to Beersheba slopes through patches of rich soil and fertile grazing land. It is a starkly beautiful drive.

## BEERSHEBA

Some 28 miles southwest of Hebron is BEERSHEBA. Also spelled Beer-Sheva, during the days of the patriarchs this was but a cluster of wells. It is the last watering hole before the desert of the Negev. Here the luster of the green hills turns to the brown of the windswept sands. Beersheba is the gateway to the Negev, once a wild and unruly city nicknamed "Dodge City." Yet today the town is being tamed by growing housing developments, subdivisions and municiple buildings. "Dodge City" has become the capital of the Negev.

The name Beersheba means "the well of seven" but it may also mean "the well of the oath." It was here that Abraham and Abimelech, king of Gerar, pledged mutual allegiance (Genesis 21:31), *"Wherefore he called that place Beer-sheba; because there they sware both of them."*

Traditionally Beersheba has not only been the southern border of Judah's territory (Joshua 15:28; Judges 20:1; I Samuel 3:20), but the southern border of the Promised Land itself, as the expression, *"From Dan to Beersheba"* indicates. Having just come from 3,042 feet above sea level at Hebron to 950 feet at Beersheba makes it seem like we have descended into the desert and the end of the world.

Like Hebron, Beersheba is a town of significant biblical importance. It was the home of Abraham for a time (Genesis 22:19). Not only did he make a covenant with Abimelech (Genesis 21:22-34) but later his son Isaac also made a covenant with Abimelech (Genesis 26:23-33). Here God appeared to both Isaac (Genesis 26:23-25) and Jacob (Genesis 46:1-7). It was from Beersheba that illusive Jacob began his flight to Haran to escape the anger of brother Esau (Genesis 28:10). And on his journey to live with son Joseph in Egypt, Jacob delayed in Beersheba long enough to offer sacrifices to Jehovah (Genesis 46:1-5). Finally, when the prophet Elijah fled from Mount Carmel before the wicked Queen Jezebel, it was here, in Beersheba, that he sat down under a juniper tree and sulked. Here too the angel of the Lord fed him in preparation for his journey of 40 days and nights to Mount Horeb (I Kings 19:1-8).

What's there to see in Beersheba today? Well, if you dig archaeology you may enjoy a visit to Tell Beersheba where these events took place. This is two or three miles northeast of the modern city. A new excavation, having begun only in 1969, the site realistically portrays the life and work of 20th century archaeologists.

But the major reason to travel to today's city of Beersheba is the BEDOUIN MARKET. Don't come to Beersheba unless it's Thursday. That's the day—Thursday. It's the only day the market is open. On this day Bedouin tribes come from out of the Negev sands to buy, sell and trade at the flavorful marketplace. If we walk through the center of town and take a left at the far edge of the old city, our noses will take us the rest of the way. What do the Bedouins sell or trade? You name it—camels, sheep, donkeys, skins, vegetables, jewelry, flour, coffee, tobacco, handwoven rugs, etc. We may even be able to join the fracas and do some haggling ourselves. But we must get there early. The Bedouin Market with veiled women and sandal-footed men opens about 5 A.M. and closes before noon. It's a experience you won't forget.

When the Israelis captured the city of Beersheba from the Egyptians in 1948, it was but a village of 3,000 people. But the stout-hearted settlers of Zionism saw this city as a particular challenge to tame the wilderness and roll back the desert. Today the city sports a population of 130,000 and is a striking contrast between the hustle and bustle of the big city and the slow moving, waterpipe-smoking nomadic life of the nearby Bedouins. It is a microcosm of Israel, some of the old, some of the new. It is the terminus of the Holy Land.

# CHAPTER 8

# The Hills of Enchantment

### THE ENVIRONS OF JERUSALEM

*"Should ye not hear the words which the LORD hath cried by the former prophets, when Jerusalem was inhabited and in prosperity, and the cities thereof round about her, when men inhabited the south and the plain?"* (Zechariah 7:7).

Although it has been said that all roads lead to Rome, in the course of human history it would be more appropriate to say that all roads lead to Jerusalem. In fact, many roads do lead to Jerusalem, literally. And in the final analysis, all of them are "up." North, east, south or west, there are roads to Jerusalem from the four corners of the Holy Land.

**Jerusalem,
city of contrasts**

The road from the north rides the mountains of the Central Highlands through Nablus and Ramallah and arrives in Jerusalem at the Damascus Gate. The Jericho Road is the famous road leading from the Jordan Valley and climbing to the heights of Jerusalem, arriving at the Kidron Valley. The Bethlehem road arrives at Jerusalem traveling north across the Hinnom Valley from Bethlehem, Hebron and Beersheba. The road east from Tel Aviv runs through the Ajalon Valley where Joshua commanded the sun to stand still (Joshua 10:12). This road is still quite new, opened July 11, 1979, and is a swift four-lane highway which passes the Ben-Gurion Airport.

The environs of Jerusalem hold many enchantments. Just being in the vicinity of Old Jerusalem breathes a special excitement. Up the hills and down the hills. Up and down. Dust on our shoes, aches in our legs and joy in our hearts. That's the environs of Jerusalem. So that we don't miss an important thing, let's approach the vicinity of Jerusalem systematically. We start with the environs north of the Old City, then east, south and west. Think of the walled city as the center of a clock. We begin at 12 o'clock and work our way clockwise around the area within five or six miles of Old Jerusalem. Let's get going; there's a lot to see.

## THE ENVIRONS NORTH

Leaving Jerusalem at the Damascus Gate, we travel the Nablus Road north until just after we pass Saint Stephen's Basilica we bear left to the Central Command Square. This is where the Mandelbaum Gate (Jerusalem's Checkpoint Charlie) stood during the partition days of divided Jerusalem. Across the square we will continue north on Shmuel Hanavi (Prophet Samuel) Street to the northern Jerusalem suburbs. At Hasanhedrin Street we enter a wooded enclosure containing the SANDHEDRIN TOMBS.

Also known as the Tombs of the Judges, these tombs were discovered in the 17th century. They received their name because the main cave con-

tained 66 tombs and the Jewish Sanhedrin, Israel's 1st century Supreme Court, which was composed of 70 members. However, another 22 of the 1st century tombs were discovered later.

The entrance to the rock-hewn tombs exhibits the best-preserved rock carving in Jerusalem. As we enter we can distinguish carvings of pomegranates, citrons and acanthus leaves. Just in front of the entrance there is a basin hollowed out in the cave floor. It was undoubtedly used as a ritual basin for the purification of the dead. Inside there are burial chambers on three levels. The chambers are in burial alcoves or niches carved in the walls of rooms off the main passageway. As we make our way back outside we leave the tombs through a vestibule with stone benches for the mourners.

There are many tombs in the area north of Jerusalem, but none of them is as impressive as the Sanhedrin Tombs.

From the area of these tombs we can see NABI SAMWIL. The most prominent feature of Benjamin's topography, rising 2,942 feet above sea level, this is the highest mountain around for 20 miles. It is named Nabi Samwil or Nebi Samwil because some believed that Samuel is buried here. The Bible, however, places Samuel's burial place at Ramah (I Samuel 25:1; 28:3).

Not much is left at Nabi Samwil and a view of it from the Nablus Road a bit to our east is usually sufficient. We see a minaret pointing to the sky like a single digit which marks the site. But it is the view from Nabi Samwil which is particularly impressive, the best view of Jerusalem in the Holy Land. In fact, after a three-year campaign, it was from this site that the Christian Crusaders first viewed the Holy City on July 7, 1099 and wept for joy. The panorama of Palestine from Nabi Samwil is absolutely astounding.

There are some who believe that this is also the site of ancient MIZPEH. Also spelled Mizpah, it was here that Samuel called Israel for prayer and rededication to Jehovah (I Samuel 7:5-7). A prominent religious center, in Mizpeh Saul was proclaimed Israel's first king (I Samuel 10:17-24). References to this site abound (cf. Judges 20:1-3; I Kings 15:22; Nehemiah 3:7-19; Jeremiah 40:8; 41:10; etc.). Others, however, hold that Mizpeh is actually about three miles farther north at Tell en-Nasbeh, Nabi Samwil being only four miles north of Jerusalem.

Perhaps instead of proceeding on Shmuel Hanavi Street out of Jerusalem we will take Eshkol Boulevard to the east and pick up the Nablus Road north out of town. Only a mile or so north is the ATAROT JERUSALEM AIRPORT. If we take that road left past the airport toward Latrun we will come to ancient GIBEON on the right side of the road. Only five miles north of Jerusalem, and less than a mile northwest of Nabi

The Church of All Nations, or the Basilica of the Agony, is in the Garden of Gethsemane. The onion-domed Russian Church of Mary Magdalene is built on the slopes of the Mount of Olives.

Samwil (although no road connects the two), Gibeon is where David defeated the Philistines (I Chronicles 14:16; II Samuel 5:25). Later, in an attempt to settle a dispute between the men of Abner and Joab, 12 men from each side killed each other at Gibeon's Pool (II Samuel 2:12-16). And still later King Solomon was here given by God the opportunity to choose anything he wanted. Choosing wisdom and an understanding heart, God also gave him riches and fame (I Kings 3:4-15; II Chronicles 1:2-17).

Perhaps the most notorious biblical event which occurred at Gibeon involved both the sun and moon. Hearing what the god of Israel did at Jericho and Ai, the Gibeonites tricked Joshua into making a league with them (Joshua 9:3-27). Subsequently, five Amorite kings joined forces against the Gibeonites and when the Israelite forces were called upon for aid they made a forced march from Gilgal in the Jordan Valley climbing the mountains of the Central Highlands to Gibeon. In the battle which ensued God sent huge hailstones hurling down from heaven and killed more of the enemy than the Israelites did. In order to complete this battle when daylight was failing him, Joshua called on the sun and moon to stand still in the nearby Ajalon Valley. They miraculously obeyed and the enemy was routed (Joshua 10:1-27).

At Gibeon, known today as EL-JIB, we will see the Holy Land's best preserved water system. It is striking. Cut entirely from solid rock the Gibeonite water system consists of a circular pool 37 feet in diameter and an incredible 82 feet deep. Take your picture of the pool so that you see the circular stairway cut out of the inside wall. The stairs have 79 steps and most are still usable although inadvisable. In addition there is a 167 foot long tunnel, similar to the ones we have already seen at Hazor and Megiddo. It too is cut from solid rock and leads to a spring outside the city. Seeing Gibeon's pool is well worth the little side excursion from the Nablus Road.

Heading back toward Jerusalem now, about two miles north of the city, we pass the ruins of GIBEAH on our left below the road. This Benjamite site (Joshua 18:28; I Samuel 13:2) was the scene of the near annihilation of the tribe of Benjamin (Judges 20:12-48). It was both Saul's hometown and became his capital after his coronation as Israel's first king (I Samuel 10:26; 11:14; 13:16; 15:34; Isaiah 10:29). Before the Six Day War in 1967 King Hussein of Jordan began a palace on the ruins of Saul's fortress. But the construction abruptly stopped due to the war.

Just a very short distance closer to the northern outskirts of Jerusalem is a road to the left which leads to ancient NOB. Here David received the sword of Goliath from Ahimelech the priest (I Samuel 21:1, 8-9). Because the Israelite hero hid from the jealous king of Israel here (I Samuel 21:1, 10), Saul slew all the priests of Nob in retaliation (I Samuel 22:6-23). Several hundred yards farther up this secondary road is the site of ancient ANATHOTH, the birthplace of Jeremiah (Jeremiah 29:27) and a place frequently mentioned in the Old Testament (cf. Joshua 21:17-18; I Kings 2:26; Ezra 2:23; Nehemiah 11:31-32; Isaiah 10:30; Jeremiah 1:1; 11:21-23; 29:27; 32:7-9).

Once we arrive back in Jerusalem on the Nablus Road we want to keep our eyes open for the American Colony Hotel on the left. Shortly thereafter the road forks and we will bear left on Saladin Street. Just ahead on our left rises a walled enclosure with a sign over the gate, Tombeau Des Rois—the TOMBS OF THE KINGS. We should not think of these as tombs of the Israelite kings. They are not. They are the tombs of Queen Helena, a wealthy queen from Adiabene on the Tigris in Mesopotamia.

Having embraced Judaism, Queen Helena and her family came to Jerusalem about A.D. 45. Here she built a palace and this necropolis. An extremely wide set of 25 steps leads to a rock-hewn cistern that was used for ritual ablutions or preparation for burial. A left turn through the archway and another left will bring us to the vestibule of the tombs. You can't miss it. It is a room cut out of the rock, the roof of which is supported on the right by two pole braces.

Enter the vestibule and look left. There you will see the real reason why we are here. The small below ground level opening to the burial chamber is only about three feet high. But look at the stone. Here is a rolling stone in a small channel or track to seal the face of the tomb. It is the very kind of stone and opening we would expect on the tomb of the Lord Jesus. This will give us an accurate and authentic representation of what a 1st century A.D. tomb was like.

If you're adventurous you can enter the chamber. A friendly fellow just inside will hand us a lighted candle (the only light source). The chamber is not very high and locomotion is uncomfortable for tall people, but 30 tombs are visible inside. As we leave the chamber, don't fail to see relief carvings of grape clusters and wreaths on the walls of the rock vestibule.

Continuing south on Saladin Street toward the Old City we join Sultan Suleiman Street at the Jerusalem post office (on the left). This is the street just outside the Jerusalem city wall at Herod's Gate. A block or more left, across from the northeastern corner of the city wall, is the ROCKEFELLER MUSEUM. Constructed by funds donated by John D. Rockefeller, Jr. and opened in 1938, the official name is the PALESTINE ARCHAEOLOGICAL MUSEUM. The sand-white block building is easily spotted by its gracious octagonal tower rising above a lovely garden of trees and flowers.

The main part of the museum is built around a rectangular cloister. The exhibits, which are chronologically arranged, depict the history of the Holy Land. Here we will see reliefs from Sennacherib's palace at Nineveh (c. 700 B.C.), the lintels of the Church of the Holy Sepulchre and an extensive and very impressive collection of Holy Land jewelry and coins. Also, from the El Aksa Mosque are intricately carved wooden panels, beams and doors. From the Caliph Hisham Palace at Jericho (8th century A.D.) are plaster statues of people and animals.

If you want to do some quick reading or heavy research on the Holy Land, this is the place to do it. The museum has a comfortable reading room with hundreds of periodicals and a library of over 35,000 volumes, all on the subjects of Holy Land history, archaeology and geography.

## THE ENVIRONS EAST

We are now at the Stork Tower, the northeast corner of the Old City of Jerusalem. To the right is the Jericho Road. Straight across is a street that dips down into the Kidron Valley so sharply that it simply disappears out of sight. It is Shmuel Ben Adaya and after dipping into the valley it climbs to the crest of the Mount of Olives. At the top we are faced with a choice, left or right. To the left is MOUNT SCOPUS. From here we get a spectacular view of Jerusalem contrasted with the stark wilderness off in the distance. From this strategic location overlooking Jerusalem many attacks have been launched on the Holy City. Here have camped the Romans under Titus in A.D. 70, the Crusaders in 1099, the British in 1917 and the Arabs in 1948.

On Mount Scopus today is the original Hadassah Hospital and the initial campus of the Hebrew University. When this area fell within the "demilitarized zone" in 1948, the Jews established a new campus at Givat Ram on the west side of Jerusalem. Hadassah Hospital as well has relocated on the west side of Jerusalem near Ein Karem.

At the head of Shmuel Ben Adaya Street we'll go right toward the central heights of the MOUNT OF OLIVES. There is the RUSSIAN TOWER OF THE ASCENSION, the most noticeable structure on the mountain. Visible from miles away and the landmark with which Jerusalem is identified at a distance, the tower rises six stories into the rarified air over the Mount of Olives. The 214 step-climb to the top provides a most beautiful view of the city below. A rock at the southeast corner of the church is the traditional spot, according to the Russian Orthodox Church, where Mary stood as Jesus ascended into heaven.

A rival site for this honor is the DOME OF ASCENSION. In A.D. 380, a round structure was built over the rock said to be the exact spot where Jesus Christ ascended. In fact, you can even see the supposed footprint of Christ left in the rock. A good imagination and a willingness to believe will reveal it to you. In 614 the Persians partially destroyed this shrine but the Crusaders restored a roofless, polygonal chapel over the rock. When the Muslims gained control of the shrine in 1187 they added the cupola, the ceiling dome characteristic of a mosque. This Christian site is under Muslim control but Jesus was considered a prophet by the Muslims as well. Like so many Holy Land shrines the site is shared by several Christian communities and denominations. On different dates different groups celebrate the Feast of Ascension here, setting up tents and portable altars. The iron hooks on the wall around the shrine mark off the areas for each community.

Nearby, to the east, is the PATER NOSTER CHURCH. This is the "Our Father" church where the Lord's Prayer of Matthew 6:9-15 is

The Dome of Ascension was built in A.D. 380 over the rock said to be the exact spot where Jesus Christ ascended.

beautifully inscribed on 44 tiles, each in a different language. This is not the site where the prayer was offered, that was in Galilee, but is best understood as the site where Jesus taught His disciples about the destruction of Jerusalem and the kingdom to come (Matthew 24—25). In 1868 the French Princess de la Tour d'Auvergne purchased the site and established a convent for the Carmelite Sisters. Favorite tiles for photographers are the prayers in the English, French and Hebrew languages.

Let's make one further stop on the top of the Mount of Olives. Continuing to the east we arrive in front of the plush pearl of the Middle East hotels—the JERUSALEM INTERCONTINENTAL built to resemble a caravansary. From here the panorama of Jerusalem is stunning. Before us is a vast Jewish cemetery clinging to the side of the mount. Behind us are the seven arches of the hotel. All around us are tour buses with eager pilgrims seeking the perfect angle for that once-in-a-lifetime picture of the Holy City. And just to add a bit of local color (and subtract a few dollars from your wallet) there is the local Arab entrepreneur with his camel. We have had other opportunities to ride a camel, but this is the only

**Giant, gnarled olive trees in the Garden of Gethsemane.**

one where the background of your photo will be the eternal city of Jerusalem.

Perhaps a word about camelriding ought to be said. First, do not, I repeat, do not pass up the opportunity to ride a camel. It's not at all like riding a horse. On a horse you bounce up and down; on a camel you rock back and forth. Camels are friendly creatures, but don't try to pet their noses as you would a horse's nose. Camels have a nasty habit of spitting; besides they don't brush their teeth. It's safer on their side.

You may need some help getting up into the box saddle. Camels are somewhat broader than horses. But once you're in the saddle and have a firm grasp on the saddle's horn, the fun is just beginning. Remember, when you mounted the camel he was on his knees. When you ride him he will be on his feet. Back legs go up first, which means that suddenly (and surprisingly) you are thrust forward. Once the front legs are up it's like sitting on the top of the world. Coming back down is quite similar. Front legs down to knees. Passenger thrusts forward in terror. Back legs down to knees. Passenger walks victoriously away to coax unsuspecting friends into a camel ride.

Now it's time to leave the mountain. There are few places in Palestine as densely populated with churches as the MOUNT OF OLIVES. More than 25 churches, chapels, convents, etc. have made their presence known on this mountain. And why not? This 2,641 foot mountain is considerably higher than Jerusalem and has played a central role in the city's history.

The mountain is actually four eminences, the northernmost and highest (2,723 feet) is called Viri Galilaei because it is thought that here the angels appeared to the disciples and addressed them, *"Ye men of Galilee, why stand ye gazing up into heaven?"* (Acts 1:11). The second mound of the mountain is the site of Jesus' ascension, where the Tower of Ascension and the Muslim Dome of Ascension are located. The third eminence is where the Church of Pater Noster stands and the final one is known as the Mount of Offense, supposedly the "Mount of Corruption" where King Solomon erected the high places for the strange gods of his foreign wives (I Kings 11:1).

Second Samuel 15:30 and 16:14 indicate that over this mountain David fled from his son Absalom. Just over the mountain to the east is BETHPHAGE. From here Jesus began His triumphal entry over the Mount of Olives and into Jerusalem (Luke 19:29-44). The traditional road crosses the mountain at the site of the Pater

Noster Church. Here Jesus cursed the fig tree (Matthew 21:17-22; Mark 11:12-14, 20-26) and here He wept over the city (Luke 19:37-44). After eating the Passover with His disciples in the Upper Room, Jesus and the Eleven went out to the Mount of Olives (Matthew 26:30; Mark 14:26; Luke 22:39).

God isn't finished with this important mountain. It figures prominently in biblical prophecy. From this very mound Jesus predicted God's judgment on the Gentile nations (Matthew 25:31-46). This judgment follows Christ's Second Coming, the Second Advent, when He comes to establish His kingdom (Joel 3:1-2). This coming to earth will actually alter the topographical structure of the Mount of Olives. The prophet Zechariah reports, *"And his feet shall stand in that day upon the mount of Olives, which is before Jerusalem in the east, and the mount of Olives shall cleave in the midst thereof toward the east and toward the west, and there shall be a very great valley; and half of the mountain shall remove toward the north, and half of it toward the south"* (Zechariah 14:4). A valley not in existence today shall come into being when Jesus returns to the mountain from which He ascended into heaven.

Descending into the KIDRON VALLEY we come to the most famous stream in the area, the Brook Kidron. Only a wadi, which is dry except when it rains, the stream and valley gain their importance from the fact that they are immediately east of the temple area, some 400 feet below. Over the centuries this valley has been a symbol of separation from Jerusalem and the true worship of Jehovah. For example, here King Asa burnt his mother's idols (I Kings 15:13; II Chronicles 15:16); here Josiah destroyed the vessels of Baal that had been erected in the house of God (II Kings 23:4-6, 12). King Hezekiah ordered Jerusalem's priests to carry all the *"uncleanness that they found in the temple of the Lord"* and dump it in the Brook Kidron (II Chronicles 29:16). Also, during Absalom's rebellion, King David separated himself from the kingdom by crossing over Kidron and seeking refuge (II Samuel 15:23).

This valley is also associated with judgment. As noted, in a valley to be created adjoining this one (Zechariah 14:4) the great judgment of the nations will occur (Joel 3:2, 12). The Valley of Kidron is also known as the Valley of Jehoshaphat. Muslims believe that Mohammed will sit by the Dome of the Rock and Jesus on the Mount of Olives. A wire will be stretched between them across which all mankind will walk. Those who have lived righteously will successfully reach the

other side; those who have not will fall into the Kidron Valley and perish.

At the bottom of the Kidron Valley road, which is the Jericho Road, there is a sharp "S" curve. To our left as we negotiate the curve is the GARDEN OF GETHSEMANE. The name means "wine" or "oil press" and our visit to the garden will show us why. The Garden is maintained by the Franciscans and contains eight severely gnarled olive trees believed to date from the 1st century. This beautifully maintained garden is undoubtedly much better manicured than it was in the days of our Lord. In fact, the Russian Gethsemane, higher on the hill than the Latin garden, is probably much more like the one Jesus visited. Nonetheless, from the Garden of Gethsemane we have a great opportunity to take a picture of the Jerusalem wall and the Golden (Eastern) Gate framed by twisted and ancient olive trees. It makes an ideal picture.

**The Tomb of Absalom in the Kidron Valley is cut entirely out of a rock cube and stands 60 feet high.**

Now let's enter the church adjacent to this restful garden of prayer. It is the BASILICA OF THE AGONY. This Roman Catholic basilica is constructed in Byzantine style and was dedicated by the Franciscans in 1924. Since it was built by funds donated from all over the world it is also known as the CHURCH OF ALL NATIONS. There is an impressive facade on the front side of the church above three gigantic arches. This colorful mosaic depicts Jesus weeping over the city in Gethsemane. The church itself features six huge pillars which support a roof of 12 cupolas or white domes covering the roof. From the Mount of Olives above, the church resembles a somewhat ornate box of table tennis balls.

Inside the church is extremely dark. The windows are of translucent alabaster and yield only soft mysterious light. We enter from the garden, through a tiled foyer and into the basilica itself. We have entered the church near the altar. Just to our left is an area encircled by a wrought iron fence resembling thorns. Within this fence is a huge rock projecting through the mosaic floor of the church. The rock, which measures approximately 25 feet square, is reported to be the site where Jesus prayed in agony in the garden (Luke 22:39-46) before His crucifixion. Above the rock is a mosaic Gethsemane scene depicting Jesus kneeling in prayer on such a rock. Since admittance to the olive-treed garden outside is prohibited, the many wooden benches in the basilica facing the lighted rock of agony provide us with an excellent opportunity to spend some minutes in prayer.

Outside the basilica and above it on the mountain we can see perhaps the most unique church in the Holy Land, at least in architecture. It is the RUSSIAN ORTHODOX CHURCH OF MARY MAGDALENE. The seven gilded onion-shaped domes or spires on the church gracefully rise out of a garden of olive trees. Built in 1888 by Alexander III, Czar of Russia, in memory of his mother, the church is maintained by the White Russian nuns. It is the Russian Gethsemane.

South of this unique church, and a bit farther up the side of the mountain, is a small, single-domed church. It is known as DOMINUS FLEVIT meaning "the Lord wept." According to tradition, this marks the spot where, coming from Bethphage on an ass, Jesus stopped to weep over Jerusalem (Luke 19:29, 41-44). The roof of the church looks like an inverted tulip but was actually designed by Barluzzi to suggest a tear drop. The four corners of the roof are styled to resemble tear-bottles. This Byzantine chapel features an austere altar backed by a glass window providing a panoramic view of the temple area.

Somewhere on the side of this mountain across the Kidron Valley from Jerusalem's Golden Gate (Luke 22:39-40), Jesus came to pray. Here He often prayed with His disciples (John 18:2). On one particular night, however, He agonized in prayer with an exceedingly sorrowful soul (Matthew 26:36-38). And to this place came a band of men and officers from the chief priests and Pharisees, led by Judas who betrayed our Lord (John 18:1-13). Here the always impetuous Peter drew his sword and sliced off Malchus' right ear (verse 10). Jesus Christ was arrested, bound and dragged away before the high priest (verses 12-13). In the quietness of the Garden of Gethsemane we can still hear the clamor as they took Him away.

Outside, the road in front of the garden presents us with a choice. The main road skirts the ridge along the upper valley, clinging to the side of the Mount of Olives. This road leads to Jericho and in just a minute or two we pass through another "S" curve. At the curve is a juice and refreshment stand, a walled garden and a large church with a high, square tower. This is the CHURCH OF SAINT LAZARUS. As we make our way through the garden we arrive at the courtyard outside the church. To our left is the Franciscan Church built in 1953 and dedicated to Lazarus. Decorated with mosaics depicting the events which took place in Bethany, the church incorporates the 4th century ruins of the first shrine on the site. To our right and adjacent to the tomb is a 16th century mosque. West of these and ahead of us is a Greek Othodox Church and the remains of a fortified Crusader tower.

Although the church is interesting, I prefer not to miss the remains of a grain mill and a spectacular olive press with a huge stone, wooden beam and turn screw. All of this can be seen in a darkened room of a 2,000-year-old wealthy home straight across the courtyard, through the door on the right and inside to the right.

Outside the church complex and a bit farther up the hill (Bethany is on the backside of the Mount of Olives) is the traditional TOMB OF LAZARUS. The tomb is less than a minute walk and on the left of the paved but sheep-spotted road. The smallish opening to the tomb is only four square stones high with a huge stone lintel over the door. Above the entrance is a large blue sign marking the site. If you enter the tomb you can take the 27 slippery steps down and folding back to the left enter a burial chamber. Whether or not this is actually Lazarus' tomb is doubtful (John 11:1-44).

The village of BETHANY was once the home of Mary, Martha, and Lazarus (John 11:1), as well as Simon the leper (Mark 14:3). This brother and sister trio were good friends of our Lord (John 11:5) and He must have made this town His Judaean "home" as He did Capernaum in Galilee (Matthew 21:17; Mark 11:11). At her home here Mary sat at Jesus' feet in adoration as Martha scurried around serving the disciples (Luke 10:38-42). And at the house of Simon the leper Judas Iscariot complained about the waste as Mary anointed Jesus with a spikenard of precious oil (Matthew 26:6-13; Mark 14:3-9; John 12:1-8).

As we return to the Kidron Valley along the Mount of Olives we can't help but remember that while returning from Bethany one morning Jesus cursed a barren fig tree (Matthew 21:17-22; Mark 11:12-14). Soon we leave the Jericho Road and take the left fork on the Silwan Road descending deeper into the Kidron Valley. SILWAN is an Arab village layered on the slopes of the southeast corner of Jerusalem's Old City. Along the left side of this narrow road are four of the oddest-looking structures in the Holy Land. They are distinctively shaped tombs, each with a unique style of architecture and an unusual story.

The first tomb we encounter, and the most outstanding, is the PILLAR OF ABSALOM or the Tomb of Absalom. A monolithic cube with a circular cap rising to a sharp point, the tomb is cut entirely out of the rock and stands 60 feet high. Although tradition ascribes this tomb to David's wayward son, perhaps even the pillar Absalom built for himself *"in the king's dale"* (II Samuel 18:17-18), nonetheless the pillar was probably erected 700 years later during the period of the Second Temple. It is Hellenistic in design. Inside the pillar is a rock-hewn burial chamber.

Behind this pillar, and almost entirely hidden by it, is the TOMB OF JEHOSHAPHAT. Cut out of the same rock to the rear left, this tomb is an alcove with eight burial chambers inside. The entrance is ornately carved in mixed Graeco-Egyptian style and features a frieze of acanthus leaves.

After a very short space the next tomb is visible. Not a free-standing edifice, the BENI HEZIR TOMBS are rather a Hasmonean portico carved in the face of the rock. This is the oldest of the four tombs, dating from the Hasmonean period (2nd century B.C.). Above the four Doric columns of the facade is a Hebrew inscription indicating that these were the burial chambers of a Herodian priestly family of the Sons of Hezir, *"Beni Hezir"* (Nehemiah 10:20). An old Hebrew tradition claims that it was here that King Uzziah (Azariah) isolated himself when he had leprosy (II Kings 15:5). There is also a Christian tradition that this site was associated with Jesus' cousin, James. In the 4th century monks found a skeleton here which they claimed to be that of James. In the 6th century a tradition arose that James hid here after Jesus' arrest and by the 15th century the tradition had grown to identify this as James' actual tomb.

The final tomb, the most recent and the second most outstanding, is the TOMB OF ZECHARIAH. It is a solid rock cube with four pillars carved on the front and a pyramid top. This 1st century tomb is believed to be that of the Hebrew prophet Zechariah. However, many Christians believe this to be the tomb of Zacharias, the father of John the Baptist. A tunnel from beneath the tomb leads to the tombs of Beni Hezir.

Since it was customary for the Jews to whitewash their tombs annually, and since the (Kidron) Valley of Jehoshaphat was a favorite burial site, it is possible that one or all of these tombs were referred to by Jesus when He alluded to the hypocritical Pharisees as being like whited sepulchres, beautiful on the outside but filthy and dead inside (Matthew 23:27).

## THE ENVIRONS SOUTH

Just beyond the Pinnacle of the Temple, the southeast corner of the Old City wall, the Silwan Road enters the village of Silwan or Siloam. Just to our right is a parking area for the GIHON SPRING. One of Jerusalem's earliest sources of water, about 3,000 years ago the Jebusite inhabitants of this ancient city dug an underground waterway to this bubbling stream. This was the "gutter" the men of David used to stealthily enter the city and capture it (II Samuel 5:6-10), thus making Jerusalem the "City of David" and his political, religious and military capital. Later it was at this Gihon Spring that Solomon's coronation as Israel's third king occurred (I Kings 1:33-45) while half-brother and rival for the throne, Adonijah, awaited crowning farther down the Kidron Valley at EIN ROGEL.

To enter the Gihon Spring, also known as the FOUNTAIN OF THE VIRGIN because of a 14th century legend that Mary washed Jesus' clothes in this spring, we must descend a set of 33 stone steps to a grilled entrance. Here is the beginning of the Holy Land's most famous tunnel, HEZEKIAH'S TUNNEL (II Kings 20:20; II Chronicles 32:2-4; Isaiah 36—37).

Because the Gihon Spring was outside the city wall it was always vulnerable to enemy attack. In 701 B.C. the Assyrian King Sennacherib invaded Palestine and threatened Jerusalem (II Kings 18:17-21). In order to secure the city's water source King Hezekiah had a conduit chiseled out of the subterranean rock of the HILL OPHEL, the southern ridge of Mount Moriah. At the end of this conduit was the POOL OF SILOAM in the Tyropoeon Valley within the walls of the Lower City. When the Gihon Spring was covered and camouflaged, the city would have ample and protected water for the entire siege.

Although the distance between the Gihon Spring and the Pool of Siloam is only 1,090 feet, the tunnel wiggles and wags its way for 1,770 feet through the solid rock. And what is really remarkable is that Hezekiah's workmen began at either end and cut toward the center. The account of this remarkable feat of engineering was engraved in the stone wall some 19 feet from the Siloam end of the conduit. In 1880 a young boy discovered this inscription in ancient Hebrew script and 10 years later it was removed, unfortunately, to the Istanbul Museum.

The tunnel averages a little more than two feet wide and six feet high. The floor is slippery and rocky because of the constant flow of water. On my last experience at wading through the tunnel the water was high, up to my shoulders in places. But if the waters are not unusually high, and if you don't mind getting wet, you can take a refreshing stroll through one of Jerusalem's oldest antiquities, almost undisturbed since 700 B.C.

Originally built by King Hezekiah as a reservoir for his tunnel, the Pool of Siloam had erected over it a 5th century church which was destroyed by the Persians in A.D. 614 and never rebuilt. All that remains today is a relatively deep, walled hole in the ground with stone steps leading down to the crystal clear waters emanating from the rounded entrance to Hezekiah's Tunnel. Also in the waters we can see the remains of a Roman bath. Above the ground is a small mosque with a slender minaret rising toward the skies out of a small grove of trees.

Probably to be identified with *"the Pool of Siloah by the king's garden"* (Nehemiah 3:15) and *"the waters of Shiloah that go softly"* (Isaiah 8:6), Luke 13:4 records that once a tower fell at this pool and killed 18 people. For Christians, however, the pool gains its greatest importance in that it was here that the blind man was instructed by Jesus to wash after our Lord spat on the ground and applied the soft clay to sightless eyes. The man's sight returned and he was taken to the Pharisees where an inane discussion followed as to whether or not Jesus was a sinner for healing him on the Sabbath. The man's classic answer simply was, *"Whether he be a sinner or no, I know not: one thing I know, that, whereas I was blind, now 'I see"* (John 9:1-25). We should not attempt to explain God's gifts to us, whether they be sight or salvation. Rather, we ought to accept them and enjoy them.

Farther down the Silwan Road, and on the same side, is the infamous potter's field known as HACELDAMA. Also spelled without the initial "H" and sometimes Hakeldema, this name means "field of blood." After Judas betrayed Jesus and began to feel uncomfortable about it, he returned to the temple and cast the 30 pieces of silver he received for his infamous betrayal at the feet of the priests. When Judas killed himself this money was used to buy a plot in the potter's field in which to bury strangers (Matthew 27:1-10). This corresponds exactly to the prophecy of Zechariah 11:12-13. Today the GREEK ORTHODOX CONVENT OF SAINT ONIPRIUS marks this site and is set among Jewish burial caves of the Second Temple period (c. 450 B.C.—A.D. 70). These caves are filled with skulls and bones of those who have been buried there. Because they were reported to be the hiding places of the apostles during Jesus' trial, these caves have also been known as the APOSTLES CAVE.

For the Christian pilgrim to the Holy land, the main attraction in the environs south of Jerusalem just has to be BETHLEHEM. With the exception of Jerusalem itself, Bethlehem is the most important city in Christendom. Immortalized in song and poetry, this picturesque village lays claim to prominence in both Old and New Testaments.

Bethlehem ("house of bread") is first mentioned in the Bible as the place where Rachel died giving birth to Benjamin (Genesis 35:16-20). Jacob marked her tomb with a memorial pillar and I Samuel 10:2 places this sepulcher *"in the border of Benjamin at Zelzah."* About one mile north of Bethlehem, on the right side of the road from Jerusalem, is the traditional site of RACHEL'S TOMB. The 23-foot square shrine has been rebuilt several times, the last time in 1841 by Sir Moses Montefiore. The tomb looks strikingly like a small mosque, with a white cupola crowning the square shrine. If you could get up there, the perfect position for a picture of this tomb would be on the rooftop across the street with the Israeli soldiers. They are always there, always watching the traffic entering Bethlehem and Rachel's tomb because it is sacred to Jews, Muslims and Christians alike.

Besides this, Bethlehem was the home and burial place of Ibzan, the tenth judge in Israel (Judges 12:8-10). The Levite's concubine abused while sojourning in the mountain of Ephraim was from Bethlehem-judah (Judges 19). The Book of Ruth is staged here. Elimelech and Naomi left Bethlehem-judah to sojourn in Moab during a severe famine. When Naomi and her daughter-in-law Ruth returned to the Holy Land it was back to Bethlehem. It was in the fields on the outskirts of this village that the beautiful romance between Ruth and Boaz blossomed. Ruth became the great grandmother of David the famous king of Israel (Ruth 4:17; I Samuel 17:12). Thus, Bethlehem is the "City of David" and the home of the Davidic family. It was to Bethlehem that Samuel came to anoint the shepherd boy David as king of Israel (I Samuel 16:4, 11-13). On the terraced slopes and grass-covered fields of Bethlehem we can still see shepherd boys tending their flocks much the same way young David once did (I Samuel 17:15).

But the great biblical importance of Bethlehem is the village's link with David's great descendant, his greater son, Jesus Christ the Lord. The prophet Micah pinpoints Bethlehem Ephratah, *"little among the thousands of Judah,"* as the birthplace of Israel's Messiah and the world's Redeemer (Micah 5:2). The "little town of Bethlehem" isn't so little as Israeli towns go today. With a population of over 40,000 it is not exactly a teeming metropolis, but it is not a sleepy little village any longer either. Micah's prophecy was fulfilled (Luke 2:4-7) and the shepherds came from the nearby fields to adore the Christ child (Luke 2:15-16). Later Herod the Great slaughtered *"all the children that were in Bethlehem, and in all the coasts thereof, from two years old and under"* (Matthew 2:15-18) when he learned that the wise men came to seek the King of the Jews. But an angel of the Lord had already appeared to Joseph and he fled with Mary and the baby Jesus to Egypt (Matthew 2:13-23; cf. Jeremiah 31:15; 40:1).

Nestled in the Judaean hills just a few miles south of Jerusalem, Bethlehem, at 2,350 feet above sea level, is several hundred feet lower than the capital. As we approach the town on the road from Jerusalem, just past Rachel's Tomb,

the road forks. To the right the road skirts the west side of Bethlehem and continues on to Hebron. About two miles south of town are three large reservoirs known as SOLOMON'S POOLS. These reservoirs supplied Jerusalem and Bethlehem with water through a conduit. Although Solomon's pools are mentioned in Ecclesiastes 2:4-6, these reservoirs are probably misnamed since two of them were built by Pontius Pilate and the third in the 15th century. We will, however, take the left fork of the road which is Manger Street. This snakes its way upward toward Bethlehem past the Holy Land Christian Mission, Saint Joseph's church and King David's Wells, each on the right side of the road. At the end of Manger Street a sharp right at the top of the hill brings us directly into the center of MANGER SQUARE. Here tens of thousands of Christian pilgrims gather each Christmas Eve to celebrate the birth of Jesus Christ.

There are souvenir shops edging the square on several sides. On the east is a large building which looks like a fort. Its high gray walls, which extend all the way to the square on the right side (although the church itself is straight ahead of us across a large square-blocked courtyard), its several belled-towers on the right extension, the fenced garden on the left of the courtyard, and the general appearance of the place make it seem cold and unfriendly. Why should the Christian visit such a prison-looking place? Because this is the main attraction of Bethlehem. This is the CHURCH OF THE NATIVITY.

**The entrance to the place of the Nativity is by way of Bethlehem Square and a very small door.**

89

The walk across the courtyard brings us to the main door of the building still unbelieving that this could be a church. The door is narrow and low, definitely a one-at-a-time entrance. Tradition says that the less than four-foot high door was constructed that size to cause all who enter to bow before the sacred spot. Another tradition holds that the Crusaders constructed the door so low to keep marauders from desecrating the

church by riding in and out on horseback. But once we are inside, the fortress appearance of the church rapidly disappears.

The Church of the Nativity is Christianity's oldest church still in use. A grotto beneath the church was identified as the birthplace of Jesus by Helena, mother of Constantine, in A.D. 325. Shortly thereafter the Emperor himself constructed a church at this site. The building we are now in was built by the Roman Emperor Justinian (527-565) who intended this edifice to be one of the finest churches in his extensive empire. The Church of the Nativity was the only church in the Holy Land not destroyed by the Persians in 614. It was completely altered, however, by the Crusaders and is a splendid example (on the interior) of a beautiful basilica of the Byzantine period.

Once we enter the diminutive entranceway we are astounded by the size of the church itself. The church is a basilica (roughly built in the shape of the cross) and is 170 feet long and 80 feet wide. It is divided into five naves by four rows of rose-brown Corinthian pillars made of the red stone of the country. To our left are double rows of pillars with 12 columns in a row. The same on the right. Each pillar faintly bears the picture of an apostle. The floor is constructed of square stone blocks. At several locations on the left side of the floor wooden trap doors can be raised exposing the original mosaic floor beneath, discovered in 1936.

Look up at the ceiling. Oaken rafters grace the ceiling much the same way rafters give a quiet elegance to any old building. The rest of the church is overornate. Hanging on long chains from this simple ceiling are several dozen gilded lamp fixtures resembling fancy kerosene lamps. Let's make our way to the front of the church.

Here we ascend several steps to the ALTAR OF THE NATIVITY. Hanging from the ceiling in the center is a magnificent gold and silver chandelier. Silver and gold abound, but the face of the altar is in typical drab-dark orthodox decor, made of hand-carved cedars of Lebanon. The area to the left of the altar is under the jurisdiction of the Armenian Church. The area to the right is the domain of the Greek Orthodox Church. Franciscan priests can also be seen tending to the needs of the basilica. You can easily identify these three different orders. The Greeks dress in long black robes, are bearded and wear their long black hair tied in a bun on the back. The Franciscans dress modestly in simple brown robes, usually with a cord tied at the waist. The Armenians are far more colorful in their purple and cream-colored robes. They are easy to identify scurrying throughout the church.

On either side of the altar are stone steps which disappear into the floor of the church. You can spot them quickly as they are just off the altar area to the back and are usually guarded by a priest with outstretched offering plate. Let's descend through the right side as it sometimes gets a bit crowded below.

When we reach the bottom of the half-dozen or so steps we enter the doorway of a cave under the altar. This is the GROTTO OF THE NATIVITY, the traditional site of the Bethlehem manger, scene of Jesus' birth. If you have come to the Holy Land, or even just dreamed about it, expecting to find a manger filled with hay, a few lowing cattle and a rustic reminder of Christ's birth, you'll surely be disappointed in what you see. What you find is a narrow room (35 × 10 feet) in a cave, with two sacred spots and enough incense in the air to make your eyes water. To our left is the place where Mary took the Christ child, *"wrapped him in swaddling clothes, and laid him in a manger"* (Luke 2:7). To the right is the place where the Virgin gave birth to our Lord. Let's enter the small room farther to get a better look.

As we face the tiny grotto in the wall of this cave we see a number of incense burners hanging over a silver star which marks the site of Christ's birth. This 14-pointed star has at its center an eternal flame burning and this inscription in Latin, "Here of the Virgin Mary, Christ was born."

The cave itself is dark, the primitive rock of the cave blackened by the smoke of the candles, oil lamps and incense. The walls of the grotto are covered with asbestos to protect against fire. But that won't dampen our spirits or the reverence with which Christians regard this place. Let's sing a Christmas carol or two before we leave the Bethlehem grotto.

As we exit up the opposite stairs into the Armenian quarter of the basilica, we will exit through the near door into an adjacent chapel. To our immediate right is a stairway descending through the floor next to the wall. Down again we go into another cave and enter the CHAPEL OF SAINT JEROME. It was here that the great biblical scholar sequestered himself in this subterranean monastery in order to translate the Bible from Hebrew and Greek into Latin. His translation is the famous Latin Vulgate. Jerome spent the last 35 years of his life (A.D. 386-420) in this cave meditating, studying, writing and translating.

Back up to the chapel and out the rear doors to a courtyard of cloisters where we see a statue of Jerome (spelled Hieronymus) placed on a high column. Once outside the courtyard we make our way left through the gardens to the stone-faced courtyard and then right back to Manger Square.

From the square we can take Shepherds Street past the Terra Sancta College to Beit Sahur and just beyond this tiny Arab village east of Bethlehem to the SHEPHERDS' FIELD. Nearby too are the fields of Boaz where the story of Ruth was enacted. *"And there were in the same country shepherds abiding in the field; keeping watch over their flock by night"* (Luke 2:8). From this pastoral setting our minds can almost relive the eventful night *"when the fulness of time was come, God sent forth his Son, made of a woman, made under the law, to redeem them that were under the law, that we might receive the adoption of sons"* (Galatians 4:4-5). As we stand under the starry hosts, the hillsides terraced with olive trees and fields glowing with golden grain, how ironic it is to think that the Son of God became a man so that men might become the sons of God. All babes are born to live; this one was born to die.

Listen carefully. Perhaps we can still hear the angels sing: *"Hail the heav'n born Prince of Peace, Hail the Sun of righteousness! Light and life to all He brings, Ris'n with healing in His wings: Mild He lays His glory by, Born that man no more may die; Born to raise the sons of earth, Born to give them second birth. Hark! the herald angels sing, 'Glory to the newborn King.'"*

Can you endure a word of caution and advice? First the word of caution. Do not plan to spend Christmas Eve in Bethlehem unless you have made special arrangements with the Israel Government Tourist Offices (I.G.T.O.) in Jerusalem, Tel Aviv or Haifa. If you have a guide he could do this for you. Because thousands of pilgrims will jam Manger Square, and because many thousands more will be turned away, admission to the Square on Christmas Eve is restricted to tourists holding special tickets only. You may find the overwhelming crowds, the noticeable presence of the Israeli military and the inclement weather sufficient reason for planning some alternative form of Christmas Eve observance.

**A view of the Bethlehem hillside. Revered as the birthplace of Christ, the small city of Bethlehem swells in size as thousands of pilgrims crowd Manger Square for the Christmas Eve observance.**

And what about the word of advice? Bethlehem has become the shopping capital of Israel, especially for tourists. On the way into town you will pass many fine shops eager to serve you. Shops are equally prevalent around Manger Square. Bethlehem is the place to buy olive wood items, carving, plaques, figurines, etc. they are world famous. Also the mother-of-pearl pins, brooches, etc. are particularly nice. And say, if you really want to please your friends, why not buy next year's Christmas cards right here in Bethlehem? You will be overwhelmed at what you can buy in sprawling shops of this sacred city. You may be overwhelmed at the prices as well, but my theory of foreign purchase is, "If you can't buy it in the States, it's not expensive here!"

## THE ENVIRONS WEST

The main gate leading west from the Old City is the Jaffa Gate. By driving away from this gate in a westerly direction we come almost immediately to Jerusalem's grandest park, Independence Park. Left on Agron Street before the park puts us on one of the main thoroughfares cutting across New Jerusalem. At the corner where King George Street intersects Argon is HECHAL SHLOMO, the imposing Seat of the Rabbinate, the supreme religious center of Judaism. Styled along the lines of King Solomon's Temple, square at the bottom with a rounded top, the building which means "palace or temple of Solomon" was named after the father of Sir Isaac Woolfson of England who donated the money for its erection. Inside is a synagogue, a library, a museum, the Abraham Wax Collection of Jewish Religions and an interesting series of dioramas depicting biblical events. Here we may purchase some authentic Jewish souvenirs.

Right next door to Hechal Schlomo is being constructed the JERUSALEM GREAT SYNAGOGUE. This multi-storied synagogue is believed by some Christians to be an interim step to the construction of the future Jerusalem Temple. But anyone who visits this synagogue will come away a bit disappointed if anything approaching Solomon's Temple is expected.

Outside, Agron Street becomes Ramban Street and continues west to the KNESSET, Israel's Parliament. The supreme legislative body of the State of Israel, the Knesset is a single-chambered house of 120 members, elected every four years in a general election. One of several government buildings in a complex, the seven million dollar Knesset building is made of peach/pink native Jerusalem stone and resembles a four-story building flattened to one story. This elegant political landmark is perched on the highest hill on Jerusalem's West Side. It features a 24-foot high mosaic by Marc Chagall in the reception hall, a synagogue, a complex of meeting chambers, exhibition halls, offices, lounges, press galleries and separate kitchens for meat and milk dishes (Kosher, you know). The Knesset has a fine library of more than 50,000 volumes. If we arrive at the Knesset on Monday, Tuesday or Wednesday between 4:00 and 9:00 P.M., we can attend a session of the Parliament.

Across the street from the entrance to the Knesset is the 16-foot high MENORAH. Carved by the British sculptor Benno Elkan, the 29 panels on this seven-branched candlestick depict scenes from Jewish history. A gift from the

To the west of the Old City is the much larger New Jerusalem. At the entrance to a complex of government buildings, including the Knesset, Israel's Parliament, stands the 16 foot Menorah, the seven-branched candlestick — a cherished emblem of Israel.

British Parliament the menorah is the symbol of the State of Israel and although it is more than twice as tall as a man, standing in front of the menorah makes a very flavorful photo.

By taking Ruppin Road across the shallow Valley of the Cross we arrive at the ISRAEL MUSEUM. Including the Betzelel Museum of Art and Folklore and the Bronfman Archaeological and Antiquities Museum, all set in the Billy Rose Art Garden, without a doubt the most famous and important section of the museum complex is the SHRINE OF THE BOOK. With its distinctive onion-shaped top, made of 275,000 glazed white bricks, and the contrasting black basalt rectangular block across the square, the museum houses the world famous Dead Sea Scrolls. The Qumran brotherhood regarded themselves as the Sons of Light in an apocalyptic battle against the Sons of Darkness. The white dome of the shrine, in the shape of the lids from the Dead Sea Scrolls' jars, represents the Qumran Essenes; the black of the basalt rectangle represents the rest of the world.

Let's make our way between the contrasting white and black, down a flight of outside stairs to the subterranean entrance of the museum. This whole unique structure is a series of symbols.

The entranceway is a tunnel-like passage with glass-faced niches on either side featuring letter fragments, household items and pieces of clothing. The main hall of the museum, under the white dome, is designed to symbolize a cave. All the while you are in the Shrine of the Book you have the feeling that you are underground, perhaps in one of the Qumran caves.

Many interesting items can be seen on the two levels of the museum. There are keys, locks, coins and even a marriage contract dated April 5, 128 A.D. Along the perimeter of the cave/museum we can peer into the walls and see fragments of the Leviticus, Psalms and Isaiah scrolls in specially treated display areas. In the center of the museum, on the upper level, is a large replica of a scroll handle rising from a cylinder around which has been stretched a copy of the great Isaiah Scroll found in Cave One. This is the central feature of the museum although artifacts and letters from the Bar Kochba years are also on display on the lower level.

As we exit the museum there is a fine bookstore to our right. There are books on the scrolls, color slides, posters and other souvenirs that can be purchased. It's worth a stop.

At the Hebrew University the Shrine of the Book Museum was built to house the Dead Sea Scrolls for preservation as well as for exhibit to the interested public.

From the Israel Museum we proceed southwest away from Jerusalem on Rav Herzog Street to the Holyland Hotel. Behind the hotel is a most interesting MODEL OF ANCIENT JERUSALEM. Commissioned by the owner of the hotel in memory of a son killed during the war, the model took seven years to construct. A team of architects, archaeologists and historians were led by noted Hebrew University archaeologist Professor Michael Avi-Yonah in planning and producing the project. On a scale of 1:50 (¼ inch equals 1 foot), this is a near perfect and painstak-

ing model of Herod's Jerusalem, the Second Temple period (A.D. 66), with opulent palaces, mammoth walls, splendid public buildings, massive fortifications, private dwellings and the magnificent Second Temple itself. Wherever possible the original materials of cut stone, marble, iron, wood, copper, etc. have been used in the model.

This is a "must see" in Jerusalem's environs for it places many of the present historic remains in the Old City and vicinity in their proper perspective. Covering a quarter of an acre, the walk around the perimeter of the model is an excellent way to become oriented to what Jerusalem must surely have looked like to our Lord.

As the highway running by the model bends to the north, we can see a world renowned institution to our left. Rising 12 stories from the top of a mountain above the village of Ein Karem is the HADASSAH HOSPITAL. Originally established on Mount Scopus, the hospital became inaccessible after the War of Independence when Mount Scopus fell within the demilitarized zone. Thus the new Hadassah was built on the West Side of Jerusalem and opened in 1961.

The $30 million Hadassah Hebrew University Medical Center is the largest medical center in the Middle East. In addition to being an 800-bed hospital, a family and community center, a child guidance clinic and the modern facilities of the Hebrew University Medical Center are located here as well. More than 2,000 students of medicine, dentistry, pharmacy, public health, bacteriology and nursing are serviced by these impressive facilities.

To the left of the main entrance of the Hadassah Hospital is a small synagogue which exhibits the world-famous stained glass windows by Marc Chagall. Each window is an abstract masterpiece depicting the Twelve Tribes of Israel. To view these magnificent windows makes the trip to the hospital well worthwhile.

Ahead of us there is a junction. The main road continues north. A second road turns left toward one of Israel's most solemn memorials. A third road slices back sharply to our left and winds into the village of EIN KAREM. Nestled enchantingly amid tall cypress trees and olive groves, on a terraced hillside, Ein Karem is remembered as the birthplace of John the Baptist. It may be identified with the Jearim of Joshua 15:60 (LXX) and perhaps even the Beth-haccherem of Jeremiah 6:1. This is also the scene of Mary's visit to Elizabeth, John's mother.

North of the center of town, against the ter-

On a central platform, under the dome of the Shrine of the Book, a replica of the entire scroll of the Book of Isaiah is displayed around a large cylinder.

raced hills, is SAINT JOHN'S CHURCH. Built over the grotto thought to be the birthplace of John the Baptist, the present church dates from 1675. The main altar of the church is dedicated to John, with a secondary altar to Elizabeth off to the right. To the left of the nave is a small stairway which leads down to the grotto. Here we see a small niche under the marble altar said to be the place of the Baptist's birth.

Just south of the main road through Ein Karem and at the bottom of the hill is the SPRING OF THE VINEYARD (Ein Karem) MOSQUE. Since Crusader times this spring has been associated with the visit of the Virgin to Elizabeth. A small mosque crowns the rock from under which the town spring bubbles forth.

Farther west along the hillside is the CHURCH OF THE VISITATION, a Franciscan church best reached up the stairway from the Russian Compound. We climb the steps, up the side of the hill, to the ornate wrought-iron gate leading to the church. The facade of the church is a bright mosaic with a scene portraying Mary's visit to the town. Inside is a grotto marking the traditional site where it is believed John was hidden during the murder of innocent children by the jealous Herod (Matthew 2:16).

To see the rest of the church we must return to the entrance courtyard and ascend a set of stairs to the east. This leads from the lower church to the upper church. Here we can see some of the country's finest floor mosaics of Holy Land flora and fauna. Also there are attractive frescoes on the walls portraying scenes from Mary's life and plaques in several languages revealing the text of the Magnificat (Luke 1:46-55).

Back down the hillside to Ein Karem and retracing our path back to the main road to Jerusalem, we arrive at the junction again. This time we take the road left, around Mount Herzl and the stark but magnificent Herzl Tomb, up to YAD VASHEM. The street which leads to this memorial is called the AVENUE OF THE RIGHTEOUS. The trees we see lining both sides of this avenue have been planted by Gentiles who risked their lives in assisting the escape of Jews from the Nazis.

On top of this hill is a complex of memorials but none here or anywhere in the world is as moving, as frightening, as solemn or as unforgettable as the Yad Vashem Memorial. Dedicated to the memory of the 6 million Jews slaughtered by the Nazis during World War II, this memorial also houses a Documentation and Research Centre with tens of thousands of pieces of microfilm relating to the Holocaust. The heavy gate at the entrance is an abstract tapestry of twisted and jagged steel designed by David Polombo to symbolize pain, agony and anguish. We can almost feel the suffering of the 6 million Jews as we peer through the gate.

The memorial itself is a plain rectangular building, sad and simple, the lower portion of which is constructed of rounded unhewn boulders. Inside is a huge crypt-like room where the flickering light from an eternal flame casts an otherworldly light on the mosaic floor in which is inscribed the names of the 21 largest concentration camps in which Jews lost their lives. No one can visit Yad Vashem and remain emotionally untouched, nor should they.

From this solemn hill we return to the main road headling north, Herzl Boulevard. We follow this all the way around New Jerusalem until it becomes Yirmiyahu Street at the extreme northwest corner of Jerusalem's environs. On our imaginary clock we are now at 11 o'clock. A left turn onto Brandeis Street brings us right to one of Jerusalem's most delightful spots. It's the BIBLICAL ZOO. Professor Aaron Shulov of the Hebrew University's Biology Department has gathered in this unique zoo almost all of the 100 animals and 30 birds mentioned in the Bible. With each bird or animal is a plaque citing the book, chapter and verse in which the animal is mentioned.

The zoo was founded in 1939 on Mount Scopus. When the War of Independence broke out in 1948 there were 122 animals in the zoo. But when Mount Scopus fell into the demilitarized zone after the war, an armored convoy brought the animals which survived the war to this present location. Only 18 animals survived. This site in the Schneller woods is perfect. It is a shaded glen with tall cyprus and fir trees all around. In 1967 the animal population had grown to 500, but in the Six day War 110 animals fell victim to the fighting. Since then the zoo has been expanding steadily.

Once we return to Brandeis Street we retrace our steps, crossing Yirmiyahu, continuing to Malchei Israel and left on this street until it becomes Mea Shearim Street. Here we enter one of the most fascinating quarters of Jerusalem. It is exotic and extreme, delightful and distressing, fascinating and frightening. It's like stepping out of the Middle East and into Medieval Europe. It is MEA SHEARIM, the super orthodox quarter of northwestern Jerusalem.

Mea Shearim is said to derive from the account of Genesis 26:12 where God blessed Abraham's son: *"Then Isaac sowed in that land, and received in*

A solemn occasion is a visit to the Yad Vashem Memorial dedicated to the memory of the six million Jews killed by the Nazis during World War II.

*the same year a hundredfold* [Mea Shearim]: *and the Lord blessed him."* One of the earliest settlements outside the Old City, this quarter was built with a one hundred-gate wall as a defense against Arab marauders. Within this quarter time has stopped. We walk down cobblestone streets and lanes lined with dingy houses with shuttered windows. Since 1887, Mea Shearim has been a bastion for the pious, a hotbed of Jewish orthodoxy.

Center of the mystical Hasidic religious sect, Mea Shearim is inhabited by descendants and immigrants from the Russian and Polish ghettos. They are orthodox Jews and dress in a distinct garb. We will recognize them immediately. The bearded men trudge through the winding streets in black gowns wearing the beaver fur hat of the Hasidic sects or else the black wide-brimmed felt hat of other orthodox sects. The boys wear short pants with long black socks reaching the bottom of their pants. And with both the men and boys we see the long, curly sidelocks falling beneath their black hats. The women dress with extreme modesty wearing long dresses covering their shoulders and arms. Their heads are always covered. In fact, when we enter Mea Shearim we are greeted with signs warning us that women dressed immodestly (by Hasidic standards) are not welcome.

This is a highly religious place. Here we see scribes painstakingly copying the Scriptures by hand. Here every other building is either a synagogue, a theological institution (yeshivot) or a seminar school (midrashim). Here we rub elbows with scholars, scribes and sages. Here we find hundreds of tiny sects, each with their own revered rabbi and private synagogue. Here we find heavy hustle and bustle before the Sabbath, but a total absence of automobile traffic and movement on the Sabbath. Here we follow hordes of the faithful making their way to the Western Wall late on the Sabbath night to offer prayers. Here is a living remnant of the Jewish orthodox faith that once was common to all of God's chosen people but it now confined to a pious parcel of present day Palestine known as Mea Shearim. It's an experience we won't soon forget.

# CHAPTER 9

# Destiny's City

◆

## JERUSALEM

*"Great is the LORD, and greatly to be praised in the city of our God, in the mountain of his holiness. Beautiful for situation, the joy of the whole earth, is mount Zion, on the sides of the north, the city of the great King"* (Psalm 48:1-2).

Have you ever walked through the streets of a city that just teemed with excitement? Perhaps you have paraded down the canyons of New York City or taken a leisurely stroll through the quaint cobblestone alleys of Paris. The glory that once was Greece may have flashed before your eyes as you wandered the streets of Athens. Or possibly the sidewalks of your hometown bring back precious memories of days gone by. But there is no city in the world which generates more excitement than the city of Jerusalem.

Sacred to the Jew, Muslim and Christian alike, Jerusalem has been the center of religious activity for thousands of years. The Jew venerates this city because it was the site of Solomon's Temple. The Muslim claims Jerusalem as the city from which the prophet Mohammed ascended into heaven. And, of course, we Christians remember the city as the scene of our Lord's death, burial and resurrection.

No city can lay claim to being the "Holy City" but Jerusalem (Isaiah 52:1; Nehemiah 11:1). Only Jerusalem is described as *". . . the city which the LORD did choose out of all the tribes of Israel, to put his name there"* (I Kings 14:21). The Bible identifies Jerusalem as the city of God (Psalm 48:1-2), the city of Jehovah (Isaiah 60:14), the mountain of the Lord (Isaiah 2:3) and the holy mountain (Isaiah 66:20). The Lord Himself refers to Jerusalem alone as *"my city"* (Isaiah 45:13) and frequently as *"my holy mountain"* (Isaiah 11:9). The 1st century A.D. Roman historian Pliny referred to Jerusalem as "by far the most famous city of the ancient Orient." Even today its importance can only be underestimated.

The first appearance of the word Jerusalem in the Bible is found in Joshua 10:1, but the city's prominence long predates that. The Tell el Amarna Tablets of the 15th century B.C. mention a city Urushalim. Genesis 14:18-20 records that the patriarch Abraham paid tithes to *"Melchizedek, king of Salem."* Salem means peace, Jerusalem is the "city of peace." But no city in the world has been coveted and conquered more than Jerusa-

The Old City seen from the west.

lem. The Babylonians, Macedonians, Ptolemies, Seleucids, Romans, Byzantines, Persians, Arabs, Crusaders, Monguls, Mamelukes, Turks, British and Jordanians are only some of the conquerors of this great city.

To understand the layout of the present Old City we must remember that this is a city accustomed to the hardship of war and the reorganization which subsequent periods of peace bring. The Walled City has existed as is for hundreds of years. In 1917 Great Britain issued the Balfour Declaration which promised the Jews a national homeland in Palestine. This brought thousands of Jews back to Jerusalem. In 1948, however, when the British left Palestine, war broke out between the Jews and Arabs and the Jews fled the Old city to the western suburbs. A year later the Hashemite Kingdom of Jordan annexed the Walled City. The Jewish Quarter was razed to the ground and 27 venerated and ancient synagogues were dismantled. For the next 20 years Jerusalem remained divided.

Then, suddenly, in 1967 Israeli forces moved on the Old City during the Six Day War and on June 28th the Old City was annexed by Israel. The wall separating Jewish West Jerusalem from Arab East Jerusalem came down. An era of urban expansion began, including restoration of the devastated Jewish Quarter. So that today, as we enter the Walled City held exclusively by the Arabs for so many years, we sense a decidedly Arab flavor but with the presence of Israeli soldiers and police. This is the new Old City.

## JERUSALEM'S WALL

The shape of and area covered by Jerusalem has changed many times. Each change necessitated a wall encircling the city. Besieged and rebuilt, the Jerusalem wall has been totally destroyed at least five times. You may remember that the great lament of Nehemiah during Israel's captivity was that *"the wall of Jerusalem also is broken down, and the gates thereof are burned with fire"* (Nehemiah 1:3).

The wall as it appears today is a conglomeration. Various periods of construction can be identified, including that of Herod's wall. Perhaps the oldest surviving section of the wall is Hasmonean, from the 2nd century B.C. We will see it at the Citadel. Most of the visible wall dates from 1542 and was built by Sultan Suleiman "The Magnificent." In general the lines of the present wall follow those of the wall scaled by the Crusaders in 1099 or those which encompassed Hadrian's 2nd century Roman colony, Aelia Capitolina.

This uneven rectangular wall, which encloses the Ir Hakodesh (the Holy City), is the most striking feature of Jerusalem. Originally all Jerusalemites lived inside the wall. But in 1860, at the southwestern corner of the Old City across the valley from Mount Zion, the first quarter outside the city wall was established. It is YEMIN MOSHE. At the entrance is one of Jerusalem's most distinctive Jewish landmarks, the MONTEFIORE WINDMILL. Although this may look like a little bit of Holland in the Holy Land, the windmill was actually built by Sir Moses Montefiore as a flour mill to provide the Jewish suburban settlers with work. Today only one-fourth of the city is housed within the wall.

The wall itself is massive, averaging 40 feet high. It is pierced by eight gates and punctuated with 34 towers. About two and one-half miles in length, the wall encompasses an area of about one kilometer square. If you are adventuresome and want to treat your camera lens to breathtaking angles of the Old City, we can walk along the top of this rampart wall and see Jerusalem in an exhilarating and distinctly unique manner. We ought to do it in the morning when the light is best and we need to allow about three and one-half hours, but it's an experience we'll treasure forever.

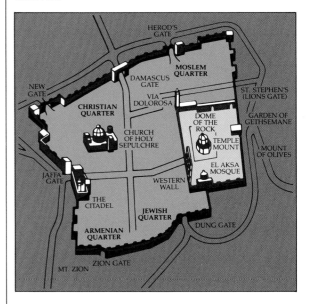

# JERUSALEM'S GATES

The stroll on top of the Jerusalem wall affords us the opportunity to become acquainted with the positioning of the city's gates. Let's start at one of the most prominent gates and proceed clockwise around the city.

*JAFFA GATE.* Again if in our minds we superimpose the face of a clock over the Old City it will be helpful. We begin at 9 o'clock, on Jerusalem's West Side. Why here and not at the Damascus Gate at 12 o'clock? Because Jaffa Gate is the only place the city wall is breached, open to the sky. So if we begin here we climb to the top of the wall at the north side of the gate and never have to descend until we return here at the south side of the gate.

Named The Gate of the Friend because of an Arabic inscription over the entrance which reads, "There is no god but Allah and Abraham is his friend," the Jaffa Gate is one of Jerusalem's busiest. From here both the road to Bethlehem and Hebron and the road to Jaffa and the Mediterranean proceed. In preparation for the arrival of Kaiser Wilhelm II in 1898, the moat between the gate and the Citadel to the south was filled in and the wall over the main entrance of the gate breached to allow a mounted procession. In contrast, when General Allenby arrived at this gate he dismounted his horse as a mark of humility before entering the city.

*NEW GATE.* Walking north, with the Christian Quarter to our right, we arrive at the New Gate, about 10 o'clock on our clock. Built in 1887 by Sultan Abdul Hamid it was subsequently known as the Gate of the Sultan. Just opposite and outside the gate is the Notre Dame de France and behind it the Russian Compound. With the growing Christian facilities outside the wall, the Sultan decided a gate was needed to give ready access to the Christian Quarter. This gate, along with Zion and Jaffa Gates, was closed during the Jordanian occupation of the city (1948-1967) as this side of Jerusalem faced territory held by the Israelis.

*DAMASCUS GATE.* Just about at 12 o'clock is the main gate of Old Jerusalem, the Damascus Gate. It is so named for here the road leading from Israel's capital to Syria's capital begins. The Jews also call it Shechem Gate for that same road passes through Nablus and Shechem.

In Arabic the gate retains two other names. It is called the Gate of Victory for it was long considered the only proper gate for royalty to enter. It is somewhat more ornate and impressive than the other gates. Also it is known by local Arabs as the Gate of the Column. When Hadrian conquered the city he celebrated that victory by building a victory column at the gate. The 6th century Madeba map of Jerusalem, a mosaic map on a church floor in Jordan, also shows a pillar just inside this gate. The pillar has long since disappeared.

In recent years archaeologists have been probing beneath the Damascus Gate. Outside the gate, at the bottom left, we can see the northern gate of Hadrian's city, complete with a Roman inscription. Deep under the street which passes through this gate is the Cardo Maximus, the main thoroughfare into the city during the Roman Empire. It was intersected by the Decumanus, a street running into the city from the location of the Jaffa Gate. Basically, these two streets effectively quartered ancient Jerusalem, today the Christian, Muslim, Jewish and Armenian Quarters.

*HEROD'S GATE.* At a bit past 12 o'clock on our Jerusalem clock we find Herod's Gate. With a name like that you would expect an impressive entrance to a bustling quarter of the city. That's what you'd expect, but this isn't so. The gate apparently received its name from medieval pilgrims who believed the tradition that inside this gate was the residence of Herod Antipas. However, it is more likely that Herod resided in the old Hasmonean Palace on Mount Zion. Nonetheless, Herod's name continues to be associated with this northern gate.

*LION'S GATE.* Known to the Arabs as Saint Mary's Gate for it leads to the Church of Mary's Tomb and the Kidron Valley, this prominent gate is placed at about 2 o'clock. It is important for the street passing through Lion's Gate leads to the Via Dolorosa. It receives its current name because of the twin lions carved in relief on either side of the entranceway. These are the emblem of the Mameluke Sultan Baybars.

Somewhere near here was the Sheep Gate or Benjamin's Gate in New Testament times. Outside this gate today there is still the city's sheep market. But in the Christian tradition the Lion's Gate has most often been identified as Saint Stephen's Gate for it was believed that through this gate (actually one below it) Stephen passed, was stoned to death outside, and became the first Christian martyr (Acts 7:54-60). However, the Church of Saint Stephen was built north of here, at the gate now known as Damascus Gate. Originally it was held that here Stephen was stoned preserving, probably, a more correct tradition.

On June 7, 1967 the advancing Israeli armies penetrated the Lion's Gate (or Saint Stephen's) and fought their way through the Old City to the Western (or Wailing) Wall. It was the first time in the city's long history that an invading force was successful in attacking Jerusalem from that direction.

*GOLDEN GATE.* This brings us due east (3 o'clock) to the only one of Jerusalem's eight gates closed tight. It is the most celebrated and most ornamented gate of the city. In fact, not only is this the oldest city gate, it is also the only one which leads directly to the Temple Mount. Sometimes referred to as the Eastern Gate, it is commonly known as the Golden Gate.

Thought to have been built by Eudocia, wife of the Byzantine Emperor Theodosius II in the 5th century, this is a double gate with twin arches. The northern arch is called the Gate of Repentance, the southern arch, the Gate of Mercy. It is believed this was the site of the Closed Gate of the First Temple and the Shushan Gate of the Second Temple. It was clearly designed as the main entrance of both Old and New Testament Jerusalem. Thus, Jesus made His triumphal entry into Jerusalem through this gate (Matthew 21:8-11) and exited the city here to pray in the Garden of Gethsemane (Matthew 26:30, 36).

Since the Kidron Valley below has long been associated with judgment, it is said that the Turks blocked the double-arched Eastern Gate in hopes of postponing the Day of Judgment. Others say it was done to prevent the entry of the Messiah. Many Christians identify the Prince of Ezekiel 44:1-3 with Jesus Christ and believe that at our Lord's second coming the Golden Gate will be unblocked and He will enter the Temple Mount uninhibitedly.

Just outside of this gate is a Muslim cemetery, overrun with dandelions and other wildflowers. It is (theoretically) off limits to non-Muslims, but for a small "tip" the keeper of the cemetery will permit us entrance. A short walk from the cemetery entrance at Lion's Gate will bring us to the base of the Golden Gate and a fantastic photo of Jerusalem's premier gate.

*DUNG GATE.* Perhaps the least impressive of the eight gates, the Dung Gate is on the southern perimeter of the Jerusalem Wall at about 6 o'clock (maybe 5:30). It is sometimes known as the Gate of the Moors for it leads to the Temple Mount through the inner Moor's Gate. Today it is our quickest route to the Western Wall. In Crusader times it was called the Tanner's Gate. But from the time of Nehemiah (Nehemiah 2:13; 3:13-14; 12:31), it has been affectionately known as the Dung Gate for through here Jerusalemites for centuries have carted their garbage for disposal in the Hinnom Valley below.

*ZION GATE.* The gate at 7 o'clock which leads from the city to Mount Zion is appropriately named Zion Gate. The local Arab population prefers the name Gate of David for the gate gives access to the TOMB OF DAVID. Suleiman's wall slices Mount Zion in half and excludes the cenotaph marking the traditional site of David's tomb from his own city.

One of Judaism's holiest shrines, the Tomb of David is also sacred to Muslims and Christians. It is located in the same complex of buildings housing the traditional Upper Room and is usually visited in conjunction with it. Making our way through the cobblestone courtyard we finally arrive at the gloomy room where the cenotaph is located. Men must don a yarmulke (traditional little round Jewish hat) to enter this holy site. Inside the miniscule room we see a cenotaph covered with a thick embroidered cloth decorated with a menorah over a star of David and bordered by lions standing on pillars. Above the cenotaph is an assortment of silver crowns and Torah scrolls.

When we round the southwestern corner of Jerusalem's Wall, turn north and make our way past the Armenian Quarter to our right, we finally end up back where we started, at the Jaffa Gate. But just before we arrive at the gate, we approach one of Jerusalem's most prominent landmarks, the Tower of David.

## JERUSALEM'S CITADEL

Just alongside of the Jaffa Gate, forming its southern side, is one of two sumptuous fortress-palaces built in Jerusalem by Herod the Great. It is called THE CITADEL. The other fortress is the Antonio, defense station for the Temple area.

Herod's Citadel was constructed with three towers, named after Phasael, Herod's brother, Hippicus, one of the king's close friends, and Mariamne, his Hasmonean wife whom he later murdered. So impressive were these towers that when Titus sacked Jerusalem in A.D. 70 he left the towers standing. But when Hadrian razed the city in A.D. 135 he destroyed most of the Citadel. Only Phasael's Tower and the fortress' foundation survived. The Crusaders and Saracens rebuilt the Citadel much as we see it today, with five towers instead of the original three. Suleiman completed the project in 1540.

All but the western side of the fortress, the

The Golden Gate, although now sealed up, is the most celebrated and ornamented gate of the city and leads directly to the Temple Mount now occupied by the Muslim Dome of the Rock mosque.

Jerusalem wall side, is surrounded by a moat. Only part of it is visible today. Access to the Citadel is gained through an eastern gate, inside the city. Up the stairs and through an arch, we cross the moat over a small bridge to the main gate. Inside the gate, straight ahead of us, is an interesting 2nd century Roman sarcophagus which is highly decorated. The stairway to the right leads to Phasael's Tower.

The large rough-cut stones which comprise the lower 60 feet of the tower are clearly Herodian. They are identical to those of the Western Wall or the lower portion of the Pinnacle of the Temple. From the top of the tower we are afforded a good view of the Old city, especially the Christian Quarter to our left and the Armenian Quarter to our right.

Now let's descend to the courtyard. We clearly see the remains of the ancient Hasmonean wall slicing across the courtyard. From here as well we can distinguish the five towers of the Citadel. We have just come from Phasael's Tower, which is also known as David's Tower because of the mistaken belief some 500 years ago that this was the original site of the City of David. It is the northeast tower. The northwest tower is adjacent to the Jaffa Gate and actually comprises the southern tower of the gate. The southwest tower sits on Crusader stones with Mameluke and Turkish restorations on top of them. The southeast tower is entirely Mameluke. Perhaps the most recognizable tower is the fifth, the southern tower. This is the Minaret Tower which can be spotted for miles and is usually, but incorrectly, identified as David's Tower. The minaret was not added until 1665.

If you visit the Citadel during the summer months (March 15th—November 15th) you are in for a special treat. Each evening, except for Fridays and holidays, a SOUND AND LIGHT PERFORMANCE is presented within the Citadel's precincts. Take your pick. At different times you can hear the performance in Hebrew, French or English. It is entitled "A Stone in David's Tower" and tells the story of 4,000 years of history at this site. It's excellent.

## JERUSALEM'S QUARTERS

As we have mentioned, in the ancient Roman Empire the city of Jerusalem was divided into quarters by two intersecting streets. From the Damascus Gate, the Cardo Maximus split the city into east and west. From the Jaffa Gate, the Decumanus sliced the city into north and south. Roughly these four quarters still exist in the 20th century. Let's take a quick look at them and the most important sites for a Christian to visit in each.

***THE CHRISTIAN QUARTER.*** If we enter the Old City at the Jaffa Gate and proceed down David Street, the Christian Quarter lies entirely to our left. This is a quarter filled with churches, hospices, chapels, monasteries, schools and missions. By the way, the best shopping on this side of town is along this street and the tiny alleys which splinter from it. The major street leading from David Street into this sector is Christian Quarter Road. It's our first left. Off this road, up the terraced street called Khan el Khubat, is HEZEKIAH'S POOL. Now surrounded by buildings and not used, the 250 foot long, 148 foot wide pool has a bed ten feet below street level. Although the pool of Hezekiah is probably located elsewhere, this 2,000-year-old pool is identified by Josephus as the Pool of Amygdalon (Almond Pool in Greek or Great Tower in Hebrew). It is probably to be associated with the nearby Citadel.

Off Christian Quarter Road on the other side is the MURISTAN, a Greek Bazaar. In Arabic, Muristan means "hospice" and during Crusader times it served as such. During the 2nd century Roman city of Aelia Capitolina this area was the Forum of Jerusalem. In 1869 the Turks divided this area between the Greek Orthodox, who built this arcade and the ornamental MURISTAN FOUNTAIN at its entrance, and the Lutherans who built the Church of the Redeemer facing us at the arcade entrance. In the bazaar we find an assortment of leather luggage, sheepskins, baskets, etc. all awaiting our leisurely stroll through the open air arcade.

***THE CHURCH OF THE REDEEMER*** was built in 1898 over the gateway to the cloisters of the Crusader Church of Saint Mary Latina. It includes some of the architectural relics of the 12th century church. In fact, the present church's northern portal is the preserved gateway to the Crusader church. But for the Christian pilgrim, and just about everyone else, the tower of this Redeemer Church is the real purpose of our stop here. This church is near the center of the walled city and the tower provides a magnificent platform from which to photograph Jerusalem. This vantage point gives us a perfect "shot" at the Temple area from the west, as the area on the Mount of Olives before the Intercontinental Hotel does from the east.

North of the Muristan is the most important church of the city, the Church of the Holy Sepulchre. Held by many to be the site of Jesus' crucifixion it will be discussed in detail in the next chapter. South of the Muristan, toward David Street, is the CHURCH OF SAINT JOHN THE BAPTIST, believed to be the oldest church in Jerusalem. It incorporates the remains of several ancient churches, the present church dating from the 11th century. Under this church excavations have revealed a crypt dating from the 5th century or earlier. Discovered in it was a reliquary, a container for religious relics, which is purported to contain a piece of Christ's cross.

**THE MUSLIM QUARTER.** At the north and northeast sector of the city is the Muslim (Moslem) Quarter. Here are found the finest examples of Mameluke architecture in the city. Here too is the Old City's most famous street, the Via Dolorosa. Several other sites are of interest to us as well.

Starting from the Lion's Gate, we enter the Muslim Quarter on Saint Mary's Street. The first building on our right is the Greek Orthodox Church of Saints Joachim and Anna. Just a few feet farther is the entry door to one of Jerusalem's oldest and most beautiful churches. Through the doorway into a beautifully shaded and delightfully cool garden, straight ahead on our right is the CHURCH OF SAINT ANNE. Designed in the Burgundian Romanesque style, this is one of the finest examples of Crusader construction in the Holy Land. We enter the Gothic doorway at the back of the church. Let's look first at the ceiling. Notice that the pointed arches divide the church into thirds. The vaulted ceiling and ahead the beautiful dome make this a spectacular though inornate structure.

Constructed in 1140 by Yvette, daughter of Balwin II, King of Jerusalem, the Saracens converted it to a Muslim seminary. Napoleon III restored the building and in 1878 committed it to the care of the White Fathers, a Greek Orthodox missionary order that wear white habits.

In the right nave of the church, about halfway to the altar, is a set of stairs which lead to a crypt under the church. As we have so frequently seen, churches in the Holy Land usually are built to commemorate something beneath them. A 4th century tradition states that in this crypt the Virgin Mary was born of Joachim and Anne. Hence, the church is named in honor of Mary's mother.

Let's go back outside to the beautiful garden. To our right, until 1956, were a number of old buildings. When they were demolished the White Fathers began to excavate the site. Here they discovered a very famous biblical pool, the POOL OF BETHESDA. According to the Gospel of John, *"There is at Jerusalem by the sheep market a pool, which is called in the Hebrew tongue Bethesda, having five porches"* (John 5:2). Here Jesus performed a great miracle.

A man impotent for 38 years lay by the pool awaiting opportunity to get into the water and be healed. *"Jesus saith unto him, Rise, take up thy bed, and walk"* (John 5:8). And he did.

Excavations have revealed a 5th century church at the site, the Church of the Paralytic. Although destroyed by the Persians in 614, the Crusaders built a chapel over the remains, the apse and entrance of which are still visible at the southern end of the pool. The water level at the pool is nearly 60 feet below the current ground level, but for the surefooted, the climb down to the "house of mercy" (which is what Bethesda means) is possible.

By the way, in case you're interested, I think this quarter has the best shopping in all of Jerusalem. Just continue into the city on the Via Dolorosa and when it turns sharply left we bear sharply right on El-Wad Road. This leads us directly to the Damascus Gate and a bonanza of things to buy. If we enter the quarter through the Damascus Gate, and descend the platform steps resembling the terraced hillsides of Bethlehem, we must soon either go left on El-Wad Road or right on Suq Khan Ez-Zeit. Take the right; shopping is much better.

Here the street narrows quickly. Men sit around smoking water pipes and playing shaishbaish, a sort of backgammon. The street is mobbed with an occasional overloaded donkey slowing our progress. You can't help but smell the aroma of the spices, the Turkish coffee, the donkey. Here we can buy Arab pastries, fruit and vegetables, mother of pearl items, olive wood carvings, brass trinkets, silver necklaces, sheepskin jackets, and just about anything else. The meat markets of the section hang raw quarters of lamb, goat or beef at the front of the market so we will be enticed to shoo away the flies and buy a rack of raw lamb.

In this delightful bazaar we can barter and bargain until we're convinced we have the "steal" of the century. But the glint in the Arab shopkeeper's eye might cause us to think otherwise. Besides, if you don't see what you want in this shop, go across the street where the shopkeeper's "brother" has "a good deal for you." Enjoy this Muslim Quarter. It's like nothing you've seen before.

Not far inside the Lion's Gate and near the Church of Saint Anne, built over the traditional site of the birthplace of the virgin Mary, are the ruins of the Pool of Bethesda where Jesus healed the paralytic man.

*THE JEWISH QUARTER.* Immediately west of the Western Wall and the Dung Gate, the Jewish Quarter is on the eastern flank of Mount Zion, overlooking the Temple Mount. This was the first suburb Jerusalem ever had. When David established his city here it was on the Ophel, the area on the slopes south of the Temple Mount. When the population filled that site the overflow settled up here. Archaeological excavations show Jewish settlements here dating to the 7th and 8th centuries B.C. This became the Upper City, in distinction from the original Lower City.

During the days of Herod this Upper City flourished and elegant Greek-style homes of the very wealthy were built here. This quarter, however, was destroyed by Titus when the rest of the city was sacked in A.D. 70. Both Rome and Byzantium barred the Jews from returning to this site. It was not until the noted biblical commentator Rabbi Moshe ben-Nachman, the Ram-

ban, arrived in Jerusalem in 1267 that a synagogue was established here. From that point on this sector of the city became the center of Jewish life in the Holy City for nearly 700 years.

In the 1948 War of Independence the Arab Legion again drove the Jews out of this quarter and began to systematically destroy their synagogues. When the Israeli forces reunited Jerusalem in 1967 they began to clear the rubble and restore it. So today as we enter the Jewish Quarter we see continuing restoration, dusty, unpaved streets and the places where important Jewish landmarks once stood.

From the end of David Street (where it becomes Chain Street), turn right on Jewish Quarter Street to RAMBAN SYNAGOGUE. We can also reach it from the Dung Gate or the Lion Gate. The oldest synagogue in the Old City, Ramban was named in honor of Rabbi Moshe ben-Nachman. Jews worshiped in this synagogue until 1585 when the Mufti of Jerusalem turned it into a mosque. Upon entering this decrepit but not destroyed synagogue in 1967, Israeli soldiers had it immediately reconsecrated.

When we come out of the synagogue we are faced with a Muslim minaret, the only one in the Jewish Quarter. South of the minaret is the YOHANAN BEN ZAKKAI SYNAGOGUE. Built in 1586 to compensate for the loss of the Ramban the year before, this has been the spiritual center for the Sephardic (Spanish) Jews for centuries. The name of the synagogue comes from the tradition that this is the site of the distinguished rabbi's school in Jerusalem. Sometimes called the Four Synagogues because there are four interconnected rooms, there was an ancient legend that says Ben Zakkai's Synagogue had a secret tunnel which led directly to the Temple. Although no evidence of a tunnel ever existed, nonetheless this indicates how dear to the Jewish heart the Jewish Quarter really is.

*THE ARMENIAN QUARTER.* Located in the southwestern sector of Old Jerusalem, on the northern slope of Mount Zion, is the Armenian Quarter. Reached through the Zion Gate or Jaffa Gate, this quarter is almost a city within a city. It is self-contained, an Armenian Compound containing a museum, library, seminary, monastery, schools, etc. If we turn on Saint James Street off Armenian Patriarchate Street (coming from either Zion or Jaffa Gates), and then left on Ararat, we arrive at SAINT MARK'S HOUSE. This is the Syrian Orthodox Monastery and the See of the Syrian Archbishop of Jerusalem. The building, which dates from the 12th century, is very important to the Armenian Church. They believe this was the house of Mary, Mark's mother, where Peter went after being delivered from prison (Acts 12:12). Here, they say, Peter founded the first church and here they believe to have been the Upper Room, not on Mount Zion.

Returning to Armenian Patriarchate Road and walking a short distance south we soon come to one of Jerusalem's most gorgeous cathedrals, SAINT JAMES CATHEDRAL. Two saints named James are associated with this Crusader structure. James the fisherman, the brother of John, was beheaded by Herod Agrippa, grandson of Herod the Great, in A.D. 44 (Acts 12:1-2). The other James is James the Less, another of the Lord's disciples.

The ornate cathedral is richly carpeted with thick oriental rugs. Hanging about are alternating lamps of gold and silver with porcelain ostrich eggs as ornamentation. On the walls and pillars are antique blue and green tiles of glazed earthenware. Around the walls hang dark canvases which are reproductions of the paintings of Armenian saints and kings painted on the walls themselves. Adjacent to the altar we can see the very ornate, onion-domed throne of Saint James (the Less) whom the Armenians believe to have been James, the first Christian bishop of Jerusalem. Most Christians identify James the brother of our Lord as the head of the early Jerusalem church (cf. Acts 12:17; 15:13; 21:18; Galatians 1:19). James the Less is reputedly buried under the great altar of the church.

As we exit the church be sure to look to your right. Here is a chapel decorated with tortoiseshell and silver gates, which is claimed by the Armenian clergy to be the spot where James the Greater was beheaded by Herod.

One final site is worth our attention. Near the Zion Gate at the extreme southern end of the Armenian Quarter is the HOUSE OF ANNAS. According to John 18:13, before He was led to the Sanhedrin for judgment, Jesus was escorted to the house of Annas, the father-in-law of Caiaphas, the High Priest. We enter the 5th century church at the site through a beautiful portico. Beautifully decorated, as all Armenian churches are, the House of Annas is adorned with gilded carvings, tiled walls, old paintings and an altar similar to that of Saint James Cathedral.

Once we leave the quarter through the Zion Gate, or any other exit, we leave behind a world unto itself. Aramaic is commonly spoken in the Armenian Quarter. You may have heard priests, bishops or archbishops pray in a strange language. That was Aramaic. This segment of Christianity has followed its own language, own customs, own calendar and own beliefs since they separated themselves from the mainstream of Christianity in A.D. 491. Our visit to their little part of the world won't bring any change to their way of life.

## JERUSALEM'S WESTERN WALL

Once again, let's return to the Dung Gate. This is the most direct entrance to Jerusalem's most famous wall, the WESTERN WALL. Formerly called the Wailing Wall, the designation changed after the Six Day War of 1967. Legend has it that early in the morning heavy drops of dew form on the wall and run down like tears. Locals say it is the wall's way of weeping with Israel in her exile. Actually it was called the Wailing Wall because for centuries, especially the 9th of Av, the anniversary of the Temple's destruc-

An elderly Hasid at the Western Wall. Stones more than 2,000 years old form the lower layers of this wall.

tion, Jews would flock to the wall to moan their treasured loss.

When the Jews were driven out of Jerusalem by the Arab Legion in 1948 they were unable to assemble at the wall as usual. For nearly 20 years they champed at the bit to get to the wall. When the opportunity presented itself during the Six Day War of 1967, Israeli soldiers cut a path right through the Old City to the wall. On June 7th, 1967, when General Moshe Dayan said, "We have returned to our holy places, never to part from them again," it was this place he had in mind. Now the Wailing Wall is known simply as the Western Wall for it has become a scene of joy, a celebration of prayer and singing, occasionally interspersed with spontaneous dancing. Israeli bulldozers have cleared a large esplanade before the wall to accommodate tens of thousands of worshipers and visitors.

As we pass through the Dung Gate, up the slight grade to the esplanade, notice the current archaeological excavations going on to our right. This is the area south of the Temple Mount where digging has been in progress since 1968. Frequent and bitter conflicts have taken place here, not between Jew and Arab, but between Jew and Jew. The Hasidim, the ultra-orthodox Jews of the Mea Shearim district, believe this area once to have been a cemetery and that the modern archaeologists are in violation of Jewish desecration laws.

Ahead of us is a checkpoint. Because this wall is extremely sacred to the Jews we must all pass through a security check opening handbags, camera bags, travel bags, etc. Once through the checkpoint, as the wall looms large to our right, we have time to ask ourselves, "Why is this wall so sacred to the Jews?" Good question.

The Temple of Solomon was situated on an enlarged Mount Moriah. The expanded area was west and south, making an almost rectangular area buttressed by retaining walls. When Herod rebuilt the Temple he extended these walls even farther using massive blocks of stone in a wall supporting the artificial perimeter of the Temple Mount. Much of this wall stands today, including the Western Wall. Many Christians mistakenly identify this wall with that of Solomon's Temple. It is not; in fact, it isn't even the wall of the Second Temple but of the retaining wall to that Temple. Nevertheless, of the Herodian walls which survived the destruction of Jerusalem in A.D. 70, this Western Wall is closest to the original Temple sanctuary and thus held as the most sacred Jewish site in the Holy Land.

Standing impressively 60 feet high and 91 feet long, each stone finely cut and beveled, no mortar was ever used in the wall. The oblong stones of Herod's wall are capped by four tiers of smooth Roman blocks and about a dozen tiers of smaller stones from a Turkish wall. We can distinguish them easily. But what is more impressive, we don't even see all of the Herodian wall. When Titus razed the Temple he ordered the rubble to be cast over the wall into the Tyropoeon Valley, between the Upper City and the Temple Mount. This means that from the level at which we stand the wall goes 60 feet lower to the bedrock. Fourteen more courses of huge Herodian stones are beneath us. Through the vaulted arch to our left is WARREN'S SHAFT, an excavation hole which permits us to see down to the base of the wall.

As we approach the Western Wall the men and women are separated by a fence. Women

Once famous as the Wailing Wall because the Jews mourned here for their loss of the Temple, it is now called the Western Wall since its restoration to the Jews in the Six Day War of 1967 and has become a scene of joy and celebration as well as of prayer.

must be modestly dressed; men must don a yarmulke (skullcap). One is provided for our use upon approaching the wall. Torah Scrolls are placed at spaced intervals along the wall. Stepping closer to the wall we mingle with the worshiping Hasidim with their phylacteries and prayerbooks, bobbing and weaving as they chant their rituals.

At the upper levels of the wall notice the sprigs of green grass growing out of the cracks in the wall. But what we see in the cracks at eye level is far different. Tiny strips of paper are rolled and slipped into the cracks. These are prayers that visitors to the site have placed there in hopes Jehovah would look kindly on them.

After spending a few minutes at the wall in utter amazement at its size, let's make our way through the arch into where we must wade through orthodox Jews, young and old, in prayer. Sorry ladies, here we have gone where you can't follow as this section is only accessible through the men's side of the esplanade. In this large subterranean hall we are actually under an arch spanning the Tyropoeon Valley. It is named WILSON'S ARCH after the British officer who explored the arch in 1850.

It's almost impossible to conceive that the flat area in front of the Western Wall was once 60 feet lower in a valley leading from the center of Jerusalem to the Hinnom Valley on the south. But to imagine that two great arches once spanned their valley is even more incredible. Did I say two arches? Yes, ladies, that's right. If we return to the base of the ramp leading to the wall at the Moors Gate, the ladies will be able to see the second arch over this intercity valley. Named for the American scholar Edward Robinson (1836), we can see a small ledge of ROBINSON'S ARCH jutting out from the wall to our right, near the corner. This tiny bit of stone projecting innocently was once a mighty bridge used to provide passage from the Temple site to the upper city, home of royalty.

Our final glimpse of the Western Wall comes as we proceed up the ramp toward the top of the wall. This entrance to the Temple Mount is the MOORS GATE. Here again we encounter an Israeli soldier who will kindly ask to inspect handbags, etc. Just a brief delay and we will enter the Temple itself. What a thrill!

## JERUSALEM'S TEMPLE AREA

Now, Christian, pause a minute, catch your breath, and thank the Lord. You are standing on one of the most sacred parcels of real estate in the world. No spot on earth has been sought after more or fought over more than the 35 acres within the walls of the Temple Compound.

You are on MOUNT MORIAH, a rocky knoll of Judaea which is much like any one of a thousand others in the Holy Land. Except it was to this knoll that Abraham was commanded by God to take his long-sought and solitary son Isaac and sacrifice him to Jehovah (Genesis 22:1-14). It was this knoll which contained the threshingfloor of Araunah, purchased by King David to build an altar and offer both burnt offerings and peace offerings unto God, staying a great plague in Israel (II Samuel 24:15-25). It was on this knoll that David gathered the materials and his son Solomon built the magnificent Temple of God (I Chronicles 21:28—22:5; II Chronicles 3:1—7:11). It was from this knoll that the treasures of the house of God were confiscated and the Temple itself destroyed by Nebuchadnezzar when he carried off the Jews in 587 B.C. to Babylonian captivity. When the exiles returned it was around this rocky knoll that Nehemiah and the people built a wall (Nehemiah 2:4-20; 6:15-16) and here Herod the Great rebuilt the Temple which is known as the Second Temple.

After the Roman general Titus destroyed Herod's Temple and the city of Jerusalem, the Roman Emperor Hadrian paganized this holy mount by erecting a temple to Jupiter. In fact, in A.D. 138 Hadrian rebuilt the city naming it Aelia Capitolina and forbade the Jews from entering the city on penalty of death. In 639 Jerusalem fell into the hands of the Muslims and Mount Moriah became a Muslim shrine. The sites we visit today, therefore, are Muslim sites of the holy area known to them as HARAM ESH SHARIF.

As we proceed from the Moors Gate the first Muslim shrine we encounter is the EL AKSA MOSQUE, ahead on our right. As we approach the entrance you may notice to your left a small sunken fountain. It is circular with a single row of pinkish marble seats at its base, each equipped with a faucet from the fountain. Known as EL KAS, The Cup, it is used by the Muslims as an ablution pool, a place to ritually wash before entering the holy places. If we were Muslims we would have to do the same before entering El Aksa. As it is, we must remove our shoes, leaving them outside before we enter. Oh yes, handbags, camera bags, etc. will be searched before entering each of the shrines on the Temple Mount. In 1969, an insane Australian tourist set fire to El Aksa and now precautions are taken to prevent further desecration of the shrines.

El Aksa, which means the "distant place" (from Mecca), is Islam's third holiest shrine, after Mecca and Medina. At the site south of the Temple where Solomon built his magnificent palaces, El Aksa was erected on the foundation of a Byzantine church and still follows the general lines of a basilica. Constructed first between 709 and 715, its architect was Caliph Al Waleed, son of Abd El Malik who constructed the Dome of the Rock. It has been destroyed and rebuilt on numerous occasions. The Crusaders captured it in 1099 and El Aksa became the headquarters for the Knights Templars. But in 1187 Saladin returned the building to the Muslims.

As we enter through the seven pointed arches of the facade facing the Dome of the Rock, we don't miss our shoes at all. The floors are covered with lush, priceless oriental rugs which present our feet with cushiony and welcome relief after pounding the stones of Jerusalem. Quickly look to your left. Here in 1951 the Jordanian King Abdullah was assassinated, his grandson, the now King Hussein, being at his side. A stray bullet scarred the pillar just inside the door to our left. But let's interest ourselves in more pleasant things, the building's design, for example.

This mosque is 280 square feet built in the basilica fashion with a large central nave bounded by triple aisles on either side. Assemblies of about 5,000 worshipers are possible. On either side of the nave, up high on the walls, is a row of 21 windows made from Hebron stained glass. The silver dome at the far end of the mosque is supported by arched columns. The gleaming whiteness of the marble pillars throughout the mosque actually make the place quite cheery in comparison to other Muslim shrines we've seen. The chandeliers hanging from the ceiling are gorgeous.

As we leave the mosque, just to the right (we can spy it while we put our shoes back on) is an enclosure containing a 16-step stairway leading to ANCIENT AKSA, a now little used mosque below El Aksa. It is much older and at least as interesting as the mosque we've just left, but is usually not open to the public.

A bit farther to the east (toward the Mount of Olives) is a strange-looking, sealed stone structure. It is known as THE GREAT SEA and is the cap to one of many cisterns under the paved surface of the Haram. Don't forget, this area was artificially placed here as an extension of Mount Moriah in order to enlarge the Temple area. The estimated capacity of these underground cisterns is ten million gallons. The 40-foot deep Great Sea has a capacity of two million gallons itself.

**The exterior of the mosque is decorated mainly with blue tile mosaic work on the upper portion of the otagonal building in a pattern resembling Indian beadwork.**

On Mount Moriah, the site of Solomon's Temple, stands the Dome of the Rock, cherished mosque of the Muslim religion.

These cisterns are not the only subterranean structures at the Temple Mount. If we continue to walk toward the Mount of Olives, to the extreme southeast corner of the Temple area, we will walk directly over SOLOMON'S STABLES. Not generally open to the public, the little building with the iron gate at the southeast corner gives access to a broad staircase descending into cavernous stables.

Misnamed, these are actually the work of Herod the Great. When the prolific builder expanded the Temple area he built up this corner with a platform supported by a series of 88 pillared arches. All of this was done 170 feet above the floor of the Kidron Valley. The external wall on the south plainly displays the blocked arches of the Triple Gate of the Second Temple. Evidently Herod did use the area under the vaulted platform for stabling horses, as did the Crusaders centuries later.

Don't be disappointed if we aren't able to enter the stables, we have something more exciting to do at this corner. A short walk back along the eastern wall will reveal a narrow stone stairway that takes us right to the top of the wall. Retracing our steps to the corner we have arrived at

the PINNACLE OF THE TEMPLE. Here the middle of the three temptations of Christ occurred. *"Then the devil taketh him up into the holy city, and setteth him on a pinnacle of the temple"* (Matthew 4:5). The devil's ploy was if Jesus truly was the Son of God He could cast Himself off the pinnacle and the angels would bear Him up in their hands (cf. Psalm 91:11-12). Go ahead. Take a look. Peer slowly over the wall into the Kidron Valley hundreds of feet below. At bit frightening, we get an appreciation of this temptation that we never had before.

Let's return to the center of the Temple Mount. Beyond El Kas is a raised platform which may be ascended by any one of eight staircases, two each on the north and south, three on the west and one on the east. Over each staircase is an arcade, arches which grace the entranceway. Muslim legend says that scales the weigh the souls of men at the Great Judgment Day will be hung from these arcades. We'll mount the platform by ascending the broad staircase to the south. The graceful structure immediately to our left is the SUMMER PULPIT erected in 1456 by Burhan ed Din. It resembles the pulpits in European Cathedrals.

Straight ahead of us is the most prominent feature of this Temple area. In fact, it is the most recognizable edifice in the Holy Land and one of the most recognizable in the world. What is it? What else . . . the DOME OF THE ROCK.

When Caliph Omar captured Jerusalem in 637 he commenced to clear the site of rubble and built a wooden mosque where the Temple once stood. Because of this many pilgrims mistakenly refer to the Dome of the Rock as the Mosque of Omar. Actually, there is a Mosque of Omar in Jerusalem, just opposite the entrance to the Church of the Holy Sepulchre. The Dome of the Rock was built by Caliph Abd El Malik in 685-705.

Just look at it. It's astounding! The mosque is octagonal in design with a huge golden dome. The base is 180 feet in diameter, each octagonal side measuring 63 feet. The dome towers impressively 108 feet into the Jerusalem air with a diameter of 78 feet. Its exterior is decorated mainly with blue tiles although green, yellow and white are also visible. This is just the upper half of the octagon. The lower half is white stone. The cylinder on the roof upon which the golden dome sits is covered with tiles in patterns which resemble the bead work of America's Seminole Indians. The dome itself is an aluminum brass alloy from Italy. There are four entrances to the mosque, each under a rounded roof supported by pillars. The entrance gates are the Mecca Gate on the south, Gate of the Judgment of David on the east, Gate of Paradise on the north and the Western Gate through which we enter the mosque. Don't forget. Off go the shoes.

Inside our eyes are dazzled. We are treated to stained glass windows, intricate mosaics of grapes, date palms, fruit, corn, etc. (no design ever repeated), painted and gilded arabesques in the flash of red, black and gold reflecting from the dome. Since Greek architects were employed in the mosque's design we should not be surprised at the definite Byzantine flavor of the interior. But between the super-plush red carpets and the golden frieze at the base of the dome inscribed with verses from the Koran, our eye is caught by the center attraction under the dome. Protruding through the floor of the mosque some seven feet is the summit of Mount Moriah. This immense rough-hewn rock measures approximately 40 by 52 feet but the wooden wall around it permits us to see the rock only on tiptoe or at the one opening at the southeast corner.

Once thought to be the center of the world (and depicted as such on maps), this rock is the focal point of both the Israelite and Islamic religions. Here Abraham prepared to offer Isaac. Here was the threshingfloor of Araunah which David purchased to be the site of the First Temple. Perhaps here was the Holy of Holies. And for Islam the site is sacred because tradition says that it was from the surface of this massive rock that Mohammed ascended into heaven.

As we make our way around to the opening in the wooden wall surrounding the brownish rock a stairs appears before us descending through an arched marble doorway. The steps lead down to a cave beneath the rock known to the Muslims as the "Well of Souls" but generally referred to as its GROTTO OF THE SACRED ROCK. Legend says that twice a week the dead meet here to pray. Actually once we are in the cave under the rock we can see a hole in the ceiling said to be the drain which carried the blood from the altar of the Jewish Temple.

Once we make our way all the way around the rock, we can file out through the tiny foyer at the western entrance. A local joke is that, with so many pairs of shoes lined up outside, now is our chance to pick out the best pair possible. Once shod, let's proceed around the Dome of the Rock to the eastern side and the DOME OF THE CHAIN. This 8th century miniature Dome of the Rock is tiled like the original and was built by Abd El Malik as well. It was used by the Arabs as a treasury for storing silver. The Crusaders used it as a church, calling it the Chapel of Saint James.

This little dome exhibits an interesting phenomenon It is constructed with six inner and 11 outer pillars and no matter where you stand you can see all 17 pillars at the same time. Go ahead. Try it. You'll always see all 17 no matter where you stand.

But enough for our curiosity. Let's leave the raised platform through the eastern arcade, down the steps, across the grassy area that leads to the Golden Gate. Here we explore the inside of the 7th century structure which looks somewhat like a square building with two rounded arches in the back and, as we know, two blocked arches on the outside wall. The little path to the right leads to the interior of the gate where we can climb to the top for a breathtaking view of the Kidron Valley. No wonder this is where Solomon built his opulent Temple. It had a magnificent view. But what would you expect? This is Jerusalem, the city of God.

# CHAPTER 10

# Eternal Places

◆

FOLLOWING JESUS' FINAL STEPS

*"And the children of Joseph said, The hill is not enough for us. . . And Joshua spake unto the house of Joseph, even to Ephraim and to Manasseh, saying, Thou art a great people, and hast great power: thou shalt not have one lot only: but the mountain shall be thine; for it is a wood, and thou shalt cut it down: and the outgoings of it shall be thine . . ."* (Joshua 17:16-18).

The date was July 20, 1969. The time, 4:17.45 Eastern Daylight Time. The place, 240,000 miles from Jerusalem. The event, the Eagle had landed. For the first time in history man had reached an "unearthly" body. Neal Armstrong stepped outside the spacecraft and said, "That's one small step for man, one giant leap for mankind." Do you remember where you were on this historic occasion?

In the excitement of the hour the President of the United States proclaimed that this was the "greatest day of our lives." Most Christians, born again by the grace of God, would have to respectfully disagree with the President. Many days in the life of the Christian supersede this one in eternal importance. As we follow the final footsteps of Jesus we will visit the places associated with days unsurpassed in importance.

The events of Christ's final week are chronologically disputed. But if we follow the traditional timetable, these events look something like this.

**The Jerusalem night skyline viewed from the Mount of Olives.**

SUNDAY, A.M. Having spent a quiet weekend in Bethany with friends (Matthew 26:6-13; John 11:55—12:11), Jesus sent two of His disciples to BETHPHAGE to fetch a colt (Luke 19:28-30). Located on the eastern slopes of the Mount of Olives, this tiny hamlet boasts of being the place where the final week began. In fact, at a Franciscan convent we can visit the STELE OF BETHPHAGE, a stone which tradition claims to be the very stone from which Jesus mounted the colt. Paintings on the cubical rock date back to the time of the Crusaders.

The tiny alley over the Mount of Olives leads past the Pater Noster Church to the Kidron Valley and the Golden Gate of Jerusalem's Eastern Wall. It's possible that a bridge spanned the Kidron in Jesus' day. Nonetheless, this was the route of our Lord's Triumphal Entry into Jerusalem. Palm branches were placed in His path. Crowds chouted, *"Hosanna: Blessed is the King of Israel that cometh in the name of the Lord"* (John 12:13). When the Pharisees called on Jesus to repudiate this unsolicited adoration the Master replied, *"I tell you that, if these should hold their peace, the stones would immediately cry out"* (Luke 19:40).

SUNDAY, P.M. When the Messiah entered the Temple the chant *"Hosanna to the son of David"* continued, angering the chief priests and scribes (Matthew 21:15). It was at this point Jesus cleansed the Temple for the second time, overturning the moneychangers' tables and exhorting, *"My house shall be called the house of prayer; but ye have made it a den of thieves"* (Matthew 21:13).

At day's end Jesus returned to Bethany.

MONDAY, A.M. Early in the morning Jesus and the disciples made the return trip to Jerusalem. While skirting the Mount of Olives they passed a fig tree. This in itself was not unusual as the mountain was literally studded with fig and olive trees. Jesus examined the tree and found it leafy but fruitless. This was unusual for a fig tree bears over a ten-month period and the fruit precedes the flower. But here there was no fruit and thus the tree promised but did not perform. Jesus cursed the tree using this to teach His disciples (Matthew 21:19; Mark 11:14). The judgment of the tree symbolized the coming judgment on the ritual emptiness of the Temple worship. Apparently He returned to Bethany again for overnight. overnight.

TUESDAY, A.M. This day found the Lord Jesus teaching in the outer court of the Temple. Here He was approached by the chief priests and the elders obviously disturbed by the events of the last two days. Their questions, *"By what authority doest thou these things?"* and *"Who gave thee this authority?"* (Matthew 21:23), show their continued spiritual blindness to the messianic claims of Jesus. Their challenge evoked the 32nd, 33rd, and 34th parables of the Lord (Matthew 21:28—22:14).

Next the Lord was assailed by a combination of Pharisees and Herodians. Their crafty question about tribute to Caesar brought Jesus' classic response, *"Render therefore unto Caesar the things which are Caesar's; and unto God the things that are God's"* (Matthew 22:21).

Then it was the Sadducees' turn with their question about the resurrection. After astonishing them with His answer, Jesus turned and spoke to the multitude at large. The pronouncement of woes upon the scribes and Pharisees and characterization of them as hypocrites, blind guides and whited sepulchers was the last straw. Violent confrontation was inevitable.

TUESDAY, NOON. He departed the Temple and walked through the Kidron Valley to the Mount of Olives. Throughout the afternoon Jesus delivered His Olivet Discourse, the sermon on the coming Tribulation.

TUESDAY, P.M. The battle lines began to form. Jesus returned to Bethany, to the house of Simon the leper. The chief priests, scribes and elders assembled themselves in secret sessions at the house of Caiaphas, *"And consulted that they might take Jesus by subtilty, and kill him"* (Matthew 26:4). Judas stole away from the Bethany assembly until he found the Sanhedrin in session. His offer to betray Jesus in the privacy of Gethsemane's Garden where the Galilean's numerous supporters would not be inflamed was met with quick approval.

That night Jesus slept, the disciples slept, the Sanhedrin slept, but Judas? How could he sleep?

WEDNESDAY. A day of silence. Perhaps for the weary Master it was a day of rest and reflection at their retreat in Bethany.

THURSDAY, A.M. Rest continues. The events of this day seem to have begun in the afternoon.

THURSDAY, NOON. Jesus dispatched Peter and John to Jerusalem to prepare for the Passover. They were told to follow a man carrying a water pitcher to *"a large upper room furnished and prepared"* (Mark 14:12-15). Have you ever asked yourself how they would know the right man bearing a pitcher of water? Easy. Look around you in the Holy Land and count how many men you see carrying water. In Jewish and Arab homes that was the task of the womenfolk. This man would easily be identified. The Passover would be ready.

THURSDAY, P.M. By evening Jesus and His disciples had entered Jerusalem and made their way to the UPPER ROOM. The traditional site of this room is on Mount Zion in the complex of buildings just below the CHURCH OF THE DORMITION, also known as the Dormition Abbey. Near the Zion Gate, the abbey stands at the supposed site of Mary's death. The Upper Room and the Tomb of David occupy the same complex of buildings nearby.

The Tomb of David, originally a Muslim shrine to the Prophet David, is housed in the same complex of buildings as the traditional site of the Upper Room.

On Mount Zion, near the Zion Gate, the traditional site of the Upper Room is a part of the Church of the Dormition. The architecture of the room, however, is of the Crusaders' period.

From the parking lot below the abbey, we enter along a path which leads to the vaulted first floor of the triple-domed complex. Through the stone arch we take a sharp left up a narrow outside stairway. Just a few years ago these stone steps, which featured deep indentations caused by repeated footsteps, were retreaded for safety. At the top we turn left, through a hallway with paneless windows, across a narrow terrace and into the traditional Upper Room.

We can quickly detect the architectural craftsmanship of the Crusaders. The massive room features a rib-vaulted ceiling supported by tree-like columns. Known as the Coenaculum or CENACLE (meaning "dining hall"), this room is one of two surviving from the Byzantine Church of Saint Mary on Mount Zion. Once sacked this building was rebuilt in 1335 by the Franciscans. In 1551 this order was expelled and the complex fell into the hands of the Muslims who consecrated it as a mosque to the Prophet David. In 1948 it returned to Israeli hands.

Tradition holds that at this site Jesus instituted the Lord's Supper, one of the great ordinances of the Christian church (Matthew 26:17-30; Luke 22:7-30). Also, here the apostles reportedly met to regroup after Christ's ascension into heaven (Acts 1:13-14). Some believe that it was in this Upper Room as well that the 120 disciples were assembled when the Holy Ghost came upon them on the Day of Pentecost (Acts 2:1-42). These things make this site one of the most important in Christendom.

After the supper was over, Jesus and the Eleven (Judas now departed) walked through the moonlit streets of Jerusalem. En route the group sang a hymn (Matthew 26:30). Also as they walked He taught them, as He had done for the three previous years. His most shocking revelation to them was that *"the hour cometh, yea, is now come, that ye shall be scattered, every man to his own, and shall leave me alone . . ."* (John 16:32). But He comforted them as well. *"Be of good cheer; I have overcome the world"* (John 16:33).

Somewhere between the Upper Room and the Garden of Gethsemane the Master uttered His most intimate prayer—John 17. Appropriately called His high priestly prayer, Christ made intercession for His disciples and for all who would trust in Him as Savior. Just where He prayed this the true "Lord's Prayer" is uncertain. The rugged streets of Jerusalem do not provide the proper atmosphere for such a solemn prayer. Dare we speculate? Perhaps He stopped for one last time in the Temple courts. When He cleansed it last and made it suitable for such a prayer as this, didn't He say, *"My house shall be called the house of prayer"* (Matthew 21:13)?

Finally Christ and the disciples crossed the Kidron and arrived at the Garden of Gethsemane (John 18:1). There He left the disciples, taking Peter, James and John deeper into the night shadows. There too He left the inner circle and went a stone's throw farther to pray (Luke 22:41). Three times He returned from private prayer to find the disciples sleeping (Mark 14:39, 40, 41).

Then it happened. Suddenly a multitude appeared piercing the quiet of the chilly night. Judas led the mob. The chief priests, scribes and elders, they were all there. With the words, *"Master, Master"* and a kiss of betrayal Judas' treachery was over (Mark 14:43-50). Brandishing swords and staves, they apprehended the Savior and led Him away.

THURSDAY, MIDNIGHT. Only the Gospel of John records that Jesus was first led to the HOUSE OF ANNAS. We have already visited it in the Jewish Quarter of the Old City. It was here that Jesus was questioned concerning His doctrine and cruelly struck by one of the officers of Annas (John 18:13-23).

From here Jesus was led to the HOUSE OF CAIAPHAS, the High Priest (Mark 14:53-72). Here the assembled Sanhedrin made a miserable and unsuccessful attempt to frame Jesus with the testimony of false witnesses. But the buffoons who were testifying against Jesus could not get the facts of their trumped-up testimony coordinated and the frame failed. In desperation Caiaphas asked Jesus point blank, *"Art thou the Christ?"* With unusual directness Jesus answered, *"I am"* (Mark 14:53-65). Caiaphas decided he had Him—Jesus would be charged with blasphemy. So ended His first trial.

There are two rivals for the site of Caiaphas' House. The first is located just north of the Dormition Abbey toward the Zion Gate. The ruins of this arched church are under the care of the Armenian Church. Nearby we can see the carved marble tombs of 15th century Armenian Patriarchs.

The other site claiming to be the location of Caiaphas' House is the SAINT PETER IN GALLICANTU CHURCH. South of the Dung Gate and on the eastern slope of a hill overlooking the Kidron and Hinnom Valleys, above the Pool of Siloam, the Assumptionist Fathers built this church in 1931. A quaint-looking building with a colorful mosaic facade, we enter through a narrow doorway on the upper side of the church.

Through the foyer is the main sanctuary, beautifully decorated around the ceiling and equipped with hard benches. Here one of the fathers will tell us the story of Jesus' first trial. Also in the foyer is a stairway leading down to a chapel below. Even when we reach here we are not at the bottom. Down another set of steps curling right and down a narrow stairway we enter the dungeon explained as the guardroom where Jesus was kept prisoner by the High Priest, Caiaphas.

As we ascend to leave the church we simply must not miss the view from the balcony which encircles this lovely church. From it we can see the Kidron Valley, the Hinnom Valley, and as we progress clockwise around the balcony we see on a little spur beneath us the field of Haceldama.

You may be asking yourself about the name of the church, Saint Peter in Gallicantu. The unusual name (Gallicantu) means "cockcrow" and the church is consecrated to commemorate Peter's triple denial of Jesus (Luke 22:54-62) and his remorse after he heard the cock crow. The church is built over the remains of a Byzantine monastery and grotto where the apostle is said to have wept over his unfaithfulness. Mark attests that *"Peter was beneath in the palace,"* denied the Lord thrice *"and when he thought thereon, he wept"* (Mark 14:66, 72).

Archaeologists have discovered at this site an ancient stone mill, an almost complete set of Hebrew measures, houses and baths and the remains of Hasmonean steps leading from the hill down to Siloam. And inside, while all these were being used, Jesus was being accused falsely and convicted unjustly by desperate men on a desolate night.

FRIDAY, A.M. During the pre-dawn hours the scene changed. The Sanhedrin reconvened and having found Christ guilty of blasphemy, sent Him next to the residence of Pilate. It is just a short walk from the southeast sector of the city (it would have been inside the wall in Jesus' day) to the palace-garrison where Pilate most certainly lodged when he was in Jerusalem. This was the FORTRESS OF ANTONIO.

Located at the northwest corner of the Temple Compound, this castle was built by Herod the Great in 36 B.C. and named in honor of his friend Marc Anthony. This huge quadrangle with massive towers at each corner was really a minute city within a city. A Roman legion was stationed here to guard against any trouble which might be sparked in the Temple area. When Paul was seized by the Jews in the Temple and was about to be killed, the chief captain took soldiers and centurions from the Fortress of Antonio to rescue the apostle from the Jewish mob (Acts 21:30-40).

When Pilate received Jesus he immediately questioned, *"Art thou the King of the Jews?"* An affirmative response provoked Pilate to admit, *"I find no fault in this man."* But further accusations by the now fiercely bitter chief priests that Jesus stirred up all Jewry from Galilee to Jerusalem provided Pilate with the perfect excuse for inaction. When he learned Jesus was a Galilean and therefore under the jurisdiction of Herod (who just happened to be in Jerusalem at the time), Pilate quickly shuffled our Lord off to the king (Luke 23:1-7).

If Herod was residing in his Jerusalem palace when he received Jesus, this means that the Lord was again forced to cross the Old City. The traditional site of HEROD'S PALACE is adjacent to the Citadel. Across the moat from the Citadel's southeast tower is a Jerusalem police barracks. This site would have been where Jesus and Herod met face to face.

Herod was in Jerusalem for the festivities of the Passover. Jesus had previously called this Herod (Antipas, son of Herod the Great) *"that fox"* (Luke 13:32) and the king was undoubtedly more anxious to meet the Messiah than Jesus was to meet the king. Luke records, *"And when Herod saw Jesus, he was exceeding glad: for he was desirous to see him of a long season, because he had heard many things of him; and he hoped to have seen some miracle done by him"* (Luke 23:8). But there would be no miracles today. In fact, when the chief priests and scribes vehemently accused Jesus, He wouldn't even respond. Thus, frustrated, Herod *"mocked him, and arrayed him in a gorgeous robe, and sent him again to Pilate"* (Luke 23:11).

A return to Pilate meant a return to the Antonio Fortress. Caught between his superstitious fears and the strident demands of the Jews, Pilate proposed a solution which he hoped would satisfy those who were calling for Jesus' blood. Christ would be scourged, flogged with leather whips tipped with pieces of metal or bone to increase the pain. Surely that would satisfy the Jews. It didn't (Luke 23:13-26).

Pilate's next ploy was to remind the Jews that it was the governor's custom at the feast to release a prisoner, thus securing the favor of the people. Mark notes that Pilate asked the crowds, *"Will ye that I release unto you the King of the Jews? . . . But the chief priests moved the people, that he should rather release Barabbas unto them"* (Mark 15:9, 11). Pilate's attempt to side-step the problem of Jesus had failed again.

To Pilate's query about what to do with Jesus, the corridors of time still ring with the chilling cry, *"Crucify him!"* But Pilate's wife revealed a dream to her husband in which she warned Pilate not to involve himself with this innocent man. Pilate had only one more option, one last opportunity to disengage himself from this politically volatile situation.

Once again, Mark writes, *"And the soldiers led him away into the hall, called Praetorium; and they called together the whole band. And they clothed him with purple, and platted a crown of thorns, and put it about his had, and began to salute him, Hail, King of the Jews! And they smote him on the head with a reed, and did spit upon him, and bowing their knees worshipped him"* (Mark 15:16-19).

FRIDAY, 6:00 A.M. This cruelty completed, Pilate again appeared before the crowds with Jesus. Declaring insistently that he still found no fault in Jesus of Nazareth, nonetheless he displayed the Lord before the crowd wearing the purple robe and crown of thorns. His declaration, *"Behold the man"* (John 19:5) must be understood as *"See what I've done to this innocent man. What more do you want?"* The response was swift and decisive. *"When the chief priests therefore and officers saw him, they cried out, saying, Crucify him, crucify him"* (John 19:6). The die was cast.

Is it possible that any of these sites can be visited today? Could we actually stand in Pilate's Judgment Hall or see the spot where Pilate presented Jesus to the Jerusalem mob? Yes we can, and we will.

From Lion's Gate we walk straight ahead into the Old City. The road beneath us is the VIA DOLOROSA, the most famous street in Christendom. Meaning the "Way of Sorrow," this street became the way of the cross. Since the 1st century, millions of pilgrims have made the trek over the stones of this sacred street. In the Roman Catholic tradition, the Via Dolorosa and Church of the Holy Sepulchre exhibit the 14 STATIONS OF THE CROSS. Every Friday at 3:00 P.M. a procession led by Franciscan priests is conducted along this route. Indulgences are awarded to Catholics who make this pilgrimage.

Although many of these 14 stations are based solely on tradition and the events which they commemorate are missing from the pages of the Gospels, nonetheless, let's trace the traditional steps from Pilate's Judgment Hall to Calvary.

***Station One.*** *Jesus was condemned to death.* The present Saint Mary's Street, which begins at the

Lion Gate and continues as the Via Dolorosa, runs directly through the center of what used to be the Antonio Fortress. Hence, the first station of the cross is to our left after we pass the Church of Saint Anne. Here Jesus was mocked, crowned with thorns and condemned. This was the Praetorium, Pilate's Judgment Hall (Mark 15:16).

The site today, over the ruins of the Antonio, is a Muslim boys' school known as El Omariye. A staircase known as the Scala Santa (The Holy Steps), reported to be where Pilate stood as he washed his hands of Jesus' case, were removed to Rome by Constantine's mother, Helena. It can be seen in a church near San Giovanni in Laterano. On the upper level of the El Omariye courtyard is a small domed Crusader chapel known as the CHAPEL OF THE CROWNING OF THE THORNS. This commemorates one of history's most dreadful acts.

**STATION TWO.** *Jesus received the cross.* Across the Antonio from the Praetorium, today across the street, are two important chapels of a Franciscan monastery. On the wall outside the entrance to the monastery is a small plaque indicating "II Statio," Station Two. Within the Franciscan compound is the CHAPEL OF THE FLAGELLATION which stands on the traditional site of Jesus' scourging.

Containing three stained glass windows by Cambellotti, this medieval structure is beautifully decorated in the Crusader style. The windows depict the flagellation, Pilate washing his hands and Barrabas' release. A crown of thorns hangs over the sanctuary. There is also an altar to Saint Paul as he too was imprisoned in the Antonio (Acts 21—23).

The other chapel in the compound is the CHAPEL OF CONDEMNATION, marking the site where Pilate sentenced Jesus. The square Byzantine building features a dome, the windows of which depict angels with instruments of torture. Here we can see ancient flagstones which made up the pavement floor of the Antonio. The largest portion of this floor is visible in the convent next door.

The CONVENT OF THE SISTERS OF ZION, located just a few yards deeper into the Old City on the Via Dolorosa, was founded by a Christian Jew, Father Alphonse Ratisbone of Strasbourg. When we enter the convent we are assembled in the room to our right where one of the friendly sisters gives an informative lecture on the events which took place here that eventful night.

From this room we are led downstairs to the chapel. As we sit listening further to the sister's explanation of the buildings, the wall over and behind the altar is pointed out to us as of special interest. Look to the right corner of the altar. There we can plainly see the outline of an arch. This arch continues through the wall of the chapel, out over the Via Dolorosa and attaches to the buildings on the opposite side of the street. This is the famous ECCE HOMO ARCH.

Named "Ecce Homo" (Behold the man) because it is believed that here Pilate presented Jesus to the crowd after flogging Him, dressing Him in a robe and crowning Him with thorns (John 19:5), actually the arch has nothing to do with this event. The arch was built by Hadrian in A.D. 135 and was part of the emperor's triple triumphal gate into Aelia Capitolina. Nonetheless the sight of the arch continues to inspire those who walk the Via Dolorosa because of the event which took place there.

We are not finished at the Sisters of Zion Convent, however. From this chapel we descend even deeper into the building, down a flight of stairs to the ground level in Jesus' day. Here, in an arched room with an exceptionally low ceiling, we reach the first century pavement of the Antonio Fortress. This was the original Via Dolorosa. John 19:13 records, *"When Pilate therefore heard that saying, he brought Jesus forth, and sat down in the judgment seat in a place that is called the Pavement, but in the Hebrew, Gabbatha."*

Some Christians believe this to be the site of the Praetorium instead of the area across the street. Others hold that Pilate's private meeting with Jesus was held there while he judged our Lord publicly here.

Known as the LITHOSTROTOS in Greek, the flagstones of this large paved square within the Antonio Fortress covered about a third of the western section of the palace. Notice the way the stones are striated. In fact, put your hand on them and feel them. Many of the flagstones have ridges or grooves in them to prevent the horses from losing their footing on the Roman streets. A bit farther along we see some stones with markings on them, circles and squares. These etchings were made as games used by the Roman soldiers to while away the hours of duty. The game "Basilicus" fits the markings of these stones and donning a robe and crown of thorns Jesus easily could have been the object of this game (Matthew 27:27-30; Mark 15:16-20).

Underneath the Lithostrotos were enormous double rock-hewn cisterns. Some of the ridges of the flagstones acted as channels for the water to flow into the cisterns. The subterranean cisterns are visible through iron grates as we leave the Lithostrotos to ascend to street level. The stairs bring us up to the Sisters of Zion bookstore where fascinating volumes pertaining to the life of our Lord and these sacred sites are sold. Other appropriate souvenirs are available as well.

**STATION THREE.** *Jesus fell the first time.* At the point where the Via Dolorosa joins El-Wad Road and bends sharply to the left is a small Polish Chapel. The relief over the door shows Jesus fallen beneath the load of His cross. Attached to the chapel is the Polish Roman Catholic Biblical-Archaeological Museum. This site marks the third station of the cross, although the event is not recorded in the Bible.

**STATION FOUR.** *Jesus met Mary His Mother.* An Armenian Catholic church named OUR LADY OF THE SPASM identifies Station Four. About 75 feet from the corner we rounded at Station Three, and on the same (left) side of the street, this station is marked by a beautiful relief over the door. Jesus, bearing cross and crown, is shown being comforted by His mother. This is the most attractive marker for a station of the cross. The church is believed to stand on the site of the Byzantine Church of Saint Sophia. In the church's 6th century crypt a mosaic shows the footprints supposed to be those left by Mary when she met the Christ.

**STATION FIVE.** *Simon compelled to carry Jesus' cross.* Mark 15:21 tells us that after releasing Jesus to the mob, *"they compel one Simon a Cyrenian, who passed by, coming out of the country, the father of Alexander and Rufus, to bear his cross."* Station Five marks this event. In fact, a small depression in the stone face of the 19th century Franciscan chapel commemorating this event is said by tradition to be where Jesus rested His hand under the weight of the cross (Matthew 27:32; Luke 23:26). Simon was a native of Libya, North Africa and was in Jerusalem for the Passover. His sons are closely associated with the Christian church.

**STATION SIX.** *Veronica wiped Jesus' face.* Again on the left of the Via Dolorosa, about halfway between the two streets which angle away from each other at the Damascus Gate, stands a Greek Orthodox Catholic chapel served by the Little Sisters. This is the traditional site where a woman named Veronica wiped the blood and sweat from Jesus' marred face. According to legend, when Veronica looked at the cloth she found the imprint of Christ's face had remained. This probably accounts for the woman's name ("vera icone" meaning "true image"). Supposedly Veronica was the woman cured simply by touching the hem of Jesus' garment. However the woman's very existence is based on tradition alone, as well as her act of kindness to the Lord.

**STATION SEVEN.** *Jesus fell the second time.* Located near the corner of the Via Dolorosa and Suq Khan Ez-Zeit (which leads directly to Damascus Gate) is Station Seven. Adjacent to the market wall upon which this station is marked are two Franciscan chapels. In one of them is a reddish stone column thought to be a marker for the crossroads of main streets in Hadrian's city, Aelia Capitolina.

**STATION EIGHT.** *Jesus conversed with some women of Jerusalem.* Luke records that a great number of women followed Jesus as He was led to Calvary. The women *"wailed and lamented him."* But the Lord stopped, turned toward them and said, *"Daughters of Jerusalem, weep not for me, but weep for yourselves, and for your children"* (Luke 23:27-28). He then prophesied the weeping and wailing which would accompany the coming destruction of Jerusalem. This station on El-Khanqa Street is marked by a cross engraved in a circle on a wall of the GREEK ORTHODOX MONASTERY OF SAINT CHARALAMBOS.

**STATION NINE.** *Jesus fell the third time.* At the entrance to a Coptic monastery, located on an alley leading west from Suq Khan Ez-Zeit, is a round Roman column. This marks the spot where tradition claims Jesus fell the third time. None of these falls is recorded in Scripture but are products of tradition. The Coptic Church itself is interesting for within its whitewashed walls Abyssinian monks live and serve and beneath the edifice is an immense cistern.

Stations 10 through 14 are located within the walls of Christendom's most prominent church. They are within Jerusalem's CHURCH OF THE HOLY SEPULCHRE. Those orders which have major jurisdiction over the church are the Roman Catholic, Greek Catholic and Armenian Orthodox Catholic. Minor jurisdiction is claimed by the Syrian (Jacobite) Catholic, Coptic Catholic and Abyssinian Catholic orders. It is evident, then, the Church of the Holy Sepulchre is a Catholic site and of the utmost importance to Catholic pilgrims. Protestant pilgrims, on the other hand, find the church somewhat of a disappointment.

When Hadrian ruled the city as Aelia Capitolina he covered this site (and most of Jerusalem) with pagan shrines and temples. It was not until Queen Helena, mother of Constantine, came here that this site traditionally became identified with Calvary. Constantine built the original church in 326, which was destroyed by the Persians in 614. Just two years later Abbot Modestos, the Greek Orthodox Patriarch, rebuilt the edifice only to have it razed by the mad Egyptian Khalif El Hakim in 1010. The Crusaders again rebuilt the church but when they were defeated by Saladin in 1187 the Christian community was permitted to use the church only if the keys to the church remained in Muslim hands. Since 1330 the right of entry to Christianity's most noted church has remained in the hands of the Arab Nuseibeh family.

Today the church is a conglomeration. Every few feet the decor changes because every few feet jurisdiction changes. Confusion, compartmentalization and clutter; this is the Church of the Holy Sepulchre. There is no theme, no architectural plan, no predominant period. Byzantine, Crusader and 19th century Greek styles are evidenced, covering 1,500 years of construction.

Fires, earthquakes and the ravages of the centuries have left the church in a deplorable state. Between 1936-44 the British installed ugly steel reinforcements in the church to prevent it from collapsing. In 1958 a program of "total restoration" was proposed but in-fighting among the religious orders which occupy the site has not made restoration what you might call "total." At best, it's an on-going task.

The two-story church with a 12th century Romanesque facade is entered through double portals with pointed arches. We enter through the left portal since the other door was walled up in Saladin's day. Directly ahead of us is a polished red slab known as the STONE OF UNCTION, the traditional site where Jesus' body was anointed for burial. If we bypass this to the left we will enter the great Rotunda of the church. The steps to the right just before the stone lead to the Latin and Greek chapels which contain Stations 10 through 13. In the Catholic tradition these second story chapels are built over Mount Calvary.

**STATION TEN.** *Jesus stripped of His garments.* We ascend the stairs to the Franciscan chapel (the southern nave). This station is commemorated by a mosaic representation on the floor, the pattern of which depicts Abraham sacrificing Isaac, symbolic of Christ's sacrifice. Tradition says it was here Jesus was stripped of His garments and given gall to drink (Mark 15:23-24; Luke 23:34).

**STATION ELEVEN.** *Jesus nailed to the cross.* In the southeast corner of the Franciscan chapel is Station 11, marked by the main altar, the Medici

Altar. Behind the altar on the wall is a mosaic scene depicting the nailing of Christ to Calvary's cross (Matthew 27:35; John 19:18).

**STATION TWELVE.** *Jesus was crucified and died on the cross.* Now we move to the Greek side of the chapel. This is the north nave and in the northeast corner the main altar marks the traditional site of the crucifixion and death of our Lord (Mark 15:25, 37; Luke 23:46). Under the altar a silver star/disc indicates where Christ's cross was dropped into the ground. Two black discs, one on either side of the altar, mark where the thieves' crosses were planted. A fissure in the rock, on the right side of the altar, is reported to have been created by the earthquake which accompanied Jesus' crucifixion.

**STATION THIRTEEN.** *Jesus' body removed from the cross.* Between Station 11 and Station 12 is an antique wooden bust of Mary, mother of Jesus. It is placed in a glass case which belongs to the Franciscans. The bust is laden with jewels and gold, votive offerings from Catholic pilgrims through the centuries. This marks Station 13 but the actual event of removing Christ from the cross, according to Catholic tradition, is under the Franciscan altar.

At this point we descend to the main level of

The climax to the 14 Stations of the Cross of Christendom is centered in the Church of the Holy Sepulchre which is shared by Roman Catholic, Greek Catholic and Armenian Orthodox Catholic, as well as some other Catholic orders. The church has been under a continuous restoration program for some years.

the church. There are numerous other chapels we could visit. For example, down the stairs at the extreme eastern end of the church is the CHURCH OF SAINT HELENA. At the far end is the main altar dedicated to Helena who first identified most of the sacred sites in the Catholic tradition. To the right of the altar is a stairway leading down to the CHAPEL OF THE DIS-COVERY OF THE CROSS. According to tradition, this place was once a cistern at the foot of Calvary into which the three crosses were tossed. Helena directed the search and found the "true cross" of Christ. It is evident, however, that most of the chapels within the Church of the Holy Sepulchre are based on one tradition or another and many visitors, Catholic and Protestant alike, quickly tire of peering into chapel after chapel.

Thus, let's make our way to the last station of the cross. On the way we pass the KATHO-LIKON, the open center of the church which is actually a Greek cathedral. Here a stone chalice centered on the Crusader floor of the cathedral is reported to mark THE CENTER OF THE EARTH. This medieval tradition arose because the site is midway between the traditional Calvary and sepulcher.

Just west of here we enter the ROTUNDA. This area under a massive 19th century dome 65 feet in diameter is enclosed by a circular corridor formed by 18 gigantic columns that support the dome. The upper galleries of the Rotunda are divided into many chapels and chambers belonging to the three major religious communities sharing the church. At the center of the Rotunda is the final station of the cross.

**STATION FOURTEEN.** *Jesus buried in a sepulcher.* The traditional tomb of Jesus is enclosed in a 19th century aedicule that is so richly ornamented that it borders on being grotesque. The decor is so extravagant that it detracts from the site it commemorates. The box-like structure is crowned with a cupola of the Muscovite style and is approached by a small chamber or vestibule known as the CHAPEL OF THE ANGEL. Supposedly here the angel sat on the stone and announced the Lord's resurrection (Mark 16:5-7). A pedestal in the center is claimed to display bits of the actual stone used to seal Jesus' tomb. Over the entrance hang three separate pictures of the resurrection, one each belonging to the Latins, Greeks and Armenians.

The entrance to the tomb itself is a low and very narrow opening. Not all Christian pilgrims easily fit through it (nor do some of the church prelates). Inside is a miniscule chamber six and one-half feet long, six feet wide. Only four or five people can fit in the tomb-chamber at a time. All about us are religious artifacts and tiny lamps. To the right is a white marble slab covering the burial niche, the stone beneath it reported to be the burial place of Jesus.

As we make our way back through the church itself (we need a guide or a map lest we get lost in the maze) we mingle among tourists from all nations and all religions. We rub elbows with monks and nuns from various orders attired in various-colored robes. And although the church is overornate and confusing, and you won't get a sense of being at Calvary or the tomb at all, nevertheless there is a certain excitement which attends our visit to the church. And if you're really looking for excitement, visit the church during the festivities of Easter week. You'll need a program to follow all the activity.

But if activity is not what you want, and if you're not much into tradition, if you want to visit the quiet solitude of a garden and a tomb much as it would have been in Jesus' day, then you owe it to yourself to visit another site. Whether Catholic or Protestant, the Christian pilgrim to the Holy Land cannot leave the land of our Lord without this final stop.

FRIDAY, 9:00 A.M. Upon release by Pilate, Jesus was driven by the crowds to *"a place called Golgotha, that is to say, a place of a skull"* (Matthew 27:33; Mark 15:22). Luke calls this crucifixion site by its Latin name, Calvary. Here Jesus was crucified in full view of the passersby. Here He died on the cross.

Although the exact location of the crucifixion has been disputed over the years, we do know that it was outside Jerusalem. The writer of Hebrews says, *"Wherefore Jesus also, that he might sanctify the people with his own blood, suffered without* [outside] *the gate"* (Hebrews 13:12). Pilate placed a title on Jesus' cross: *"JESUS OF NAZARETH THE KING OF THE JEWS."* John explains, *"This title then read many of the Jews: for the place where Jesus was crucified was nigh to the city"* (John 19:20). So while Jesus' cross was placed outside the gate of the city, it was nevertheless not far from that gate and where many travelers could see the shame of the cross.

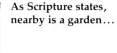

**As Scripture states, nearby is a garden...**

We don't have to wander far from the Damascus Gate to see such a site today. From the famous gate, across the street, we walk up Salah ed Din Street less than a block and on our right is a stone wall through which an alley leads to a beautifully restful compound. It is the GARDEN TOMB. Here are no altars, no orders, and no chapels. Here rather are trees, and birds, and flowers.

Entering through a bookstore foyer, when we step down into the garden we are usually invited to take a seat on benches where the warden of the garden explains the history and importance of the site. To the right is a long but pleasant path which leads to a platform at the far southeastern edge of the garden. From the top of the platform we have a grand view of what is said to be THE PLACE OF THE SKULL.

As we stare at the scarp of rock, a line of cliffs produced by faulting or erosion, we can clearly see the deep-set sockets of skull eyes without much imagination. We must erase from our minds the Muslim cemetery on top the hill and the noisy bus station below. The station has been there for some decades now, but originally this was a broad area across the road from the Jerusalem wall. Critics of the site say that the eye sockets were just cisterns broken out when quarrying was done in the area. Advocates of the site say that the quarrying was the northern extremity of the same operation that extended under the city to SOLOMON'S QUARRIES. Just north

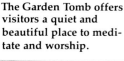

The Garden Tomb offers visitors a quiet and beautiful place to meditate and worship.

of the Damascus Gate is a seven-foot fissure in the bedrock of Jerusalem. Through an iron gate we can see this fissure open into a cavernous quarry from which stone was taken to build Solomon's Temple (I Kings 5:15; 6:7).

If the advocates are correct, the face of the skull would have been present in Jesus' day. And if so, we are viewing CALVARY, the place of crucifixion, the Place of the Skull. On this hill, or perhaps on the level area before it, Jesus Christ bled and died to atone for man's sin.

For centuries there have been skeptics about the authenticity of the Church of the Holy Sepulchre being situated over Skull Hill. Questions have periodically surfaced about whether or not the church was really outside the 1st century wall. At the same time there are snatches of information placing Calvary at other locations. One early author from Bordeaux, France (called Anonymous for his name is not known) wrote in A.D. 333:

As you leave there and pass through the Wall of Zion towards the gate of Neapolis [Nablus or Damascus Gate] . . . on your left is the hillock Golgotha where the Lord was crucified, and about a stone's throw from it to the vault where they laid his body and he rose again on the third day.

The site before us fits this description. Although others have identified it with Skull Hill,

in 1883 General Charles Gordon became convinced that this was indeed the Place of the Skull. Gordon's death at Khartoum in the Sudan a short time later made him a hero and thus this Skull Hill site became popularly known as GORDON'S CALVARY. Most Protestants accept Gordon's identification as a possible alternative to the Church of the Holy Sepulchre.

FRIDAY, NOON. From the time He was lifted up on the cross (cf. John 3:14-18) at about 9:00 A.M. until noon the Lord spoke just three times. He prayed for the Father to forgive His tormentors (Luke 23:34; cf. Isaiah 53:12); He forgave the thief and gave him assurance (Luke 23:43); and He spoke to His mother and to John (John 19:26-27).

Then suddenly it happened. Each of the Synoptic Gospels records the strange phenomenon. From noon until 3:00 P.M. there was an inky darkness that filled the land. This was the first of six supernatural events which took place while our Lord hung on the cross (Matthew 27:45, 51-53).

FRIDAY, 3:00 P.M. The silence is broken as light returns. The Savior cries to God in the language of Psalm 22 (Matthew 27:46); quietly He refers to His thirst (John 19:28; cf. Psalm 69:21); victoriously He shouts, *"It is finished"* (John 19:30); finally He commends His life unto God (Luke 23:46). Jesus is dead.

Let's not leave this platform too quickly. Meditate on the hill before us. After all, knowing the site of the Savior's crucifixion is not as important as knowing the Savior Himself. Whether here or at the Church of the Holy Sepulchre, the fact remains that God has always demanded a blood sacrifice in payment for sin. He demanded it of Adam (Genesis 3:6-7, 21). He demanded it of Cain (Genesis 4:3-5). He demanded it of the Israelites (Exodus 12:12-13). But for us He demanded it of Christ. *"God commendeth his love toward us, in that, while we were yet sinners, Christ died for us"* (Romans 5:8). Speaking of Jesus, the Apostle Peter said it this way, *"Who his own self bare our sins in his own body on the tree, that we, being dead to sins, should live unto righteousness"* (I Peter 2:24).

There is a green hill far away
 Without a city wall
Where the dear Lord was crucified
 Who died to save us all.

Let's steal away now, down the path and through the garden. The fact that this is a restful spot now, the type you would expect to find Jesus buried in, doesn't necessarily mean it was a garden in the 1st century. But the ancient wine or oil press located along the path proves that this indeed was an ancient orchard. There is also a huge cistern near the upper path which indicates the site was a garden.

At the north end of the garden, somewhat submerged from the rest of the ground, is a tomb hewn out of the scarp. The tomb and the lovely garden in which it is located are meticulously maintained by the Garden Tomb Association of London. There is perhaps no more peaceful setting in all of Jerusalem than the Garden Tomb. Here we can shut out the hustle and bustle of the city and quietly meditate on the Lord's death, burial and resurrection in our behalf.

FRIDAY, 5:00 P.M. The tomb of Jesus receives only cursory description in the Gospels. John records that Joseph of Arimathaea, a secret disciple of the Lord, was joined by Nicodemus and *"then took they the body of Jesus, and wound it in linen clothes with the spices, as the manner of the Jews is to bury. Now in the place where he was crucified there was a garden; and in the garden a new sepulchre, wherein was never man yet laid. There laid they Jesus therefore because of the Jews' preparation day; for the sepulchre was nigh at hand"* (John 19:40-42).

Inside the Garden Tomb is seen a burial site that fulfills all the details given in Scripture about the burial and resurrection of Jesus Christ.

123

**Truly, this may be the very place where the Lord lay! Most remarkable is that the tomb, when discovered, was empty.**

The tomb of Jesus was in a garden. It was near the place of crucifixion. It was a new sepulcher, never used. Luke adds that the tomb was *"hewn in stone"* (Luke 23:53). He also notes that Jesus had to hurriedly be placed in the sepulcher because the Sabbath was approaching (Luke 23:54). If the Place of the Skull is above the present bus station, then perhaps this is the tomb of Jesus. The authenticity of one is not dependent upon the authenticity of the other. But the association can hardly be coincidental.

Critics of the Garden Tomb have identified it as 3rd or 4th century. Others have said it may be Byzantine. Still, one noted and respected archaeologist, Dame Kathleen Kenyon, affirms that it is typical of a 1st century Jewish tomb. The debate will continue.

Meanwhile, we'll enjoy the tomb. Notice the face of the sepulcher thus sealing off the entrance.

Our hearts begin to pound as we approach the doorway to enter the tomb. The smallish opening (five feet high, two feet four inches wide) is a little above the sepulcher floor and we must step down when we enter. It is obvious that this was no simple tomb, no peasant's sepulcher. There are two distinct chambers in the tomb. We have entered the first which is ten feet long and eight feet wide. There is a grave trough at the back or northern end. To our right is a doorway with a barred gate. Through this doorway is an eastern chamber. There, against the back wall is a near perfect burial site. The back and ends are formed by the rock-hewn walls of the tomb. The front slab of the site is missing but a "sitting" stone is visible on either end representing pieces of the top of the box-like structure (John 20:11-12). The rock is a brownish color and bears the chisel marks of being carved out of the rock.

What we are looking at is a tomb, maybe even THE tomb, the tomb of Jesus. It forces us to stop and think. The remarkable thing about the tomb is not its craftsmanship, not its remarkable state of preservation, not even its quiet restfulness. The remarkable thing about the tomb is that it's empty. *"And the angel answered and said unto the women, Fear not ye: for I know that ye seek Jesus, which was crucified. He is not here: for he is risen, as he said. Come, see the place where the Lord lay"* (Matthew 28:5-6). This is what makes a journey to the Holy Land holy. The personal discovery that: HE IS NOT HERE: FOR HE IS RISEN.

# INDEX